INNOVATION IN PRACTICE IN THEORY

**INNOVATION
IN PRACTICE IN THEORY**
POSITIONING ARCHITECTURAL
DESIGN AND ITS AGENCY

Edited by (A-Z):

Caterina Barioglio
Daniele Campobenedetto
Andrea Alberto Dutto
Valeria Federighi
Caterina Quaglio
Elena Todella

THE PROBLEM OF INNOVATION. ARCHITECTURE, DESIGN, AGENCY, EXAPTATION

Caterina Barioglio, Daniele Campobenedetto, Andrea Alberto Dutto, Valeria Federighi, Caterina Quaglio, Elena Todella (A-Z)

In a time of supra-national economic, political, and social crises, architectural design is acknowledged as necessitating a fundamental restructuring in order to gain renewed relevance both as a discipline and as a practice.

In what we think is a most crucial time for discourse around issues that are concerned with the political, institutional, and social shape of worlds to come, this book explores the agency of the project of architecture and its processes of innovation by constructing an opportunistic and contingent map of positions.

The book is the result of a tripartite academic trajectory dedicated to the issue of innovation in practice. It gathers material produced for and during an international PhD course, an international Summer School for Master's students, and an international PhD seminar, all held at Politecnico di Torino with the participation of students and faculty from TU Berlin, University of Belgrade, Architectural Association, KTH Stockholm, Sciences Po, Centre Jean Pépin, CNRS Paris, and Ecole National d'Architecture Paris Val de Seine. These three events also coincided, in temporal terms and in the general hypothesis being tested, with the fifth issue of the journal *Ardeth (Architectural Design Theory),* guest-curated by Andrés Jaque and dedicated to the theme of "Innovation as it happens."[1] These academic experiences are part of a wider thrust towards the consolidation of a growing network of schools and research groups working on the issue of innovation in the project of architecture: what does it mean to innovate the practice of architecture? Can we understand the project of architecture as a socio-technical object that, as much as other socio-technical objects, is susceptible to processes of innovation? Which paradigms of innovation can we refer to as architects? What is the role of critical theory in the research for innovation in the project? And, on the other hand, what is the contribution that pragmatist approaches can make when looking at day-to-day practice?

Any understanding of innovation, in design as well as in other fields, is not absolute, but rather contingent: the use of artificial intelligence in design processes, for instance, which is rapidly developing in China where the number of architects is relatively low, and the real estate market demands the construction of consistent numbers of new residential units in equally numerous newly-built settlements, would arguably not fit as well in the Italian market, where the number of architects is highest in the world, and very little demand exists for new residential units or new developments in general.

On the other hand, if we concern ourselves with the understanding of innovation—that is, if the understanding of innovation is our objective—we need to define at least some degree of commensurability across contingent situations. How can we go about managing the variables at play to isolate recurrences and differences? The contingency of the market that is interested in new AI design technologies is sufficiently large (as large as China, in fact) to justify substantial investment on the part of research, as it is fairly sensible to imagine that such technology can be used enough times to justify its costs, before it is made less profitable by changing contingencies.

This book deals with questions that are crucial with respect to the debate on architectural design and its agency. It aims to look at the ways in which we understand, tell, capitalize, and possibly reproduce "innovation." To introduce the book and its contents, we propose two sets of questions that define a two-axes diagram that we employ to navigate the different positions expressed by different authors.

The first set of questions concerns itself with the distinction between built objects and actions as the focus of observation, and as objects that are susceptible to innovating, or being innovated. Should discourse deal with the built matter of architecture: buildings—and their effects on our societies? Or, on the contrary, should it deal with the system of practices that, together with other systems of practices (that of engineers, contractors, but also sociologists and philosophers) contributes to the production of built objects on a daily basis? Both positions recognize the built world as part of a stratified entanglement of social, economic, and political instances. Agency is not a prerogative of human beings: buildings, documents, people, norms, can have different types of agency within processes of innovation. If we look to buildings as the object of analysis and the locus of innovation, it is possible, for instance, to make an attempt at defining measures of effectiveness that have to do with different types of performance, such as environmental or economic ones (Batty, 2017; Bertaud, 2018), or to develop critical approaches to address the relationship of cause and effect between built space and society at large (Borden, 2003). Also, it is possible to develop retrospective narratives that make comparable types of innovations that develop in different times and places (Forty, 2004; Cohen, 2012). The articulation of this last set of positions is represented in architecture schools around the world within "History and Theory" pedagogical frameworks. On the other hand, if we look to design as the object of analysis and the locus of innovation, the aim/focus of the observation shifts to defining the effectiveness of the practice, rather than the products, of design. The time of observation spans the time of production of design documents, rather than the time of production of built objects; the place of observation is the laboratory of design practice, rather than the worksite, the city, or practiced space. The articulation of this emergent set of positions includes ethnographic observations that attempt to give a definition of what a laboratory of practice is (Yaneva, 2018) as well as neomarxist attempts at locating design practice within the market (Deamer, 2015), or critical analyses of the agency of design within wider social trajectories of change (Awan et al, 2009; Doucet, 2015).

The second set of questions concerns itself with the understanding of the relationship between theory and practice, and is defined by two positions: one that looks to theory as a result of practice, another that looks to practice as subsequent to theory. The difference is notable: on one end, we find the cartesian argument that makes ontology a product of epistemology, and locates the distinctive trait of human nature in our ability to think and formulate complex thoughts—which makes us fundamentally different from other animals, but also from machines. On the other end, we find the pragmatist claim that ontology leads to technology, which, in some cases, leads to epistemology: technology is developed in the course of action, and exists even without a full comprehension of its functioning. According to philosopher Maurizio Ferraris, "You don't need to know what you're doing to do it successfully; even more, you don't need to know your physiology to feel the pangs of hunger. Understanding is a luxury; competence and action are a necessity [...] Nevertheless, in most cases competence is a necessary step toward understanding." (2021: 201, translation by the authors). If competence can precede comprehension, knowledge is produced *in practice*: as in Gould's and Vrba's account of evolutionary exaptation (1982), the interval of possibilities is narrowed down in the course of action and reaction, and effects emerge as a consequence. If, on the other hand, comprehension must precede competence, actions in practice should follow a definition of desirable effects: actants preliminarily define their field of agency, and then act accordingly.

The two sets of questions thus presented give shape to two gradients that can be arranged along two axes: built objects (architecture) or actions (design), and competence as preliminary to comprehension (exaptation) or rather comprehension as preliminary to competence (agency)? The essays included in this book are arranged in the four quadrants that exist as a result of these two gradients. Essays include long position essays (written by scholars and researchers), shorter case-study essays (written by PhD students) and visual essays that are primarily image-based. Together, these three formats and these four quadrants attempt to offer a wide spectrum of positions that integrate, oppose and complement each other.

Caterina Barioglio, Daniele Campobenedetto, Andrea Alberto Dutto, Valeria Federighi, Caterina Quaglio, Elena Todella - The Problem of Innovation

The first quadrant (architecture-agency) displays essays that are concerned with exploring the relationship between different types of agency as a conscious effort toward a specific effect, and different types of built space: Hélène Frichot operates a critique of the very concept of innovation, and challenges the relationship between built object and design process by looking at two critically acclaimed installations at the Venice Biennale. The following two essays are first concerned with defining the research field and tools: Ozan Soya proposes the concept of tectonics as a key to reconciling technological and cultural aspects in exploring the concept of innovation "as a total experience"; while Matheus Cartocci starts from an analysis of John Ruskin's writings to identify the collective interest as the field of application of innovation in architecture, concluding that "innovation in architecture can be considered as such when it is an anonymous addition to the line of historical events." Melek Pinar Uz Baki, whose essay opens a theoretical inquiry into the concept of *techné*, reflects on and traces the project of architecture and its agency for a critical and innovative act, conceptualizing then architecture as a *technopoietic* system. Finally, Jörg H. Gleiter problematizes the effects of digital design methods in the constitution of architectural knowledge, exploring the role of the modeling chain in creative design processes and in theory-building.

The second quadrant (agency-design) contains essays that explore the relationship between agency and design as a field of research: Snežana Vesnić explores the semantic potential of words, and traces their relationship with practice through a series of designs that represent the movement between "object" and "concept." Pierre Caye points out how the architectural project has been neglected from the theoretical point of view and shows under which conditions and in which form it can prove to be a critical tool of "liberation" rather than an instance of order and organization. Andrea Alberto Dutto wonders whether the overcoming of the avant-garde—i.e., the logic of the new at all costs, and of *tout court* breaking with the past—can be a way to innovate, with particular reference to the legacy of diagram-making. Also working on the tools of design, Klaus Platzgummer argues that innovations are never creations ex nihilo: rather, they can be found in the materiality of cultural techniques—specifically, of drawing as material expression. Moving to the dimension of exchange, Petar Bojanić unfolds the temporal nature of the word "project" as a way to assess its potential agency within social processes, while Federico Cesareo and Valeria Federighi explore the relationship between narratives of innovation as retrospectively constructed by practitioners, through the collection of 75 stories of innovation and the observation of recurrent narrative structures. Then, reconstructing the origin of architectural terms and (de)constructing projects, Petar Bojanić and Snežana Vesnić examine the potential of language in architectural theory and practice, and focus on how to render architectural conceptualization visible.

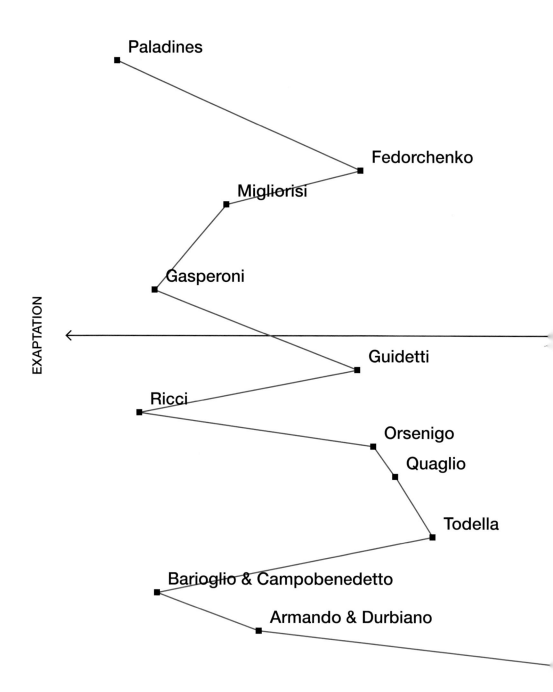

EXAPTATION

Paladines

Fedorchenko

Migliorisi

Gasperoni

Guidetti

Ricci

Orsenigo

Quaglio

Todella

Barioglio & Campobenedetto

Armando & Durbiano

DESIGN

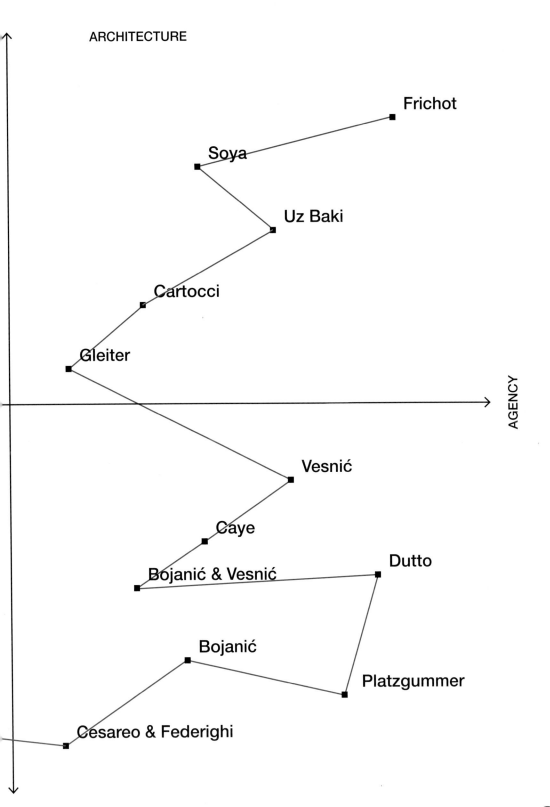

ARCHITECTURE

Frichot

Soya

Uz Baki

Cartocci

Gleiter

AGENCY

Vesnić

Caye

Bojanić & Vesnić

Dutto

Bojanić

Platzgummer

Cesareo & Federighi

In the third quadrant **(design-exaptation)** we can find essays that unpack the mechanisms of design innovation as they evolve within situated systems. **Alessandro Armando and Giovanni Durbiano** try to frame the range of possibilities for innovation in architectural design: by entering the folds of a real architectural design process, the authors propose a method to recognize more effective design strategies, based on the "instability" of both the architectural process and the architectural product. From a similar perspective, **Elena Todella** explores a mapping tool tracing architectural design practice as a taxonomy of multiple entities that interact in a multi-sited and large-scale decision-making process, while **Caterina Quaglio** retraces the history of area-based initiatives to investigate the relationship between individual learning and collective capitalization in order to assess the actual conditions and modalities of innovation in design practices. **Caterina Barioglio and Daniele Campobenedetto** explore the echoes produced by the anthropic modification of the spatial environment, in terms of urban rules, technical requirements, cultural shifts, and behaviors that travel beyond the place in which the modification occurs. Through four case studies in New York and Paris, the authors investigate the possibility of considering localized design as a means of representing and addressing general and comprehensive issues. **Gianfranco Orsenigo** reflects on the role of architecture and architectural innovation to address uncertainty and complexity in marginal contexts, through a reflexive critique of two personal research experiences, while, starting from the concept of "potential" as an operational category to act on existing assets, **Elena Guidetti** points out how an evaluation of the transformative "potential" of buildings could open up possibilities in architectural practices of adaptive reuse. In closing the section, **Donato Ricci** tries to unfold the specificities of a design approach to repurposing online images to study, inquire, and intervene in urban issues. The scope is to extend and further the role of large image corpora visualizations beyond pure analytical or critical purposes.

The fourth and last quadrant **(exaptation-architecture)** defines a field of observation that refers mechanisms of innovation to built space and its forms of evolution. **Lidia Gasperoni** elaborates on the notions of mediality and performativity in architecture and on the way in which these concepts can affect the practice of the environmental architect, namely an architect who embodies complex social and political challenges. **Ambra Migliorisi** reflects on the need for a new legal context of reference to contemporary urban practices, reducing the power of traditional urban design instruments and proposing gaps for experimentation as a possible paradigm change within the existing regulatory grids. In the essay by **Marco Paladines**, the recent transformations of the city of El Alto, Bolivia, become opportunities to study innovation in architecture as the confluence of different accumulation processes, while for **Maria Fedorchenko** the contemporary city represents a reservoir of experimentation with her students at the Architectural Association in London. Her reflection is concerned with the representation of the city as a space in constant transition both physically and conceptually.

Notes

1 *Ardeth* is funded by the Department of Architecture and Design (DAD) at Politecnico di Torino, the Department of Architecture and Urban Studies (DAStU) at Politecnico di Milano, and the Department of Architecture and Design (DiAP) at Roma La Sapienza, and is edited by a group of researchers from Politecnico di Torino, Politecnico di Milano, Roma La Sapienza, and ETH Zurich.

References

Awan, N., Schneider, T., Till, J. (2009), *Spatial agency. Other ways of doing architecture,* Abingdon, Routledge.

Batty, M. (2017), *The New Science of Cities,* Cambridge, MIT Press.

Bertaud, A. (2018), *Order Without Design: How Markets Shape Cities,* Cambridge, MIT Press.

Borden, I. (2003), *Skateboarding Space and the City; Architecture and the Body,* Oxford, Berg Publishers.

Cohen, J. (2012), *The Future of Architecture Since 1889,* Londra: Phaidon Press.

Deamer, P., ed. (2015), *The architect as worker: Immaterial labor, the creative class, and the politics of design,* London, New York, Bloomsbury Academic.

Doucet, I. (2015), *The Practice Turn in Architecture. Brussels after 1968*, London, Routledge.

Ferraris, M. (2021), *Documanità: filosofia del mondo nuovo* (Documanity. A philosophy for the new world), Roma-Bari, Laterza.

Forty, A. (2004), *Words and Buildings: A Vocabulary of Modern Architecture.* Londra: Thames & Hudson.

Gould, S. J. and Elisabeth S. Vrba (1982), "Exaptation - a missing term in the science of form," *Paleobiology,* vol. 8, n. 1, pp. 4–15.

He, W. and Xiaodi Yang (2019), "Artificial Intelligence Design, from Research to Practice," in Philip F. Yuan et al (eds.), *Proceedings of the 2019 Digital Futures,* Singapore, Springer, 189–98.

Yaneva, A. (2018), "Editorial. New voices in architectural ethnography," *Ardeth 2*, pp. 17–24.

Yuan, P. F., Hua Chai and Weiran Zhu (2019), "Experimental Construction Community," *Time+Architecture,* vol. 6, pp. 6–13.

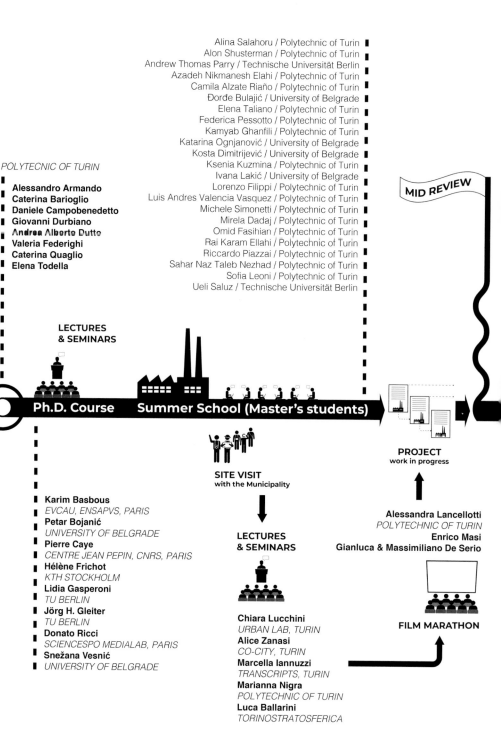

Alina Salahoru / Polytechnic of Turin
Alon Shusterman / Polytechnic of Turin
Andrew Thomas Parry / Technische Universität Berlin
Azadeh Nikmanesh Elahi / Polytechnic of Turin
Camila Alzate Riaño / Polytechnic of Turin
Đorđe Bulajić / University of Belgrade
Elena Taliano / Polytechnic of Turin
Federica Pessotto / Polytechnic of Turin
Kamyab Ghanfili / Polytechnic of Turin
Katarina Ognjanović / University of Belgrade
Kosta Dimitrijević / University of Belgrade
Ksenia Kuzmina / Polytechnic of Turin
Ivana Lakić / University of Belgrade
Lorenzo Filippi / Polytechnic of Turin
Luis Andres Valencia Vasquez / Polytechnic of Turin
Michele Simonetti / Polytechnic of Turin
Mirela Dadaj / Polytechnic of Turin
Omid Fasihian / Polytechnic of Turin
Rai Karam Ellahi / Polytechnic of Turin
Riccardo Piazzai / Polytechnic of Turin
Sahar Naz Taleb Nezhad / Polytechnic of Turin
Sofia Leoni / Polytechnic of Turin
Ueli Saluz / Technische Universität Berlin

MID REVIEW

POLYTECNIC OF TURIN

Alessandro Armando
Caterina Barioglio
Daniele Campobenedetto
Giovanni Durbiano
Andrea Alberto Dutto
Valeria Federighi
Caterina Quaglio
Elena Todella

LECTURES
& SEMINARS

Ph.D. Course   Summer School (Master's students)

PROJECT
work in progress

SITE VISIT
with the Municipality

Karim Basbous
EVCAU, ENSAPVS, PARIS
Petar Bojanić
UNIVERSITY OF BELGRADE
Pierre Caye
CENTRE JEAN PEPIN, CNRS, PARIS
Hélène Frichot
KTH STOCKHOLM
Lidia Gasperoni
TU BERLIN
Jörg H. Gleiter
TU BERLIN
Donato Ricci
SCIENCESPO MEDIALAB, PARIS
Snežana Vesnić
UNIVERSITY OF BELGRADE

LECTURES
& SEMINARS

Chiara Lucchini
URBAN LAB, TURIN
Alice Zanasi
CO-CITY, TURIN
Marcella Iannuzzi
TRANSCRIPTS, TURIN
Marianna Nigra
POLYTECHNIC OF TURIN
Luca Ballarini
TORINOSTRATOSFERICA

Alessandra Lancellotti
POLYTECHNIC OF TURIN
Enrico Masi
Gianluca & Massimiliano De Serio

FILM MARATHON

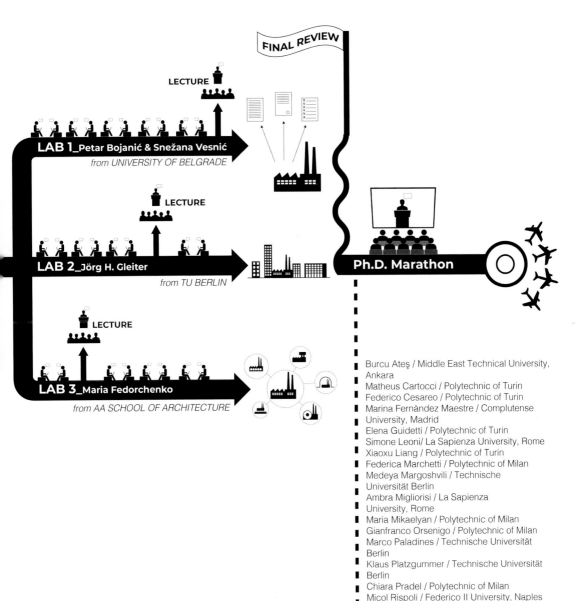

FINAL REVIEW

LECTURE

LAB 1_Petar Bojanić & Snežana Vesnić
from UNIVERSITY OF BELGRADE

LECTURE

LAB 2_Jörg H. Gleiter
from TU BERLIN

LECTURE

LAB 3_Maria Fedorchenko
from AA SCHOOL OF ARCHITECTURE

Ph.D. Marathon

Burcu Ateş / Middle East Technical University, Ankara
Matheus Cartocci / Polytechnic of Turin
Federico Cesareo / Polytechnic of Turin
Marina Fernàndez Maestre / Complutense University, Madrid
Elena Guidetti / Polytechnic of Turin
Simone Leoni/ La Sapienza University, Rome
Xiaoxu Liang / Polytechnic of Turin
Federica Marchetti / Polytechnic of Milan
Medeya Margoshvili / Technische Universität Berlin
Ambra Migliorisi / La Sapienza University, Rome
Maria Mikaelyan / Polytechnic of Milan
Gianfranco Orsenigo / Polytechnic of Milan
Marco Paladines / Technische Universität Berlin
Klaus Platzgummer / Technische Universität Berlin
Chiara Pradel / Polytechnic of Milan
Micol Rispoli / Federico II University, Naples
Ozan Soya / Technische Universität Berlin
Melek Pınar Uz Baki / Middle East Technical University, Ankara

Innovation, Enervation...
Experiments in the Swiss Pavilion
Hélène Frichot

Innovation, which demands the perpetual production of the new, too often seeks out nov-elty for the sake of novelty alone, resulting, finally, in a sense of affective enervation. This chapter argues that innovation needs to commence from the point of view of problems worth addressing, and questions worth asking. Sometimes, the result might not be to pur-sue innovation at all, but to slow down and undertake a careful reconsideration of a state of affairs by acknowledging what most urgently confronts us in a contemporary world. To question and critique the thoughtless push for innovation, I look to the controlled and circumscribed event and exhibition space that is the Venice Biennale of Architecture. To enable focus and specificity, I address the 'innovative' architectural experiments on display in the Swiss Pavilion in the 15th and 16th Biennale of Architecture, in 2016 and then 2018 respectively. After placing these architectural experiments in critical dialogue, I conclude by introducing Isabelle Stengers and Didier Debaise's "speculative pragmatism" as a rem-edy to the presumed good of innovation.

On the Tectonic Threshold of Innovation.
Between Architectural Object and Architectural Act
Ozan Soya

Should we need to think about innovation in architecture through the object of architecture or the act of architecture? In other words, should we look at buildings and architectural products, or accept these objects as results of several changes that occurred in processes that architects are involved in? A contemporary tectonic theory may have the answer. The term tectonics derives from the word "tekton," referring to carpenter or builder at its Greek origin. However, throughout the 19th century, the term was used by architectural theorists to refer to architecture's coordination of structural/constructional aspects with systems of decoration/ornamentation. Today, its potential, providing various perspectives on the rela-tionships between the major aspects of architecture, gains even more importance.

John Ruskin, Architectural Innovation in Anonymity.
The Creative Process of a Discipline
Matheus Cartocci

If innovation is a term applied to an instrument that is set to perform a *work,* this short pa-per proposes to define a hypothetical work field and goal for architecture as a discipline. Writings of John Ruskin (1819–1900), theoretical scholar of the Victorian period, will here be used for their clear definition of architecture as a tool for an expressed purpose: the establishment of a better society and the formation of personal character through an act of education. Once the objective of the work to pursue has been clarified, this paper presents the characteristics of *innovation* in architecture when utilized as a practical instrument, through the theoretical classifications of different scholars of the 20th century.

A Critical Investigation into the Technopoiesis of Architecture
Melek Pinar Uz Baki

This paper presents a theoretical inquiry into the concept of *techné* and traces the project of architecture and its agency for a critical and innovative act. The conventional account of making trajectory in architecture within the scope of a design problem, maker(s), and alternate possibilities has been enhanced through the changing nature of design thinking, tools, and methods. Besides its practical appeals and evolving discourse, developing tools, technics, and technologies have caused the disciplinary transformation of architectural thinking as well as the ways of practicing, transferring, and interpreting experiments. On the transformation of tools into technologies, *technopoiesis* will be introduced as a contemporary explication of *techné* to remind the significance of knowledge production generated from the current interrelationship of *poiesis* and technology. Architecture will be conceptualized as a *technopoietic* system that offers pluralistic participation, multiplicative operations, and particular solutions for architectural thinking and making.

The Promise of an Object.
Design Processes as Processes of Theory Construction
Jörg H. Gleiter

Digital design methods pose major problems to architecture. Rapid prototyping, digital fabrication, or BIM and other forms of computer-aided design, are possible without clearly scaled model spaces as introduced by Leon Battista Alberti (1404–72). Alberti was the first to insist on architectural design in the form of concrete, scaled drawings. Accordingly, Alberti's innovation was to transform the design process into a series of modeling processes, each at its own scale, each with its own promise of an object. With Alberti, the process of designing became a process of theory building. But today, digital design processes interrupt the modeling chain. In doing so, they interrupt nothing less than the creative design process and thus further theory building. Despite the possibility of creating fantastic new forms and figures, theory building is short-circuited in strictly algorithmic design processes. The crisis of creativity as it can be observed today is basically a crisis of theory building, triggered by the partial interruption of the modeling chain.

INNOVATION, ENERVATION...
Experiments in the Swiss Pavilion
Hélène Frichot

Hélène Frichot is an architectural theorist and philosopher, writer and critic; she is Professor of Architecture and Philosophy, and Director of the Bachelor of Design, Faculty of Architecture, Building and Planning University of Melbourne, Australia. In her former position she directed Critical Studies in Architecture, School of Architecture, KTH Stockholm, Sweden. Her recent publications include *Dirty Theory: Troubling Architecture* (AADR 2019), *Creative Ecologies: Theorizing the Practice of Architecture* (Bloomsbury 2018), and *How to Make Yourself a Feminist Design Power Tool* (2016). She is editor on a number of collections, including with Catharina Gabrielsson and Helen Runting, *Architecture and Feminisms: Ecologies, Economies, Technologies* (Routledge 2017) and more recently with Naomi Stead, *Writing Architectures: Ficto-Critical Approaches* (Bloomsbury 2020), and with Marco Jobst, *Architectural Affects After Deleuze and Guattari* (Routledge 2021).

Innovation performs the act of conceptual and material prowess that brings something new into the world, including, as a following step, the presentation to a willing audience of wondrous things previously unimaginable, unthinkable, until now. Innovation and industry go together like shock and awe to provide technological solutions to invented problems, some of which were perhaps not problems that really needed solving in the first place, some of which are perhaps problems inadequately posed. You deserve the problems you choose, suggests philosopher of science Isabelle Stengers, setting your thinking track toward anticipated ends. Nevertheless, "a problem must matter in order to get a possibly relevant answer" (2011: 374). Or more urgently, a problem must stir in us the power to think. Stupid, environment-destroying solutions usually presume poorly posited problems, and yet we are compelled to innovate, to invent. Inside the initial gesture of composing a problem, determining its outline and possible direction forward, there is packed great ethical responsibility, resulting in the ethical imperative: Take responsibility for the problems you invent and decide to resolve.

For research in the sciences, in the humanities, in design, a circumscribed field needs to be framed, and a suite of problems relevant to that field identified, or invented. Gilles Deleuze and Félix Guattari describe the situation like this: "all concepts are connected to problems without which they would have no meaning and which can themselves only be isolated or understood as their solution emerges" (1994: 16). A research infrastructure is required to test the limits and outlines of problems. Think for instance of laboratory spaces, workshops, design studios: all are controlled spaces for experimentation.

Then there are the attendant spaces in which innovation or new ideas might be placed on display. In the era of colonization these were raised as magnificent exposition halls, an archetypal instance being the famed Crystal Palace and all the wonders it sheltered, the spoils collected from a vastly colonized empire. Today, these spaces of display include event spaces such as to be found in the environmentally precarious city of Venice, where art and then architecture in alternate years place all their most recent innovations on display. The Venice Biennale of Architecture was first launched in 1980 with a curated theme dedicated to the temporal conundrum of the persistence of the past in the present, entitled *The Presence of the Past*. More than just a style of pastiche and collage, Postmodernism here could be seen to be issuing cautions around assumptions concerning the universal march of progress. This was the Biennale where Aldo Rossi's much-loved *Teatro del Mondo* rocked gently at its moorings promising to drift away. What an innocent world. There was to be found the cut-out architectures of the *Strada Novissima* at the scale of 1:1, producing as Leá-Catherine Szacka explains "a series of Potemkin-like facades: a highly theatrical display, which produced a new and very impressive type of exhibition space" (2012: 14). This installation was based, as it turns out, on a German Christmas market, only here a collection of architects was selling its baubles.

Because of the convenience of the circumscribed event space that is the Venice Biennale of Architecture, I'll use this opportunity to critique the notion of innovation here, with a specific focus on the Venice Pavilion in the years 2016 and 2018, at the 15th and the 16th Venice Biennales of Architecture. This is a highly contrived experiment undertaken in a fully controlled space, but I take these steps wilfully, arguing that innovation as a process tends to be highly cultivated. As Brett Steele writes in the Preface to *Architecture on Display: On the History of the Venice Biennale*,

> "The biennale's importance today lies in its vital dual presence as both register and infrastructure, recording the impulses that guide not only architecture but also the increasingly international audiences created by (and so often today, nearly subservient to) contemporary architectures of display" (2010: 7).

It takes the pulse of contemporary architectural experimentation, and hence innovation, placing that "architectural life" on display. More than this, as Alex Brown and Leá-Catherine Szacka explain, Venice offers opportunities to move beyond the mere display of objects toward "immersive and experiential environments." (2019) All the more likely to captivate and reformat the visitor.

So, two consecutive Biennales, themed in turn by Alessandro Aravena under the title *Reporting from the Front*, and then by Yvonne Farrell and Shelley McNamara with *Freespace*. The 2016 event expressed an earnest socio-political concern, while the 2018 event favoured a vague phenomenological emphasis, gesturing broadly to a sense of humanity, and the generosities of free space, extending to desire and questions of embodiment. Returning to these events I commence by locating the reader inside the unassuming Swiss Pavilion, constructed in 1952 by Bruno Giacometti.

Incidental Space, 2016

> "The latter too occurs much less through rapt attention than by noticing the object in an incidental fashion." (Benjamin, 1968: 240)

Reputation preceded the wonder that it professed to shelter, and a special issue of the German magazine *ARCH+* (2016) is dedicated to it, but what exactly is it? What was it supposed to be or do? Through the entry portal, turning a corner, passing walls significantly wallpapered with intimations of it, the thing itself is finally revealed. There, in an otherwise unobtrusive exhibition space lit from above, a thing, cloud-like yet lumpen, suspended somewhat uncomfortably, an alien object from one vantage point, an inviting grotto from another: this is what is to be discovered. A museum ribbon stretched between two stainless steel posts invites and cautions visitors. It is even possible to enter the thing itself, to climb into it, to get a feel of its substantial stuff under socked toes. Shoes have to be removed before climbing aboard. Grown adults are found exploring its crevices. Giggling children clamber in it. The rarefied thing so presented goes under the title *Incidental Space* and is authored by the Swiss architect Christian Kerez who explains that what is on offer is "a pure encounter with architecture" (Mairs, 2016). This begs the question: an encounter purified of what exactly?

What was especially peculiar about the thing in question, *Incidental Space*, was the non-response it appeared to offer to the curatorial ambitions of the 2016 Venice Biennale of Architecture, which under Aravena's curation was aimed at considering points of view on architecture that emphasized its social and political capacities to increase quality of life for diverse peoples. Where other pavilions explored simple construction techniques that might be managed by those with meager resources and few skills, the thing in the Swiss pavilion appeared to be preoccupied with quite another agenda. Innovation here was not about extending the remit of architecture toward issues of "segregation, inequalities, peripheries, access to sanitation, natural disasters, housing shortage, migration, informality, crime, traffic, waste, pollution and participation of communities," (Aravena, 2016) instead, disciplinary autonomy, even a retreat from worldly concerns was on offer. It was merely incidental, effectively disinterested. Hence the work of 'purification' in the encounter on offer. Architecture for the sake of architecture, pure non-representational form, the interplay of digital techniques and technologies with the work of manual modeling extended a retort to the soft-hearted socialists eager to make architecture undertake its social work. It is hard not to read *Incidental Space* as anything but a disciplinary call to order, a retraction of architectural responsibilities in the face of mounting social and environmental struggles.

Exactly because the thing refused interpretation, or because it invited an unfurling, open-ended play of interpretations, I propose here that it lends itself to being read as a parable. *Incidental Space* can be read as a parable of the excesses of architecture where it cares only for itself and its internal disciplinary concerns. How were these pretensions toward autonomy purveyed? On display was the conceit of a single authorial gesture, signed by Kerez, hiding behind it the mostly unattributed labour of design students at the ETH whose task it was to produce a series of non-standard forms that begged decryption. There was the black-boxing of architecture as process, instead inviting the phenomenological mystification of the arcane art of the architect. Peter Zumthor, a second-generation phenomenological architect, celebrated Kerez's thing for its sumptuous indications of the ongoing relevance of hand-modelled stuff (Mairs, 2016). At the same time, the thing was celebrated for its technical achievement, that is, as historian of the digital Mario Carpo excitedly explains, the project took a thing of irregular shape and form the size of a shoebox and scaled it up (Carpo, 2016: 70-72). This challenge of exactly reproducing a small, highly complex object into a larger sculptural form that might occupy the pavilion was deemed an act of considerable technical achievement. Curiously, between phenomenological wonder and digitally augmented technical prowess there is the collapse of the distinction between what Walter Benjamin once described as the 'aura' of the original, on the one hand, and the reproducibility of a work of art facilitated by way of industrial development, on the other. More could be said concerning the implication of this collapse. I'll only reflect briefly on the final passages of Benjamin's famous essay, *The Work of Art in the Age of Mechanical Reproduction*, where between 'aura' and technological reproduction (advanced in the case of Incidental Space through digital means of reproduction) Benjamin finally warns of the politics in which forms of fascism are rendered aesthetic, reminding us

Figure 1
Incidental Space in the Swiss Pavilion,
Venice Biennale of Architecture, 2016.
Photography by the Author.

of the dictum *"Fiat ars – pereat mundus"* (242) that is, make art though the world may perish. These tendencies, Benjamin explains, run alongside the conjunction of creativity with genius, and eternal value with mystery (218).

From all this what can be concluded concerning the role of innovation? That it maintains the pre-eminence of the architect and 'his' aesthetic gesture as sole genius thereby mystifying design knowledge; that it withholds access to knowledge, but for an affect-driven phenomenological encounter: remember, Kerez has characterized the encounter with architecture as purified. It refuses politics, placing the stupefied wonder of the passive onlooker to the fore. Still, as Isabelle Stengers points out, to wonder is both "to be surprised and to entertain questions" (2011: 374). This might be obvious to an English speaker, but what it suggests is that we cannot rely on the passivity of wonder enduring, for questions must eventually be asked. In that the thing itself "looks like" something formed by "natural" means, a rock, a grotto, but is in fact molded by human hands, nature, finally, is denatured. Distinctions between nature and culture are placed into crisis, but not in the sense that Donna Haraway or Bruno Latour might encourage (Haraway, 2008; Latour, 1993). Rather than reflecting upon natures-cultures and their entanglements, it is the pre-eminence of human industrial activity over and above nature that is celebrated. Anthropogenic design without environmental or social consideration.

House Tour: Svizzera 240, 2018

Two years later, in 2018, something altogether different took up temporary residence in the Swiss Pavilion. Where the thing that was *Incidental Space* had sat alone as a rarefied apparition in the gallery space, distinctly an object around which a visitor would circulate if said visitor was not daring enough to crawl inside, in 2018 the interior of the same pavilion was rendered near unrecognizable.

In 2018 a pop-up fun palace invaded the interior of the Swiss pavilion, but a fun palace bleached of the candy-striped colors one might expect of a fairground. Like Alice in Wonderland, visitors found themselves either too small or too large relative to doorways and door handles, corridors, and rooms. Abrupt spatial leaps in scale required the body to bend down low, or else the neck to crane, looking up toward looming, over-sized details. *House Tour: Svizzera 240* took up the Venice Biennale curatorial theme of *Freespace* to interrogate the contemporary state of the real estate market in relation to architecture with its homogenous white-on-white interiors colonizing European residential housing stock from Zurich to Stockholm. The focus, truth be told, was the Swiss context, but there was much to be learnt more generally about the regulation of interiors toward a bare minimum of habitability.

While the interior of *House Tour* aroused joy and a sense of playfulness for those who engaged with it, the message conveyed was a serious one. This project, as the design collective composed of Matthew van der Ploeg, Ani Vihervaara, Li Tavor, and Alessandro Bosshard explained, was about the success of a variety of ordinary architecture that is "hidden-in-plain-sight" that is, the interior of contemporary housing (2018: 150). Ordinary, banal, everyday architectures within which the contemporary urban dweller ekes out their daily existence. One of the greatest successes of modern architecture, the design collective explains, is in the role it plays in the production of what might be called a continuous interior that routinely consists of "a volume 240cm in height, dressed with white walls, parquet or tiled flooring, and off-the-shelf fittings" (150): a mass industrial production of the interior rolled out across vast urban territories. What they want to interrogate is an interior of a specific kind, one that is unfurnished. As they explain, images of designed interiors have been gaining page space in journals of architecture, often in the form of the uninhabited interior presented to an architectural audience in advance of the architect losing 'organisartorial' control and having to give over to the unruly, possibly messy, and worse still, taste-challenged occupant. By organisartorial I nod toward a portmanteau conceptual construction that places together an organisational logic with sartorial flair, something like the fashioning of the interior for best effect. It is a concept hatched in collaboration with Helen Runting; in fact, I acknowledge her as its primary author (Runting and Frichot, 2017). What the concept does is draw attention to the great amount of labour dedicated to the dressing of interiors for display, whether that be for presentation in industry journals, or more insidiously, across the many digital platforms that support the circulation and consumption of the spatial products of real estate. The preparation of the interior followed by the framing of the image, just so, is key. Beyond the special interests of the architectural industry, it is toward real estate that the creators of *House Tour* draw attention, going so

Figure 2
Project team for the Swiss Pavilion at the 16th International Architecture Exhibition - La Biennale di Venezia, May 2018.
Left to right, Alessandro Bosshard, Li Tavor, Matthew van der Ploeg, and Ani Vihervaara.
Photo: Christian Beutler / KEYSTONE

far as to argue that when it comes to the genre of real estate the "interior shell not only looks back at you, but starts to ask questions" (151).

What kinds of questions are the proliferating images of the unfurnished interior asking? In addition to the industrial mass production of interiors and the homogenizing effects they must surely be having on the formation of contemporary subjectivities and the social lives of urban denizens, there is the question of representation. One of the aims of the *House Tour*, with its humorous allusions to the house-proud, is the ubiquitous role of image-making practices in architecture and the multiplying platforms across which such images are purveyed and consumed. As Charles Rice wryly observes in his contribution to the catalogue that accompanied the exhibition, these days our smart phones support real estate apps that attempt to match us with our perfect home, much as Tinder purports to match us with our perfect mate (Rice, 2018: 129). To reflect on the power of the image, to flip its prevailing logics, the design collective explains that: "Instead of *representing building*, we *build representation*" (van der Ploeg, Vihervaara, Tavor and Bosshard, 2018: 152). The installation that is *House Tour* is based on an archive of anodyne interior images cut and paste together into something of a *cadavre exquis*, following the premise that images are scale ambiguous. They have been collaged together and the collage has been taken seriously, the result composing a constructed interior that ranges in scale from 1:5, 1:2, 1:1.6, 1:1.3, 1:1.2, 1:1, 1.1:1, 1.3:1, 1.5:1. What results is a sequence of confounding scalar shifts that produce the spatial effects of the fun palace I described in the opening. Here exhibition has become constructed environment (see Brown and Szacka, 2019). You've got to experience it, but in experiencing it you might also find you are encountering something of a return of the repressed.

In architecture we are always at risk of dismissing the interior as not being worthy of serious architectural consideration. What the exhibition *House Tour* draws attention to is the question of scale in relation to the image and how scale needs to be understood in a number of ways. Yes, there is the play of scales of the interior that the visitor to the Swiss Pavilion at the 2018 Biennale could take pleasure in, but there is also the broader issue of the scale of industrial production of the interior and the way it is rolled out across urban environments. The design collective provocatively explains that when you venture into their *House Tour* you become a new subject, a House Tourist (152). But whether we are architects or else consumers immersed in the real estate market, we are already reconstructed as house tourists, and often unwillingly so. The darker message that we are left with is that we all live here in these banal, homogenized interiors, and here is where any sense of public and private has been addled. Here is where the home is less home sweet home than a spatial commodity prepared in advance for inevitable resale.

What of innovation? Innovation is quite literally "on display" in *House Tour*, but it is not to be found where you might be tempted to go looking for it. Even though the design collective responsible for *House Tour* went to considerable trouble to work with industry to produce door furniture that would function across their featured suite of scales, even though the construction of the interior was taken seriously as a design challenge in its own right, innovation operated more like a question mark addressed to the "standardisation of life" (Macarthur, 2018: 112). The idea of a display home, a house tour, incorporating the real estate hungry or design-fascinated punter greedily perusing images, is reflected back at us as though from Alice's looking glass. Once we venture through the looking glass strange effects can be observed to erupt, affecting us, the hapless house tourist, but also provoking us to think again. The concerns that are raised in this encounter with the interior turn out to be environmental in scope; from the door handle to city planning the effects of the standardization of the 240 cm floor to ceiling fundamentally affect how we plan, construct, and inhabit constructed environments (Macarthur, 2018: 113). Innovation comes into play as the way in which a standardized approach to construction is distributed at a massive scale, but again, to what effect? The question of the relation of private to public is also ventured, a question that has become urgent in these times of COVID-19, where more often than not we find ourselves, by necessity, working from home. The interior presses in threatening to smother rather than to sooth, the white walls close in threateningly, and the fun palace begins to stir up something closer to the *unheimlich*.

What is worth mentioning finally is the collective who came together for this spatial experiment: Matthew van der Ploeg, Ani Vihervaara, Li Tavor, and Alessandro Bosshard. It's a team effort, and the emphasis on this collaborative spirit, including the diverse essays available in the accompanying publication (Jasper, 2018), dispense with the conceit of sole authorship. We are all in it together in our design work as in our interiors, and we need to establish the best ways of continuing to learn and work together collaboratively. Today, no less than the environment is at stake. The thing is, I'm not sure whether the collaborative spirit falls under the mantle of innovation, or whether innovation instead encourages each to selfishly venture out on their own. Do experiments such as the *House Tour* automatically assume innovation as a "good"? Is experimentation, as such, always already an act of innovation? Or not?

Innovation or Enervation?

By now my hesitation over the assumed good of innovation as process, as drive, as aspiration, has probably become clear. Innovation for the sake of innovation demands a tireless pursuit of the novel in answer to problems that appear only when the solution presents itself. I'm concerned about what futures innovation propels us toward and what investments it requires. There is a tirelessness required of innovation and very often an assumption that industry should set the agenda. The designer, technologist, scientist as innovator is obliged to exhaustively attend to what is possible, even to exhaust the possible. This does not

Figures 3-4: Installation views of "Svizzera 240: House Tour" at the Swiss Pavilion at the 16th International Architecture Exhibition - La Biennale di Venezia, Photo: Christian Beutler / KEYSTONE

always require either invention or experimentation, it can merely be a new organizational logic, a new arrangement of things. The new of innovation is usually not so very novel, and the shock of the new wears off over time, at which juncture, the innovators return and change things up again. What happens when fatigue sets in, what about the limits of exhaustion? What happens when available resources are threatened with depletion, when innovation places its own pursuits over and above environmental concerns, which must be conceived as entangling mental, social, and environmental ecologies (Guattari, 2000)? I have argued elsewhere that at its limit exhaustion might yield something fruitful, and that by persisting through our collective exhaustion we might yet find the means to achieve creative answers to pressing problems (see Frichot, 2018), but what I wonder is whether innovation is what is needed here? Despite its motivational mood and can-do demeanour, is innovation simply enervating?

And yet, we need to think new things, or rather, we need new ways for thinking to take place in response to contingent problems as they emerge. This is a distinct formation of the problem discussed at the opening of this essay. Where I commenced with the idea of the invention of problems, and the importance of taking responsibility for the problems you invent, here I am introducing another kind of problem, the one that hits you in the face. The global spread of COVID-19 would be a good example here, for this is a problem that intrudes upon our daily lives and demands a response. I hasten to add that even amidst the most constrained life there are contingencies, encounters that demand responses, that might appear to call for "innovation." We must answer to things, this is what life demands, simply put, we must do something, we must respond somehow, we must make the best of things. To take the thinking part seriously we require an adequate interplay, a relay, between theory and practice. Checks and balances, theory and practice, question and answer, in open dialogue. Although it would require more space and time than I have available in this essay, I want to conclude by taking a pragmatic turn. I want to conclude by offering an alternative to innovation, something that might be called speculative pragmatism.

In his introduction to Joan Ockman's edited collection, *The Pragmatist Imagination*, the result of a workshop at the Temple Hoyne Buell Centre, Columbia University, New York, John Rajchman explains that: "Pragmatism is a philosophy that, for certainty and invariable method, substitutes experimentation and belief in the world" (2000: 11). Belief in the world comes straight out of the Deleuze and Guattari playbook: we've got to believe in this world, they urgently implore us (1994). Deleuze was famously keen on the American pragmatists, especially William James, and was partially responsible for drawing attention to the work of A.N. Whitehead, a mathematician who came to philosophy late and who arguably expanded on a pragmatist position, if in his own singular way. Didier Debaise, a frequent collaborator with Isabelle Stengers, places pragmatism and speculation together and commences by explaining that pragmatism is a method for inventing ideas. Importantly, what Debaise, after A. N. Whitehead, stresses, is that creativity does not come first, instead it is the encounter in all its radical contingency that calls on creativity to commence its work.

Encounter first, creativity as a response to the situated encounter (see Frichot, 2020). In *Nature as Event*, Debaise argues: "What is needed is a philosophy that, in its very form, its ambition and its manners of relating to things, can grant due importance to the deeply plural experience of nature" (2017b: 77). Together, Debaise and Stengers call forth what they call a 'speculative gesture,' which must be promptly distinguished from the avaricious forms of speculation we are familiar with in architecture and design where it collaborates with property development interests. Vinciane Depret, who co-wrote *Women Who Make a Fuss* with Stengers (2014), connects the pragmatic stance with learning how to follow practices to learn with them (2018: 65). There is very much the sense of a collaborative spirit here. Ockman explains that: "Most simply defined, pragmatism is a theory of practice" (2020: 271), perhaps even the means of securing a rapprochement between theory and practice in architecture. At least, this is what Ockman's original ambition appeared to be when she convened her workshop at Columbia University in New York, though by the time she comes to reflect on this event 17 years later, she seems somewhat wearied by the experiment (Ockman, 2020). But perhaps that's another story, concerning how innovative theoretical conjunctions become too easily exhausted in the discipline of architecture, sometimes without being given enough of a chance.

So, finally, why this conceptual construct that is speculative pragmatism, rather than the heady rush toward innovation? Where the speculative gesture leaps forward, the pragmatic one ties us to the empirical ground, simply, "We experience...we experiment" (Deleuze, 2003: 1). Experience leads us toward experimentation, and it is what equips us to confront problems, and then cautions us with respect to those problems we choose to invent. In this way we create practical relations that answer to the contingency of our encounters amidst unpredictable global and everyday events. The risk I am attempting to draw attention to is how far innovation answers to demands that lose sight of the empirical ground. Innovation for the sake of innovation deranges the possible and always risks asking for too much, more than the Planet Earth is able to give. With this distinction between problems, confronted or invented, and this notion of a speculative pragmatism as a near paradoxical formula that ties us to the ground while supporting us as we leap forwards, I'll return briefly to the two events at the Biennale of Architecture introduced earlier.

With Kerez's *Incidental Space*, it is plain to see the invention of a problem that speculates on little more than the ingenuity of technical prowess with the aim of producing wonder as an output, as well as entertaining the manifestation of greater levels of formal complexity in design. What remains unclear is what such formal complexity, performing under the disguise of a nature-culture conundrum, contributes; what further thoughts it provokes; what better modes of living it invites. While I acknowledge it is risky to undertake an exercise in "compare and contrast," for the outcome can be crude, when considering the second case, that of the collaboratively conceived project *House Tour: Svizzera 240*, I suggest something begins to unsettle the controlled space of the Biennale. As the design collective explains, the interior "not only looks back at you, but starts to ask questions" (van der Ploeg, Vihervaara, Tavor and Bosshard, 2018: 151). The complacency of architecture is troubled. *House Tour* performatively demonstrates the wide-spread issue of the mass industrialization of housing and the intersection of this with the avarice of the real estate marketplace with its own speculative gestures, speculative here in the negative sense of speculating on the profit to be gained from pre-packaging spatial products. Here the problem is less invented than one that intrudes on the concerns of the design collective, who greet the problem with critical humor and serious consideration when they create their installation and their critical creative response.

The speculative gesture is tied up with contemporary urgencies: we must respond, we are obliged to. The speculative gesture is flung forwards only to arc backwards again, becoming ingested into the body (human, animal, mineral) that strives to learn, transforming it, that body that propels itself always inevitably forwards, onwards—we must go on, to make the gesture—the body advancing, retreating, responding, recoiling, shock, and then on again. What choice is there really? You choose the problems you deserve, Stengers wryly observes when she states that the philosopher, to which we could add the architectural theorist or practitioner, becomes "both the creator and the creature of his own passionate construction" (2014: 192), and when innovation goes awry, you have no one to blame but yourself. Finally, you are responsible for the problems you invent, and bound to respond, response-ably, to the problems that confront you.

References
Aravena, A. (2016), *Curators Proposal*, "Venice Biennale of Architecture." Available at: https://www.labiennale.org/en/architecture/2016/intervento-di-alejandro-aravena [Accessed: November 4, 2021].
Benjamin, W. (1968), *The Work of Art in the Age of Mechanical Reproduction*, "Illuminations," trans. Harry Zohn. New York, Schocken Books.
Brown, A. and Szacka, L. C. (2019), *The Architecture Exhibition as Environment*, "ATR (Architectural Theory Review)," vol. 23, n. 1, pp. 1–4.
Carpo, M. (2016), *Christian Kerez's Art of the Incidental*, "Arch+ Journal of Architecture and Urbanism, Release Architecture," edited by Anh-Linh Ngo, pp. 70–76.
Debaise, D. (2017a), *Speculative Empiricism: Revisiting Whitehead*, Edinburgh, Edinburgh University Press.
Debaise, D. (2017b), *Nature as Event: The Lure of the Possible*, Durham, Duke University Press.
Debaise, D. (2018) *The Minoritarian Powers of Thought: Thinking beyond Stupidity with Isabelle Stengers*, "SubStance," vol. 47, n. 1, issue 145, pp. 17–28.
Debaise, D. and Stengers, I. (eds.) (2015) *Gestes spéculatifs*, Dijon, Les presses du réel.
Debaise, D. and Stengers, I. (2017), *The Insistence of Possibles: Towards a Speculatve Pragmatism*, "Parse Journal," issue 7, Autumn 2017. Available at: https://parsejournal.com/article/the-insistence-of-possibles%E2%80%A8-towards-a-speculative-pragmatism/ [Accessed: November 4, 2021].
Deleuze, G. and Guattari, F. (1994), *What is Philosophy?*, trans. Graham Burchell and Hugh Tomlinson. London, Verso.
Deleuze, G. (2003), *The Three Kinds of Knowledge*, "Pli: The Warwick Journal of Philosophy," vol. 14, pp. 1–20.

Frichot, H. (2018), *Creative Ecologies: Theorizing the Practice of Architecture*, London, Bloomsbury.

Guattari, F. (2000), *The Three Ecologies*, London, Athlone Press.

Haraway, D. (2008), *When Species Meet*, Minneapolis, University of Minnesota Press.

Jasper, A. ed. (2018), *House Tour: Views of the Unfinished Interior*, Zurich, Park Books.

Latour, B. (1993), *We Have Never Been Modern*, Cambridge MA, Harvard University Press.

Macarthur, J. (2018), *The Banality of 240cm*, Adam Jasper ed. "House Tour: Views of the Unfinished Interior," Zurich, Park Books, pp. 112–5.

Ngo, A. L. (2016), *Editorial*, "Release Architecture," "Arch+ Journal of Architecture and Urbanism," pp. 3–4.

Ockman, J. (2020), *Consequences of Pragmatism: A Retrospect on 'The Pragmatist Imagination'*, Sebastiaan Loosen, Rajesh Heynickx, Hilde Heynen, eds. "The Figure of Knowledge: Conditioning Architectural Theory 1960s to 1990s," Leuven, Leuven University Press, pp. 269–97.

Oehy, S. and Kerez, C. (2016), *Incidental Space*, Anh-Linh Ngo ed. "Release Architecture," "Arch+ Journal of Architecture and Urbanism," pp. 12–15.

Rajchman, J. (2000), *General Introduction*, Joan Ockman ed. "The Pragmatist Imagination: Thinking About 'Things in the Making'," New York, Princeton Architectural Press, pp. 6–25.

Rice, C. (2018), *Antagonistic Exchange*, Adam Jasper ed. "House Tour: Views of the Unfinished Interior," Zurich, Park Books, pp. 128–31.

Runting, H. and Frichot, H. (2017), *White, Wide and Scattered: Picturing Her Housing Career*, Teresa Stoppani, George Themistoekleous, Giorgio Ponzo, eds. "This Thing Called Theory," Abingdon, Oxon, Routledge, pp. 231–41.

Steele, B. (2010), *Preface*, Aaron Levy and William Menking, eds. "Architecture on Display: On the History of the Venice Biennale of Architecture," London, AA Publications.

Stengers, I. (2014), *Speculative Philosophy and the Art of Dramatization*, Roland Faber and Andrew Goffrey, eds, "The Allure of Things: Process and Object in Contemporary Philosophy," London, Bloomsbury, pp. 188–217.

Stengers, I. and Despret, V. (2014), *Women Who Make a Fuss: The unfaithful daughters of Virginia Woolf*, trans. April Knutson, Minneapolis, University of Minnesota Press.

Szacka, L. C. (2017), *Exhibiting the Postmodern: The 1980 Venice Architectural Biennale*, Marsilio Editori.

Szacka, L. C. (2012), *The 1980 Architecture Biennale: The Street as Spatial and Representational Curating Device*, "OASE Journal for Architecture," pp. 88.

Mairs, J. (2016), *Christian Kerez creates cavernous cloud to offer "a pure encounter with architecture,"* "Dezeen," May 27. Available at: https://www.dezeen.com/2016/05/27/christian-kerez-cavernous-cloud-installation-swiss-pavilion-venice-architecture-biennale-2016/ [Accessed: 4 November 2021].

Van der Ploeg, M., Vihervaara, A., Tavor, L., Bosshard, A. (2018), *Svizzera 240: House Tour*, Adam Jasper ed. "House Tour: Views of the Unfinished Interior," Zurich, Park Books, pp. 150–3.

ON THE TECTONIC THRESHOLD OF INNOVATION.
Between Architectural Object and Architectural Act

Ozan Soya

Ozan Soya is an architect, trained at Izmir Institute of Technology. After completing his master study in History of Architecture at Istanbul Technical University, he developed an academic career and taught at Başkent University in Ankara. Since 2019, he is a DAAD Doctoral Research Fellow at TU Berlin Department of Architectural Theory. His doctoral study focuses on the contemporary evolution of tectonic thinking in architecture and its relationship with architectural historiography.

Structure, Construction, and Tectonic Culture

Should we need to think about innovation in architecture through the object of architecture or the act of architecture? There are two basic concepts that we need to look at to give a better answer to this question. These are the fundamental concepts: *structure* and *construction*. Architectural theorist Eduard F. Sekler in his 1965 article *Structure, Construction, Tectonics* describes the difference between them, defining the concept of structure as a resulting product and construction as a *process* (Sekler, 1967).

In light of this clear definition, a structure is a sum of load-bearing elements or principles that sustain the standing against gravity. From a mathematical point of view, it is the sum of three-dimensional geometric values. According to Sekler's understanding, the concept of construction, on the other side, is a collection of information and methods on how a building or an architectural product comes into the real world. In other words, by adding the dimension of time to the concept of structure, architecture performs a real-world physical action.

It is pointless to talk about performing an architecture that can't stand. For this reason, the concept of structure remains a prerequisite when it comes to architectural practice. Therefore, contemporary technological advancements in properties of building materials and methods of construction both affect architectural products and their applications. High-strength and lightweight materials offer structurally wider design opportunities, while technical advancements in montage and assembly enable fast, error-free, and complicated architectural productions.

However, according to Sekler, there is one more area of knowledge within the architectural practice that cannot be explained by the conceptions of structure and construction. Sekler introduces *tectonics* as an interrelated term: "a certain expressivity arising from the statistical resistance of constructional form in such a way that the resultant expression could not be accounted for in terms of structure and construction alone"(ibidem). This definition, by its very nature, describes tectonics as a transcendent area of knowledge above the concepts of structure and construction. It surpasses, leaves them behind, and enters an area that we cannot access directly by objective methods. Thus, the field of tectonic architecture goes beyond the concepts of structure and construction and is moved to a cultural domain.

The cultural aspect of architectural object is also widely discussed by British architectural theorist Kenneth Frampton in his book *Studies in Tectonic Culture* (1995). Frampton's ideas on tectonics strongly depend on the ideas of 19th-century architectural theoretician Gottfried Semper (1989), who believes that art begins with simple and practical acts that are directly related to the natural laws of objects. For instance, the ornamentation of a textile begins with its practical production, precisely with a knot; and the knot becomes the ontological starting point of the aesthetic profoundness of the textile. Semper here proposes that ornamental systems of architecture derive from architecture's functional and structural needs. Frampton basically takes over Sekler's way of

thought which corresponds more than mere building, concerning thoughtful construction, and elaborates on the concepts "structural-technical" and "structural-symbolic" presented in Semper's *Bekleidung* (dressing) theory (2004). Over this fundamental distinction of Semper, Frampton establishes his own duality by positioning the two opposite aspects of building: *representational* versus *ontological*. He also extends this distinction to a new category by slightly shifting the duality to (*representationally*) *atectonic* vs. (*ontologically*) *tectonic*,[2] where atectonic is utilized to "describe a manner in which the expressive interaction of load and support in architecture is visually neglected or obscured" (1995).

These distilled dualities simply propose that architectural innovation cannot be easily reduced to the technical production of objects, where all objects come from the heritage of the ethnographic and cultural world that existed within architectural practice as an intrinsic intertwinement.

Innovation Through Today's Tectonics

Frampton's definitions of (*representationally*) *atectonic* and (*ontologically*) *tectonic*, basically fit the idea of perceiving architectural practice as more than an object, accepting it as a cultural activity that holds the potential to fill semantic gaps in broader symbolic contexts. With this regard, if we turn back to our very first question on whether to think of innovation through the object of architecture or the act of architecture, applying this question to tectonic theory creates two nutritious areas of discussion.

On the one side, a call for authenticity with a significant focus on architectural detail and ethnography provides broader cultural contexts for the object of architecture, which is expected to sustain its semantic features. With this understanding, an honest craft of detailing is seen as the rescuer of the semantic aspect of architecture. Accordingly, today, many architects conceive tectonic expressivity as a virtuous struggle for filling the semantic gaps within the practice, with a particular focus on the object of architecture (Fig. 1).

On the other side, contemporary socio-cultural tendencies provide opportunities for adaptations and ad-

vancements to the act of architecture. This second area of discussion refers to a pluralistic notion that brings fragmented cultural tendencies into architectural practice. With this, external strategies fight for space within architectural discourse. Contemporary socio-cultural and technological issues including neo-liberalism and digital technology are in this group of debates that contextualize the practice of architecture (Fig. 2).

These independent areas have been melting their strict borders, starting to penetrate the domains of each other with the growth and adaptation of technologies, however presumably we are in a transition period. Regarding the innovative practice in archi-

Figure 1
Herzog & de Meuron's design for Olympic Stadium of Beijing, 2008. The building represents an ultimate condition of craft detailing with ethnographic connotations. (Wikimedia Commons. Accessed March 15, 2021.
https://commons.wikimedia.org/wiki/File:Beijing_national_stadium.jpg)

Figure 2
OMA's CCTV Headquarters, 2012. One of the iconic buildings of the neo-liberal regime of
complexity, with the integration of technological devices into the architectural program.
(Wikimedia Commons. Accessed March 15, 2021.
https://commons.wikimedia.org/wiki/File:China_Central_Television_Headquarters_1.jpg)

tecture, oscillating between these two tendencies shows that today's architecture can not be easily reduced to a singular understanding. Perhaps, an innovative architectural practice would be inevitably open to both cultural and technological interactions. Neither the virtuous crafting to accept the object of architecture as a focus, nor the notion for adaptations of the act of architecture to socio-cultural tendencies is solely capable of giving a singular notion to an expected *socio-technological* architectural practice.

By progressing through a tectonic threshold, as architects, we need to think even more extensively about the reconciliation of all technological and cultural content into a total experience of architectural innovation.

Notes
[1] Semper classifies four elements that he consideres to have existed in all primitive cultures. Through these elements, he connects architectural style to oldest practical craftsmanship and past artistic expressions of existed cultures.
[2] Frampton, Studies, 20. For the term atectonic, Frampton cites a subsequent essay of Eduard F. Sekler, which deals with Josef Hoffmann's masterwork Stoclet House built in Brussels in 1911. See Eduard F. Sekler (1967), "The Stoclet House by Josef Hoffmann," in Essays in the History of Architecture Presented to Rudolf Wittkower. London, Phaidon Press, pp. 230–1.

References
Frampton, K. (1995), *Studies in Tectonic Culture: The Poetics of Construction in Nineteenth and Twentieth Century Architecture*, John Cava ed., Cambridge, The MIT Press.
Sekler, E.F. (1965), *Structure, Construction, Tectonics*, "Structure in Art and in Science," Gyorgy Kepes ed., New York, George Braziller Press, pp. 89-95.
Sekler, E.F. (1967), *The Stoclet House by Josef Hoffmann*, "Essays in the History of Architecture Presented to Rudolf Wittkower," London, Phaidon Press, pp. 230–1.

Semper, G. (1989) *The Four Elements of Architecture and Other Writings*, trans. by Harry Francis Mallgrave and Wolfgang Hermann, Cambridge, New York, Cambridge University Press.
Semper, G. (2004), *Style in the Technical and Tectonic Arts; or, Practical Aesthetics*, trans. by Harry Francis Mallgrave and Michael Robinson, Los Angeles, Getty Publications.

JOHN RUSKIN, ARCHITECTURAL INNOVATION IN ANONYMITY.
The Creative Process of a Discipline
Matheus Cartocci

Matheus Cartocci is currently an architect and PHD fellow in Architettura. Storia e Progetto at Politecnico di Torino. He graduates in Politecnico di Milano with the Master's thesis Ontology of the Void, being awarded with a cum laude grade. After his intense working experience in Milan on large scale projects for urban transformations, he is interested in researching through his PHD fellowship the relation between Architecture and Morality: starting from the historical questions addressed in the XIX century with figures such as John Ruskin, Gottfried Semper, Lev Tolstoj to come the contemporary scenario of architecture.

Figure 1
Image elaboration by the author

Innovation is associated to a certain idea of performativity and positive advancement, usually in the sphere of technologies and controlled actions. The scientific methodology is considered to be the most efficient method to study and foresee these actions.

Cambridge Dictionary defines innovation as "the use of a new idea or method" (dictionary.cambridge.org), which implies a vague notion of instrumentality towards a determined goal and a specific usage.

When a third object is mechanical and capable of a specific work, it can be subjected to innovation and when the energy required to produce that given work diminishes, innovation is associated to *performance*.

Once a final objective is set, innovation is a *new way of doing*[1] an action in order to achieve the results. This paper identifies in John Ruskin's writings, a precise definition of the objective of any social being with transformative capacities: the betterment of the collective society through individual revision.

Moreover paraphrasing Ruskin, architecture is defined as a highly efficient tool for this type of work, *when applied in the direction* intended.

The Objective of an Action

In 19th-century Victorian London, during the highest peak of England's second industrial revolution, in an era of great scientific advancements and technological innovations, the scholar John Ruskin stands as one of the central figures of the century. His visions are different to the newly compartmentalized academic subjects. His interests begin with geology and grow through art and architecture, to finally land in economics and sociology.

In *The Stones of Venice*, with his most famous chapter *The Nature of Gothic*, Ruskin tackles in 1851 the very idea of innovation related to the new conditions of labor in the industrialized Victorian London, and brings the focus not on the goods' production yet on its producers:

"We have much studied and much perfected, of late, the great civilised invention of the division of labour; only we give it a false name. It is not, truly speaking, the labour that is divided; but the men divided into mere segments of men—broken into small fragments and crumbs of life; so that all the little pieces of intelligence that is left in a man is not enough to make a pin, or a nail" (Ruskin, 2009: 165).

In 1866 John Ruskin publishes *The Crown of Wild Olive* where he groups a series of lectures delivered in 1864 and 1865. Among these, the author re-proposes with *Traffic* the lecture that took place in Bradford (England) in 1864.

In this paper he presents his views about architecture and its role in society, after maturing his new beliefs on political economy and social innovation. When invited by the wealthy businessmen of the town of Bradford to suggest an architectural style for a local exchange building that was to be built, Ruskin suggests rather to reconsider the initial reasons and questions that called for a new public construc-

ARCHITECTURE – AGENCY

Matheus Cartocci - John Ruskin, Architectural Innovation in Anonymity. The Creative Process of a Discipline

tion. He affirms that a specific architectural style is of no meaning whatsoever if the community that builds it does not live in accordance: it would produce just a superficial image of a building and not a true manifestation of a collective intentionality, and fade rather quickly in time. In this occasion, one of the most famous Victorian defenders of gothic architecture—Ruskin became well known for his thorough apology of Venetian architecture (Ruskin, 2009)—affirms "the Gothic rose also to its loveliest, most fantastic, and finally, most foolish dreams; and in those dreams was lost" (Ruskin, 1997: 240). In the century of harsh dispute between gothic revival and neo-classicism, the author invites his audience to go beyond minor stylistic choices and actually focus on the social relevance of erecting a truly collective building. Ruskin advocates for a more equal and just society, where architecture is necessarily the tool to achieve this goal, since it is the final manifestation of all arts, and among all arts it is the only that can stand the passing of time, and memory (Ruskin, 2007: 211).

John Ruskin's work can be of great use for today's understanding of social and political justice not for his aphorisms and answers yet for the clarity of his questions: for his capacity of setting a communal target that can justify the expenses of a collective endeavor.

"But if you can fix some conception of a true human state of life to be striven for—life for all men as for yourselves —if you can determine some honest and simple order of existence; following those trodden ways of wisdom, which are pleasantness, and seeking her quiet and withdrawn paths, which are peace;—then, and so sanctifying wealth into "commonwealth," all your art, your literature, your daily labours, your domestic affection, and citizen's duty, will join and increase into one magnificent harmony. You will know then how to build, well enough; you will build with stone well, but with flesh better; temples not made with hands, but riveted of hearts; and that kind of marble, crimson-veined, is indeed eternal." (Ruskin, 1997: 249).

The Instrumental Use of a Tool

In the second half of the 19th century John Ruskin advocated for a usage of designing and building that went beyond architectural styles and mere symbolic decorations.

One hundred years later several thinkers and practitioners, such as Rafael Moneo, address the instrumental use of typologies and models in architecture along with their efficiency in the contemporary practice. With his essay *On Typology* (Moneo, 1978), Moneo writes of architecture and its types related to the large span of time and history, for a better understanding of *innovation* in the practice. Some of the questions that implicitly seem to arise are: When does the discipline encounter a leap forward that is characteristic of an innovative change (Britannica Encyclopedia)? What are the conditions that need to occur in order to have a significant transformation in the linearity of history, in evolution? What are the instruments architects may use to foster this shift and is it possible to recognize it during the action?

In the paper Moneo suggests two very interesting characteristics that could reveal if a contribution by a single or collective are truly significant in its innovation: *generality* and *anonymity*. Two features that were very dear to Ruskin's understanding of the original gothic architecture (Ruskin, 2009).

"By looking at architectural objects as groups, as types, susceptible to differentiation in their secondary aspects, the partial obsolescences appearing in them can be appraised, and consequently one can act to change them. The type can thus be thought of as the *frame within which change* operates, a necessary term to the continuing dialect required by history. From this point of view, the type, rather than being a 'frozen mechanism' to produce architecture, becomes a way of denying the past, as well as a way of looking at the future.
In this continuous process of transformation, the architect can extrapolate from the type, changing its use; he can distort ... he can overlap ... The list of different mechanisms is extensive - it is a function of the inventiveness of architects.
The most intense moments in architectural development are those when a new type appears. One of the architect's greatest efforts, and thus the most deserving of admiration, is made when he gives up a known type and clearly sets out to formulate a new one. Often, external events—such as new techniques or changes in society—are responsible for impelling him toward this creation of a new type, in accordance with a dialectical relationship with history. But sometimes the invention of a new type is the result of an exceptional personality, capable of entering into architecture with its own voice.
When a new type emerges—when an architect is able to describe a new set of formal relations which generates a new group of buildings or elements —then that architect's contribution has reached the level of generality and anonymity that characterises architecture as a discipline." (Moneo, 1978: 27–8).

This last sentence is particularly relevant since it associates to the discipline of architecture the universal characters of anonymity and generality and by writing this, the author seems to understand it differs from the arts and their history of personal achievements related to the artists; it rather comes closer to the sciences and their objectivity in method and goals.

This anonymity could also be intended as impersonality and detachment from the results of one's work: belonging no longer to a single's experience, yet to history's major timeline. As Simone Weil writes so well in her *Écrits de Londres et dernières lettres*,

"What is sacred in science is the truth. What is sacred in art is the beauty. The truth and the beauty are impersonal. This is all too evident. If a boy makes a mistake in a math-

Matheus Cartocci - John Ruskin, Architectural Innovation in Anonymity. The Creative Process of a Discipline

ematical addition, the mistake carries a trace of his person. If he proceeds in a perfectly correct manner, his person is absent from the entire operation. Perfection is impersonal. The person within us corresponds with the part of us that is error and sin. All the efforts of the mystics were always directed to remove any part of their soul that said 'I'" (Weil, 2012: 19).

Learning from John Ruskin, architecture becomes truly innovative, not just in style, when it is used as a tool for a collective endeavour that is larger than any personal aspiration or temporary fashion. Innovation can be seen as a happening that occurs on a truly singular and subjective sphere, springing from the awareness of single people that take part in a larger collective, and only in a second moment arises to a state of anonymity and impersonality.

As Siegrfied Giedion has coined the term *anonymous history* in *Mechanization Takes Command* (Giedion, 1970: 2–4), we could conclude: innovation in architecture can be considered as such when it is an anonymous addition to the line of historical events.

Notes
1 "Innovation, the creation of a new way of doing something, whether the enterprise is concrete (e.g., the development of a new product) or abstract (e.g., the development of a new philosophy or theoretical approach to a problem)," Britannica, accessed January 12, 2020, https://www.britannica.com/topic/innovation-creativity.

References
Giedion, S. (1970) (1948, first edition), *Mechanization takes command*, New York, Oxford University Press.
Moneo, R. (1978), *On Typology*, "Oppositions," MIT Press, n. 13.
Ruskin, J. (1997) (1860, first edition), *Unto this Last and other writings*, ed. Wilmer C., London, Penguin Classics.
Ruskin, J. (2007) (1849, first edition), *Le sette lampade dell'architettura*, Milano, Jaca Book.
Ruskin, J. (2009) (1851, first edition), *The Stones of Venice Volume II (of 3)*, "The Project Gutemberg eBook," December 31, 2009 (release date), [eBook #30755], Available at: http://www.gutenberg.org/files/30755/30755-h/30755-h.html.
Weil, S. (2012) (1943, first edition), *La persona e il sacro*, Milano, Adelphi Edizione Editore.
Cambridge Dictionary [online], Available at: https://dictionary.cambridge.org/dictionary/english/innovation [Accessed January 12, 2020].
Britannica [online], Available at: https://www.britannica.com/topic/innovation-creativity [Accessed January 12, 2020].

A CRITICAL INVESTIGATION INTO TECHNOPOIESIS OF ARCHITECTURE

Melek Pınar Uz Baki

Melek Pınar Uz Baki is an architect and a PhD candidate, affiliated at Middle East Technical University (METU), Architecture Faculty. Her doctoral research investigates architectural making with its expanded means in philosophy of technology, technics and aesthetics. She has received various awards due to her academic performance while conducting several research projects, architectural & urban practices, theoretical & archival works. Currently, she is working as an instructor at Başkent University, Department of Architecture.

Architecture as a Creative Making and a Critical Act

Architectural work connects knowledge and imagination through exploration of form, new technics, articulation of materials, and new contexts informed through making within cultural, environmental, and political discourse. This physicality can be considered as an end product following a notational, mechanical, or digital progression that developed with different modes of representation as to the repositories of a design idea(l). The variability of hand-making in craftsmanship has transformed into a literal production of identicality by the innovation of machine making (Carpo, 2011). It has brought into two other challenging notions; material possibility and standardization. However, it also transforms the ways of thinking; from self- esteem into social awareness. The production of particular small-scale solutions emerged with the intersection of digitalization and socio-cultural circuit. In digital-making, technology and *poiesis* as the indispensable components of *techné* construct a close dialogue between human and machine as never seen before. The emergent digital technology in making activity opens up new ways of thinking on new materiality, new possibilities of different modes of making, machine learning, social integration, and relatedly, different alternatives on different modes of living and particular design solutions for generic problems. Beyond being just a mere construction of a building, an architectural project is a both innovative and interpretive action that offers a translation from an inquiry into an act by the aid of critical thinking, design, and production of knowledge. Architectural making with its process, tools, and actors can be interpreted as a disciplinary work and a knowledge production in which theoretical and creative approaches are readable.[1]

Architectural Making as Techné

The word *techné* is "a state involving true reason concerned with the bringing into existence of production"[2] (Aristotle, 1999). The *logos* of making is a long-established yet significant notion in questioning and tracing the possibilities of alternative ways of making in both the discipline of architecture and different related fields.[3] *Techné* denotes not only the technics of making yet signifies building of unique knowledge. It is an expedient agent to generate alternative design solutions through the project of critical, innovative architecture and its agency.

Techné proposes generative processes in circumventing limits, learning experimentation on physical specialty, material conditions, tectonics, and orientation of tools. Unique knowledge can be comprehended by the physical engagement (either of the human actor(s) or machine) in the act of making. The potential of innovation is hidden in mistakes, errors, unexpected results in the process that can open a new perspective for re-projections. Concerning learning by making, *techné* is an operative notion in the production of particular knowledge. Constructed on the relationship between revealing and doing, architectural work is a non-static process that is open to explorations of unique traces, new alterations, and interventions.

As a practice of inquiry, architectural innovation is the production of responsive meaning, which subordinate to both constant and ever-changing conditions. The conventional account of making trajectory in architecture within the scope of a design problem, maker(s), and alternate possibilities have been enhanced through the changing nature of design thinking, tools, and methods from hand-making to digital turn. Besides its practical appeals and evolving discourse, developing tools, technics and technologies have caused the disciplinary transformation of architectural thinking as well as the ways of practicing, accumulating, and interpreting architectural knowledge and experiments. As each technological development invalidates the previous one, the change in technologies and technics accompanying human action becomes a sign for future transformations that can be more effective than previously thought. Architecture within the current information age has become an inseparable part of an emergent system of flow. As a matter of discursive, practical, and theoretical setting, architecture has gained an openness for pluralistic participation, multiplicative operations, variable end products, and learning processes generated from an immediate presence of technology and *poiesis*.

Technopoiesis of Architecture

Technology as an integral constituent of *techné* has constantly evolved and activated various disciplines together while encouraging new perspectives for generative making. It offers alternative possibilities as an initiator for expressive technics, the generator of new forms, alternative solutions, and different modes of architectural production. Assuming each technological development corresponds to both a theoretical and a practical novelty one can claim that architectural interventions through technological or technical advancements have the power to direct the processes of making through design or production of new spaces. Besides socio-cultural admissions, contemporary developments and new approaches affect the ways that architects think and make as they are effective on theoretical elaborations and practical applications. Tool, technic, and technology in the process of revealing are significant enablers for the production of specialty and unique knowledge. Furthermore, technology as an ultimate tool for an architect provides recording architectural knowledge and a collection of experiences that can exist only if collected, accumulated, transmitted, and communicated with.

The term *technopoiesis* can be interpreted as a contemporary explication of techné to remind the significance of knowledge production that is generated from the current interrelationship of *poiesis* with technology. By the digital technologies within the changing courses of revealing, material condition, systems of making, the orientation of technics and physical specialty, *techné* has gained a *technopoietic* dimension that refers to a dual existence of technology and revelation through explorations of unique traces, new alterations, interactions, and social consolidations. It can be claimed that technopoiesis has developed a more integrative dialog with the process, the result, and tuehe maker(s) in digital-making when compared with two other modes of making; industrial production and craftsmanship (Carpo, 2011). *Technopoiesis* permits the production of technical alternatives and poietic identities together. The production of particularity relies on proprietary techniques for unique conditions and authorial decisions of different actors. Despite the changing interface, the production of uniqueness still relies on learning activity, interpretation, and manipulation of matter rather than a direct transformation of an ideal. Innovation is now based on digital *poiesis*, machine learning, unpredictable results, and collaborative work.

Conclusive Remarks

By nature, *techné* indicates an emphasis on both the engagement (both human actors and machine) in the act of making (*poiesis*, a process of creation, generation) and also the technical, technological appointments (*episteme*, theoretical knowledge). The theoretical discussions on *techné* in the 21st century through changing and challenging modes of production are still instrumental for architecture to mediate between machined abundance and the modestly humane references. The term *technopoiesis* reminds the innovative sense of knowledge production generated from the unpredictable changes and the interrelationship of *poiesis* and technology. The architectural project as a technopoietic system for innovative thinking and making manifests an innovative dialogue between humans and machines, between experts and users without distorting their hypotheses. The *technopoietic* phenomenon of architectural work refers to something that is open to participation (either machines or individuals), as well as spontaneous in it, but that at the same time

Melek Pinar Uz Baki - A Critical Investigation into Technopoiesis of Architecture

is planned, worked, and premeditated within a disciplinary framework. The generative and innovative potential of *technopoiesis* is hidden in unpredictable variation and facultative qualification resulted from a dialogue between revelation and development. Thus, architecture in the current information age has an expressive and innovative language, relatedly as a part of the historical, cultural, and sociological accumulation. It can act as a *poiesis*, as it is supposed to act, reconstruct an innovative particularity, or resist as a part of a social construct.

This paper as a theoretical inquiry addresses *technopoiesis* in digital making in which the ways of thinking, designing, theorizing, and making architecture have gained an openness for pluralistic participation, multiplicative operations, and particular end products generated from an immediate presence of technology and *poiesis*. It has been both expanded and altered on a more concrete comprehension of the ongoing dynamics of meaning construction hidden within the conception of technopoiesis. It claims that architecture as a *technopoietic* system has the power to transform the project of architecture from a static physical object into an accumulation of knowledge that can move, transform itself for future works, and be interpreted by individuals. Through a search for cooperative associations and generative technologies, the project has the potential to contribute to current architectural theory and practice.

Notes

[1] The ongoing PhD study by M.P. Uz Baki on architectural making in relation to the notion of techné has been conducted since 2016 at Middle East Technical University, Department of Architecture, Ankara, Turkey.

[2] The book is a compilation of 10 books of Aristotle, written on several topics.

[3] For the definition of antique techne see. Plato. Complete Works, John M. Cooper (ed.), Indianapolis: Hackett Publishing Co., 1997, Aristotle. Nicomachean Ethics, second edition, translated by Terence Irwin, Indianapolis: Hackett Publishing, 1999, (originally published in 349 BC), The book is a compilation of 10 books of Aristotle, written on several topics, Robert W. Hall. "Art and Morality in Plato: A Reappraisal," Journal of Aesthetic Education, vol.24, no:3, Autumn 1990, pp. 5–13, http://www.jstor.org/stable/3332795, Accessed October 29, 2017, David Roochnik. *Of Arts and Wisdom: Plato's Understanding of Techné*, University Park: The Penn State University Press, 1996, p. 19, Xenophon. Memorabilia and Oeconomicus, translated by E.C. Marchant, Loeb Classical Library, Cambridge: Harvard University Press, 1979.

References

Aristotle (1999) (Originally in 349 BC), *Nicomachean Ethics*, trans. T. Irwin, Hackett Publishing.

Cooper, H. M. (eds.) (1997), *Plato, Complete Works*, Indianapolis, Hackett Publishing Co.

Hall, R.W. (1990), Art and Morality in Plato: A Reappraisal, "Journal of Aesthetic Education," vol. 24, n. 3, Autumn 1990, pp. 5–13.

Roochnik, D. (1996), *Of Arts and Wisdom: Plato's Understanding of Techné*, University Park, The Penn State University Press.

Xenophon (1979) *Memorabilia and Oeconomicus*, trans. by E.C. Marchant, Loeb Classical Library, Cambridge, Harvard University Press.

Ingold, T. (2013), *Making: Anthropology, Archaeology, Art and Architecture*, London, New York, Routledge Press.

Carpo, M. (2011), *The Alphabet and The Algorithm*, London & Cambridge, The MIT Press.

Sennett, R. (2008), *The Craftsman*, London, Yale University Press.

THE PROMISE OF AN OBJECT.
Design Processes as Processes of Theory Construction

Jörg H. Gleiter

Jörg H. Gleiter is the head of the Chair of Architectural Theory at Technische Universität Berlin. From 2005–12 he was professor of semiotics of the image and aesthetics at the Faculty of Arts and Design of Free University of Bozen-Bolzano (Italy). He holds a PhD in theory of architecture and habilitation in philosophy of architecture, both from Bauhaus-University Weimar. He held guest professorships at Venice International University (Italy), Waseda University (Japan), Bauhaus-University Weimar (Germany), Brown University (USA), and Politecnico di Milano. He has worked as an architect at Eisenman Architects (New York), Leeser Architecture (New York), and at various architects' practices in Italy and Germany. He is the founder and editor of the book series *ArchitekturDenken*. His research topics include: critical theory of sustainability, knowledge transformation, Anthropocene studies, ornament theory, architecture philosophy, and semiotics.

The towering achievement of Leon Battista Alberti (1404–72), the most important theorist to emerge from the Renaissance, was that he single-handedly turned architecture from an autographic art into an allographic art. He insisted on the importance of *lineamenta*, that is to say, on the fixed notation of an architectural design in the form of concrete, scale drawings. However, the decisive innovation was not that an edifice could now be built on the basis of exact drawings without the architect having to be present on the construction site; the real innovation was that, by insisting on allographic notation, Alberti turned the design work into a series of modeling processes, each with its own promise of an object. Ever since then design processes have always moved forward, step by step, from one modeling stage to the next—from the first sketch of an idea through a series of scale models to the realization of the original idea in the finished building. Of course, the design process is shaped by constant shifts between different scales, but whatever that may mean, the overall process advances in a chain of individual modeling stages from the largest to the smallest scale, with the scale of 1:1 as the final model space. Even though this has long since become common practice and an everyday routine, the consequences of designing using particular scales are far-reaching and can scarcely be overestimated.

First Thesis: Alberti's introduction of the notation of designs in fixed, scale drawings saw architecture advancing beyond its purely material-constructional processes and situative presence to the point where it became open to a new intellectualization of its knowledge praxis.

The architectural design process turns, in its own particular way, into a process of theory-construction, in the sense that the design-discovery process (as a creative act) and the theory-construction process (as a reflective act) now become closely interlinked.

Second Thesis: The introduction of design using different scales opens up architecture to the transformation of architectural substance. For every scale has its own specific design potential. At the outset of every modeling process on a particular scale there is a design hypothesis with a specific promise of an object; each also ends with the notion of an object in its actual, realized form. As the design progresses to the next scale, the ensuing new possibilities and insights ensure that the precise form previously arrived at is re-opened and becomes a hypothesis for the new model space.

Third Thesis: As a consequence of this chain of modeling processes architecture is able to absorb the cultural dynamics of its own time. The status of the chain of models comes to the fore, insofar as this is the prerequisite for the absorption of dynamically changing, cultural logic—in all its complexity—into the substance of architecture. This in turn is the prerequisite for the modern concept of architecture that has steadily been evolving since Alberti. This modern concept sees architecture as the main, symbolic form by means of which people—in dynamically shifting cultural force fields—are able to create an environment that is appropriate to their own time, that is meaningful, uniquely suitable for human beings, and different from nature.

The above statements lead to the significant, central thesis for architecture in the digital age, namely that the currently evident crisis in design is not primarily a crisis of creativity but rather a crisis for theory. With rapid prototyping, 3-D printing, BIM, and other forms of computational design making it possible to skip different stages in the scale modeling process and to progress directly from the initial parameters to the 1:1 model, the chain of models has been broken and, consequently, the process of theory-construction has been short-circuited. As a consequence, the likelihood of the current cultural logic being absorbed into the substance of architecture is reduced, if not removed altogether.

Model

Before we go any further, it would be useful to clarify exactly what a model is. In so doing I will make reference to Bernd Mahr and his essay "Das Wissen im Modell" (Mahr, 2014). In Mahr's view, it is models that make the connection between contents and form possible in the first place. They structure this connection with the aid of "symbolic generalizations." And it is through them that knowledge can emerge and become effective. Models are, in his view, "vehicles and benchmarks" for knowledge, without themselves laying claim to knowledge as such. Models constitute an ordered system by which—in any disciplinary matrix, such as architecture—things can advance to the point of recognizability.

It is models that provide a means for connecting contents and form. As such they are the vehicles for the knowledge associated with a disciplinary matrix. Or to put it another way: knowledge is realized—with reference to the disciplinary matrix—in the model. In the model it comes to light, by dint of symbolic generalizations, and is subsequently exemplified in a tangible mass-model or in a tangible drawing. We must therefore distinguish between

1. *the disciplinary matrix.* Architecture as a specific knowledge-praxis is a disciplinary matrix of this kind;

2. *model spaces* with their generative potential for architectural knowledge. These model spaces could take the form of hand-done sketches, outline drawings, or perspectival drawings;

3. *symbolic generalizations*, through which knowledge becomes representable. Examples of symbolic generalizations could be lines, continuous or dotted, thick or thin, colored or just black; and

4. an actual representation in the sense of an *exemplification or an exemplar.* That is the actual drawing or the actual wooden model on a particular scale. In this knowledge is expressed and exemplified; it becomes visible and legible.

It should be noted that in the model spaces pertaining to a particular disciplinary matrix, there is an objectification of personal, intuitive, implicit knowledge and mere opinions alike. With the aid of the model, knowledge develops in the transition from the original subject-reference and becomes "liberated thought-content that is both storable and communicable," as Mahr puts it. It is no longer purely subjective, because it is now tied to the realm of operation of a particular model space and its symbolic generalizations. Knowledge owes its objectification to the structuring achieved through the model. Accordingly, there can be no knowledge without a model. However, if knowledge can only be rendered visible with the aid of symbolic generalizations in connection with a model space, then it should also be noted that within any given model space it is only possible to represent certain forms of knowledge. And the model space both determines the level of freedom and potential for the creative process and sets the limits for the latter. This could be described as the pre-structuring or pre-determination of knowledge by the model.

This is what Friedrich Nietzsche meant when he talked of tools being involved in our thought processes: "You are right—our writing utensils contribute to our thoughts," as he put it in a letter to his friend Heinrich Köselitz (Nietzsche, 1986). This is interesting in epistemological terms, insofar as Nietzsche conveys the idea that tools are themselves model spaces, within which knowledge attains structure and visibility. Tools have a certain generative potential for certain forms of knowledge, in the same way that they exclude others. In other words: the epistemic structure of tools informs the knowledge that is attained through them. And this explains references to the "knowledge within the model." But architects know only too well that creative intuition cannot be separated from their drawing materials. A 6B pencil can be exactly the right tool for a quick sketch of an idea. It belongs within the model space of quick sketches, but not in the model space of detailed planning, where an HB pencil or even a 2H pencil would be much more useful.

And this is precisely what happens in the design stages in various model spaces, for instance on the scale of 1:1000, 1:100, 1:10, and even 1:1. In each of these there is a transition from subjective ideas to their objectification. The knowledge that can be represented is tied to the given model space, to the relevant scale and the corresponding symbolic expressions or means of representation. Each scale provides the possibility of transferring cultural contents into architectural substance, which is then linked and articulated in architecture through materials, forms, and situations. On a scale of 1:500, for instance, spaces with approximate sizes and proportions can be related to each other. However, in discussions of a tiling layout or the precise construction of a wall or a ceiling, the scale 1:500 provides little useful insight, because there is no form of representation that works on this scale and hence no possibility of symbolic generalization. Be they load-bearing or not load-bearing, be they cast in concrete in situ, brick-built, or constructed as partition walls, all walls look more or less the same on a scale of 1:500. On the next scale up, 1:200, it is possible to discern differences in the thickness of walls, on a scale of 1:100 or 1:50 the construction of the wall can be shown, different layers are visible and it is possible to show how walls, doors, and windows relate to each other. On any given scale only one set of knowledge can be rendered visible.

However, a problematic area has emerged for architecture in the digital age. It concerns the matter of the constitution of architectural knowledge in computational design. What happens when—during the computational design process—the hand-done sketch and its potential for knowledge no longer have a part to play? What does it mean—in a parametric design process—if the initial parameters transfer directly into their materialization in a 3-D model? If certain scales and models can be skipped, the customary chain of the modeling process is broken. In these circumstances, how can the transfer of cultural logic into the substance of architecture now be achieved? Or: in the context of a digital process, which cultural knowledge is expressed and rendered visible in architecture?

Pictoriality

Having sketched in the relationship between model, knowledge, and the chain of modeling, let us now take a look at the processes within the individual model spaces, that is to say, let us turn to the actual design process. And this is where the concept of pictoriality comes into play. Our point of reference here is the work of Ferdinand Fellmann. In "Wovon sprechen die Bilder," which might be literally translated as "What are the pictures talking about?" Fellmann discusses the notion of pictoriality in terms that are also relevant to any modeling process, which always involves some form of pictoriality—in all its "provocative indeterminacy" (Fellmann, 1997: 151).

Fellmann regards pictures as more than just a "subordinate class of signs" (Fellmann, 1997: 147). The fact that they are different from linguistic signs does not mean that they are subordinate to the latter. The function of linguistic signs, and others, is communication and description; as a rule, they point to that which is absent, while they themselves are almost nothing. That is to say, signs are not the thing itself, they merely point to it. The word "tiger" is not a tiger, it only represents that animal. Pictures, by contrast, are notable for their presentness. Their prime task, as images, is not to point to objects. Pictures are distinguished from pure signs by the fact that they are what they are, in their presence in a particular place. And the picture ensures that that which is given in the picture is present, no more and no less. Fellmann describes this as the "state-of-being" of pictures.

As Fellmann shows, pictures "articulate the field of the visible according to a different principle to that which applies to concepts" (Fellmann, 1997: 147). In contrast to words, which, as a rule, are used intentionally, pictures do not talk of intentions to the same extent. And Fellmann's suggestion is that this applies not only in the case of painters who paint badly; on the contrary, it is in the nature of pictures that they are not entirely beholden to the author's intentions. The reason for this is that by definition and due to the material nature of pictures, their various qualities cannot be separated and combined at will, as the uninitiated often imagine. The painted picture always retains a certain openness with regard to the painter's intentions. A painting never wholly matches the painter's intentions. Fellmann thus talks of a unique, open realm of "pictoriality." And this pictoriality indicates the state-of-being of the paintings in their visibility.

The decisive factor is that a painted view of an object only becomes a picture when it is seen in isolation from the other three views. Bearing in mind Edmund Husserl's "Analysis of Perception" it could be said that in a painted picture a certain "irrealization of objectivity" ensues. For the object, which can be shown perspectively in up to three views in the painting (but no more than that) is not defined in its other views. As Charles Sanders Peirce has said, it is not quite *fully determined*. We can fantasize all sorts of things into it, because we cannot know how the painter imagined the back of the object. Paintings present us with almost endless possibilities in that respect. In other words, the object in the painting promises more than the real object that it is referring to could ever keep. This is why Fellmann talks of the "provocative indeterminacy" of paintings in their pictoriality and of the promise of the object as a sign of pictoriality.

And this is what distinguishes the design process at every stage of modeling: the fact that the sketch or the drawing is initially determined by this degree of openness and provocative indeterminacy. In every model space the object is initially provocatively open. It formulates the promise of an object that is defined with ever greater precision during the course of the design process. At the outset everything in a model space is provocatively open; at the conclusion—depending on the knowledge potential of that particular model space—everything is fixed. Then the scale is changed. What was fixed and precise on the previous scale now—with the new scale—regains the status of pictoriality and, in this new model space, is once again provocatively open.

Abduction

In light of what has been said so far, the basis of the creative design process is within the chain of models, and what has been "established" in one model space becomes a "surprising event" in the subsequent model space. It is a surprising event because it does not yet conform to the rules of the new model space. In the context of the new model space, that which was previously concrete turns into a hypothesis and a surprising event. And as a hypothesis of this kind it becomes the point of departure for the creative design process in the new model space.

However, we only describe this as a creative process if, in the subsequent stage of the design process, the removal of the surprise is not achieved merely by ironing it out, by standardizing it, and adapting it to the existing system of rules. We describe it as a creative process if the removal of the surprise is achieved by introducing a new rule within the disciplinary matrix. This form of creative approach is described by Peirce as abduction. The process of abduction creates a new system of symbolic connections, a new order. It creates new relationships between the elements of architecture, and also ensures that architecture itself enters into a new relationship with the prevailing cultural dynamics.

In the context of his *theory of logical operations* Peirce defines abduction as a form of argument that arises from a "puzzling fact" (Wirth, 2000: 137), that is to say, from an experience that is at odds with an active or passive conviction. "Abduction is the process of forming an explanatory hypothesis. It is the only logical operation which introduces any new idea" (Peirce, 1931: 171). The abductive process consists in the generalization of the surprising experience, in other words, in the formation of a new theory that does not reinforce the old rules but contributes to the creation of a new system. Various architects have referred to comparable processes. Oswald Mathias Ungers meant something similar when—using the terminology of classical rhetoric—he talked of designing with metaphors and—very much in the spirit of Peirce's abduction or Mahr's model theory—saw pictorial metaphors as a means to transpose subjective associations into plausible arguments. In his book *Morphologie, City, Metaphors*, Ungers (1982: 11) states that "a model [is] itself a theoretical complexity, which introduces either a visual form or a conceptual order into the components of complex situations."

Ungers recommends a metaphorical design process, in the spirit of pictoriality, through which possible solutions can be pre-structured. Or, as Gerhard Kurz puts it in *Metapher, Allegorie, Symbol*: "Metaphors function as action- and knowledge-orienting models. They have the capacity to create new realities and to change our system of concepts" (Kurz, 2004: 23). In that sense, metaphors serve in the design process as hypotheses, which instigate the epistemological process of abduction, where abduction is the "first step of all processes of sign interpretation that seek to couple observation and theory."

Theory

It is important to note that the process of abductive theory-construction is a creative process, not for the sake of the subjectivity of the architect and not for the sake of the new, but as a means to incorporate a changing cultural logic into architecture. The actual creative process thus resides not in the free combination of images and metaphors, but precisely in the extrapolation of rules that, in the spirit of abduction, make it possible to integrate metaphors into the model space—by extending existing theories. The processes of modeling are processes of theory-construction specifically if, on the basis of an initial hypothesis, the changed cultural logic finds its way (through abduction) into the substance of architecture and changes the theoretical conception of the latter.

This new insight allows us to make a direct connection between Peirce's *theory of logical operations* and Mahr's *Wissen im Modell*. Both are underpinned by a triadic model of epistemology. Mahr talks of the three states of being-a-model or the three identities of an object as model, which, on closer examination, correspond to the three logical operations described by Peirce. Mahr distinguishes firstly the "*object in itself* (qualified as a model), that has its own form of appearance" (Mahr, 2014: 11), for instance, as a text, a body, a house, and so on. Secondly, Mahr talks of the *model of something* which is the result of "what can broadly speaking be regarded as induction, whereby views, experiences, measurements, features...come to be part of the model...through selection, generalization and by being tied to a new form and representation" (Mahr, 2014: 12). Thirdly Mahr talks of a *model for something*, whereby, in the sense of Peirce's deduction, "the contents embodied in form and representation are set free again, by the use of the model, and can be transferred to another object" (Mahr, 2014: 12). Importantly, in order to be able to justify any judgment of the state of being-a-model, there have to be "factors that confirm this threefold identity" (Mahr, 2014: 12). Interestingly Mahr associates the *model of something* and *model for something* with Peirce's operations of induction (model of something) and deduction (model for something). If one takes the threefold nature of the state of being-a-model seriously (Mahr does not mention this fact), then it seems eminently reasonable to make the connection between the third form of the *object in itself* and the third operation described by Peirce, namely, abduction. The *object in itself*—in its purest form—stands for the hypothesis, for pictoriality, for a pre-theoretical standpoint in the modeling process, that is to say, for the surprising event that, as we have to conclude, first has to create its own new legality through induction, as defined by Peirce. In order to lead to the construction of a theory, it must first be a *model of something* (induction), so that it can become, in the next stage, a *model for something* (deduction), that is to say, it lays down the law and hence becomes theoretically binding.

A normal modeling process, one could say in conclusion, is dominated by deduction and induction, in other words, by the model for something and the model of something. Nothing new comes of this: the outcome is already familiar, in keeping with familiar rules. The stage of the hypothesis falls by the wayside, the object in itself is repressed. It is only abduction, on the basis of a hypothesis, that can set in motion the creative process with is potential to absorb new parameters into the model space of a particular disciplinary matrix, such as architecture, that is to say, to introduce new cultural contents into architectural substance.

If we therefore come to the conclusion that digital design processes interrupt the modeling chain, then the process of abduction, the creative design process, and hence the continuing construction of theory in architecture will also be interrupted. Contrary to some opinions and despite new forms and figures, the construction of theory is short-circuited in strictly algorithmic design processes. In that sense parametric-algorithmic design processes are distinguished by a lack of theory-construction. With reference to computational design processes the crisis in creativity basically proves to be a crisis in theory-construction, triggered by the partial interruption of the modeling chain, that is to say, by the interruption of the process of abductions. Without these, the processes of the absorption of cultural logic into the substance of architecture may not be halted altogether, but they will certainly be made more difficult.

Translated from the German by Fiona Elliott

References

Fellmann, F. (1997), *Wovon sprechen die Bilder. Aspekte der Bild-Semiotik*, in Recki B., Wiesing, L. (eds.), "Bild und Reflexion," Munich, Wilhelm Fink Verlag.

Kurz, G. (2004), *Metapher, Allegorie, Symbol*, Göttingen, Vandenhoeck & Ruprecht.

Mahr, B. (2014), *Das Wissen im Modell*. Available at: https://www.flp.tuberlin.de/fileadmin/fg53/KIT-Reports/r150.pdf [Accessed: March 12, 2014].

Nietzsche, F. (1986), *Letter written in late February 1882*, trans. from idem, in Giorgio Colli and Mazzino Montinari (eds.) "Sämtliche Briefe, Kritische Studienausgabe in 8 Bd.," Berlin, Walter De Gruyter, vol. 6.

Peirce, C.S. (1931), *Collected Papers of Charles Sanders Peirce*, vol. 5, P. Weiss, C. Hartshorne, & A.W. Burks (eds.), Cambridge, MA, Harvard University Press.

Ungers, O. M. (1982), *Morphologie, City, Metaphors*, Cologne, Verlag der Buchhandlung Walther König.

Wirth, U. (2000), *Zwischen Zeichen und Hypothese: Für eine abduktive Wende in der Sprachphilosophie*, in Wirth, U. et al (eds.), "Die Welt als Zeichen und Hypothese. Perspektiven des semiotischen Pragmatismus von Charles S. Peirce," Suhrkamp, Frankfurt am Main.

Time and Technology of the Architectural Concept. (Sur)réalité Virtuelle
Snežana Vesni⊠

In this text, I thematize the creation of the (architectural) concept and creation with the concept, in order to present a new argument that the production of the object of architecture is a consequence of the creation by concept. The concept translates one form of reality into another. In these deconstructions of reality and the object, we find the potential for ever-novel creation and an always new reality. In the changes of *modes of reality*, the object always has a new reality. The non-identity created among various forms of existence of a single object creates new '*potency*' for new objective reality. In the text, I present the phrase *"surréalité virtuelle"* to express my idea of the creation of the new conceptual potential at the point of absence, lack, or inexistence of the architectural object.

The Poietic and Symbolic Place of the Project in the Contemporary Architectural Situation
Pierre Caye

Contemporary architecture is in a paradoxical situation. The project, which played such an important role in the Modern Movement, has been neglected from the theoretical point of view, even though in practice architecture cannot do without it for legal and economic reasons as much as for constructive reasons. But architecture as an art form no longer depends on the project. The project is no longer the condition for its symbolic establishment. However, I do not believe that the deconstruction of the architectural project is an expression of its freedom, particularly in relation to the construction industry. This article shows under which conditions and in which forms the project can prove to be a critical power of liberation even more than an instance of order and organization.

Diagrams beyond the Avant-Garde.
Several Reasons Why Diagrams Are (Still) Worth Making in Architecture
Andrea Alberto Dutto

Making diagrams beyond the avant-garde means recognizing in the ordinary use of these representational tools an architectural competence. The essay presents some reasons why making diagrams is not a matter of style but a technical and epistemological issue. The diagram can be considered as an innovative tool insofar as one renounces to recognize a value in temporary architectural trends. The essay proposes a reflection on the diagram as a contingent medium. Unlike the avant-garde: making diagrams does not constitute a value in itself.

Documents, Monuments, Lineaments.
on Pre-existing Elements of Innovation in Construction Drawing
Klaus Platzgummer

This paper argues that innovations in architectural practices can be found in the materiality of cultural techniques—in this case, in the materiality of the cultural technique of drawing. This is rendered visible by two historical moments in the development of construction drawing: the transition from stone to paper as sign carrier in the early modern period and the transition from paper to complex electronic sign carriers in the second half of the 20th century. Ultimately, the paper attempts to show that innovations are never creations ex nihilo but are always constituted in pre-existing elements, such as material expressions and traditions of thinking.

On the Temporality of the Project
Petar Bojani⊠

This essay will attempt to systematize a few difficulties and present a few conditions that have to do with revealing the future, that is, the temporal nature of the project. First, I would like to insist on a weakness in languages spoken by a great number of people, which is that the future is difficult to linguistically stabilize and document: German and English do not have a future tense, using instead auxiliary verbs, respectively, "werden" (to become), "will"/"be going to." I will argue that when the project is no longer—there is no longer any future. The project ensures the future. To achieve complete circularity, I will introduce a third element: without the future, a group (in studio) or a "we" (in love) cannot possibly exist. In this essay I would like to unreservedly insist that the idea of a project, or perhaps a sketch of any future theory of the project (or concept), was provided at the beginning of the last century, within an imaginary exchange between Henri Bergson and Georg Simmel.

Narrating Innovation. Some Stories in the Voice of Practitioners
Federico Cesareo and Valeria Federighi

Starting from a research on the topic of innovation in architectural practice, the essay attempts to analyze the epistemic level of the relationship between the events of a design practice and the way of narrating them. Beyond specific contingency factors that a practitioner may point out, it can be argued that the concept of innovation in architectural design practice is conveyed through communication based on comparable narrative constructs. In accordance with Bruner, the research shows how the actions and events narrated by designers are part of legitimation processes that require a correctness of the choices made, not in absolute terms, but relative to a thematic-value focus. Through the presentation of some of the stories collected, it is possible to find a coexistence of three levels of signification on which the design narrations act. By parametrizing these planes, the essay introduces a comparative representation capable of making explicit the relationship between the components of innovation in the tales of architectural design practice.

Architecture & Terminology
Petar Bojani⊠ and Snežana Vesni⊠

As the first and most important institution, language institutionalizes all institutions, gives them the power to become disciplines and produce knowledge. In architectural theory and practice, language defines the processes of architectural design, while in architectural philosophy it reveals conceptualization and thematization. The main goal of this project is to extensively study architectural concepts. By introducing the philosophical text into the process of architectural design, this project aims to examine the relation between architectural concept (philosophy), architectural design (technology), and architectural project (process). Furthermore, this research will attempt to assemble an architectural dictionary of technical terms and notions, and then apply them to deconstruct architectural concepts.

TIME AND TECHNOLOGY OF THE ARCHITECTURAL CONCEPT. (SUR)RÉALITÉ VIRTUELLE

Snežana Vesnić

Snežana Vesnić, PhD is an architect and Assistant Professor at the Faculty of Architecture, University of Belgrade. She is a founding partner of the architectural studio Neoarhitekti (Belgrade) and award-winning author, twice nominated for the Mies van der Rohe Award (2009, 2019). Vesnić held the position of postdoctoral fellow at the Center for Advanced Study of the University of Rijeka, where she conducted research in the field of aesthetics and philosophy of architecture. A project on which she is currently working is the RTS Memorial kinetic sculpture "Sixteen." She is the author of Architectural Concept: Object of Reality, Subject of Illusion (2020).

Figure 1
Projections: *National Museum,* Belgrade, project by Neoarhitekti, Architectural Competition (2010) & *Opéra au Carrousel*, Étienne-Louis Boullée (1781)

Figure 2
National Museum, Belgrade, project by Neoarhitekti, Architectural Competition, (2010)

Figure 3
The First and the Second Object of Architecture: Commercial Building Textil, Uzice, Built 2007, project by Neoarhitekti, Nomination for Mies van der Rohe Award, (2008)

Figure 4
Between Present and Absent: Villa Pavlovic, built 2017, project by Neoarhitekti, Nomination for Mies van der Rohe Award (2018)

My intention is to thematize the creation of the concept, by concept, and in the process, I would like to document some reflections on these processes. (Re)constructing the layering and complexity of the architectural understanding of the processes, acts, gestures, and documents that the architect uses to produce the object of architecture will yield a new idea: the methodological necessity of simultaneous creation and overcoming the existence of the object.

The title of the text comes in three parts. The first, *Time and Technology,* refers to the production of and with the architectural concept. The technology of translating the architectural object from one form of existence into another, in successive and simultaneous projections, gives the methodology of the architectural project a hyper-specificity.

The third part of the title, *(Sur)réalité virtuelle,* indicates a possibility of a different understanding of the terms virtual and realism in the sense of destabilizing the reality of the virtual and introducing the novel into the very notion of the virtual. *Surréalité virtuelle* refers to my idea of creating a new conceptual potential at the point of absence, lack, or inexistence of the architectural object.

The middle part of the title, however, *Architectural concept,* not only offers an explanation of the concept as generator of all these processes, but is my suggestion for the deconstruction of reality through the use of the architectural concept. This innovation in architectural philosophy is also an innovation in architectural practice, and is only seemingly paradoxical.

Snežana Vesnić - Time and Technology
of the Architectural Concept. (Sur)réalité Virtuelle

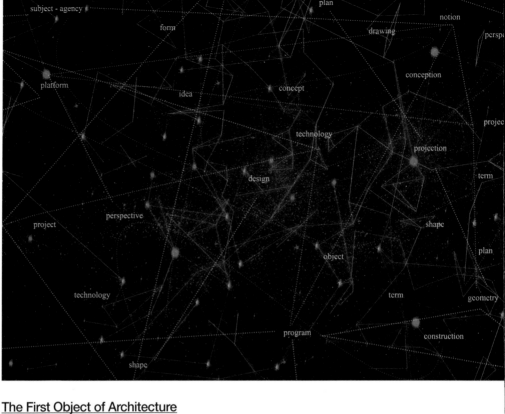

The labels visible in the image: subject - agency, form, plan, notion, drawing, perspe, platform, idea, concept, conception, projec, technology, projection, projec, design, term, project, perspective, shape, plan, object, technology, term, geometry, program, construction, shape

The First Object of Architecture

Let us begin from the object—or better, objects—of architecture. By projecting the "concept of the object" and "objectivization of the concept" (Vesnić, 2020: 85—94), my aim is to simultaneously structure the relations between concept, design, and project. In this methodological reconstruction of the architectural project, I wish to explain that the creation of "new concepts" (Deleuze, 1994: 55) is the condition of creation of the new in architectural theory and practice. Architecture is a discipline of creating the new through theory and practice. First, the primary dialectic of architecture concerns the relationship between the subject as an agent or agency and the object of architecture. Specifically, the subject as an agent is a being with the capacity to act, and having agency indicates a manifestation of this capacity. I emphasize here that agency may be "an entity or institution endowed with a power of acting."[1] The architectural act is directed toward the production of the object (the physical object in space and time), making the relation between the subject-agent and the object (of architecture) one of the most important ones in architecture. Second, much like philosophy, architecture is the creation of concepts, which at first glance seems like an entirely and completely Deleuzian definition. Yet, beyond this, I insist that architecture is creation of concepts and creation with concepts.

As a word adopted from philosophy, concept is a most delicate term in architecture, since it problematizes not only language and philosophy, but also architectural production. Concept destabilizes the shifting field of architectural terms, but also has the capacity to project systems, structures, and relations. And much like ideal or other geometries, it provides a basis. Not only does "correct reading"—a phrase by Peter Eisenman (Bojanić and Djokić, 2017: 13)—determine architecture as a discipline, but the concept is a complete (comprehensive) instrument in the architectural project.

Figure 5
Space of (Architectural) Notions

The word *conceptus* literally means fetus, a product of interior gestation. But as of late Roman Antiquity, the grammarians begin to use it metaphorically along the lines of designating intellectual representation taking place in the mind. It enters philosophical vocabulary, and following its etymology of *con-capere* (to take together) indicates a unification of a plurality in a common apprehension. It thus acquires the status of notion, which in the epistemological sense refers not only to the product or process of the mind's engenderment, but to the collection of a multitude of elements in a single perception. The lexeme's layers and its polysemy across Europe's linguistic plurality are not reducible to a signification of a purely logical act; rather, they indicate a further moment of figuration and metaphor within thought, and a capacity of productive imagination. Pellegrino wrote a tract in dialogue form entitled *Del concetto poetico* (On the Poetic Concept) (1971). Several persons in it, among whom the philosopher, poet, and rhetorician, discuss what is the concept and what is its role and place in the creation of a work of art. It is initially described as an image of the object (*idem*). Variations of the German term *Begreifen*, meaning understanding of an intellectual act, intellectual grasp of a thing or idea, to seize, catch, or capture, as well as reflections of *con-capere* (to take together) derived from the Latin *conceptus*, literally meaning fetus, both indicate that this is a term that resists a well-rounded definition. The Italian word *concetto* further complicates matters by introducing capacities of figurability of conceptual content and intention, figurability of ideas and intellectual abstractions.

Using myriad philosophical tools and both philosophy and practice of architecture, I define the architectural concept as "the first object of architecture," containing the ideality projected through the project into the *real object*, which in turn I call "the second object of architecture." The essential value of the concept for architecture is its further productive and creative potential for a new creation, coming up with new concepts and conceptions, new objects, philosophies, and aesthetics of the future. The concept is essentially real only when it produces, when it allows new creation, when its forms and formlessness overcome the object positions through new, engaged roles with the potential and power of acting (Vesnić, 2020). The concept is a unified whole, and the object of architecture always appears in two modalities, as *aistema* or the object of aesthetics, and *noema* or the transcendental object of logic. More simply, the concept and the object always have a philosophical and aesthetic projection. Peter Eisenman privileges the aesthetic aspect because "presence in the object means that the aesthetic takes primacy" (Eisenman, 2004a: 204), as well as that "the idea of presence and the representations of presence represses all other interpretations" (Eisenman, 2004b: 230). The architectural object, although it has an immediate aesthetic and function presented in its presence, can never completely overlap with its materialization, and always indicates its own absence, since it also contains its own other (an absence). If presence is understood as existence, then its taxonomic opposite, absence, is defined as inexistence. Absence is what can be called into question, due to its ambivalent nature. However, this does not mean that presence assumes only the notion of existence, which is to say the known or the certain; rather, the absent is also present in the body.

(De)Construction of Reality

The architectural object would be much more easily explicable if merely a question of (its) presence and absence. However, matters become more complicated when we introduce the following questions: what is the reality of the present and/or absent, and what are other modalities of existence or forms of reality that exist and in which the architectural object exists? Both the object and its objectivization are impermanent, primarily because what is present materializes the absent, just as the absent renders corporeal the present. That which is absent allows for the openness of the object for further reading, gestures, and specifications. Following Eisenman, absence always implies a transfer, but such that there is nevertheless a hidden but present reality of an object in its own presence (Eisenman, 1971: 1—5).[2] The existence of the entire object requires a whole range of transfers and acts through which the existence of the architectural object takes place. Architectural objectivization at the same time structures and deconstructs complex forms of reality through presences, absences, present absences, and through dissolution of presence. As the object is never a constant entity, its reality is transient. But these changes and transitions from various "states" or modalities of reality explain the life of the object of architecture and its complex existence. Therefore, the architectural project is a process of projections and transformations from one shape to another, one form into another, one technique into another—from one (form of) document to another.

To elaborate the processes of translation and projection, I will reconstruct the terms that explain the modalities of reality and then construct a system in which I can explain the conceptualization as a process of simultaneous and continuous projections (of presences and absences) across the architectural project. Drawing on German philosophy and language, Jean-François Courtine makes the following distinction: 1) the actual [das Wirklichkeit] (what is given in sensation or has an effect on me, and on which I have a retroactive effect; 2) the being-there [das Daseiende] (what is there in general, that is, in space and time); and 3) being [das Sein] (what is purely and simply by itself, independently of any temporal condition) (Courtine, 2014: 885). The Medieval philosopher Duns Scotus uses the notion of reality in reference to the thing, res, what exists in itself. It is interesting that this conception simultaneously implies a possibility of several realities,[3] and thus reality itself must be defined more closely. The subtle distinction of the German terms Realität and Wirklichkeit is the potential germ of architectural conceptualization. Following Hegel, I would like to emphasize the difference between the real and reality, that is, *Realität* and *Wirklichkeit*. For Hegel, *Realität* was close to Dasein and Erscheinung, mere existence or objective reality. Realität—the real—is pure, brute fact, simple appearance. *Wirklichkeit*, on the other hand, is seen as actual, effective reality (that which emerges as a consequence of action on *Realität*). *Wirklichkeit*—actuality—is the effect and independent actuality, which once produced is capable of generating effects of its own. Hegel further differentiated between the terms *Wirklich* and *Wirken*. The former designates the actual, while the latter is active and can draw on effectiveness and act. In the case of the verb Wirken—meaning action or activity, as well as to work and to act on something—it is the basis for understanding the terms action and reaction, having an effect, being effective. What is important here is that each actualization implies two things, effect and further action, or act and further acting.

Hegel's term *Wirklichkeit* aligns with Aristotle's term *energeia*. Aristotle set up the duality *dynamis* and *energeia* (in Latin, *potentia* and *actus*). The Latin actualis is analogous to reality, that is, the German *Wirklichkeit*. Thus, in Latin, the distinction *potentia* and *actus* is used to translate the Aristotelian distinction between *dynamis* and *energeia*, presenting the difference between potential and act. These dualisms indicate that there is potentiality (*dynamis*) that is opposed to actuality (*Wirklichkeit*, *energeia*). Moreover, dynamis designates both potentiality as 1) the not yet of the act and 2) power that results from it. Latin expresses this difference through the terms *potentia* and *potestas*, which translate to the English dynamic and power. Throughout these gradations, "potentiality can…become not the absence of the act, but rather its eminent quality and the mark of the human, which makes the act a work." (Baschera and Lichtenstein, 2014: 9).

<u>Construction of the Object</u>

Allow me to now place these terms into a structure and then project it across three planes: one plane will contain the duality *potentiality* and *actuality*; one plane *actuality* and *reality*; and finally, *actual* and *virtual*. Then, I would like to demonstrate the generation and acting of the object of architecture through these modalities of reality. (Architectural) realization assumes constraints within which potentialities are considered thwarted, while on the other hand, not being realized, they pass into reality. In architecture, this transfer will always take place between the actual, real, and virtual. The *actual* is defined as *existing in act or reality*, *not just potentially, really acted or acting*. As supplement to the actual, the real means true, genuine, not merely nominal or apparent, or that which can be characterized as a confirmation of truth, while effect or expression of something depends on the capacity or contingency of the act itself. Finally, the virtual is what possesses all the conditions for actualization, or what exists without manifesting, has not yet become actual through the act. The category of the virtual does not have to be realized, but rather actualized; however, the concepts forces it to create its actualizations, even if the actual does not have to look like the virtual it renders corporeal. For Deleuze, both the actual and the virtual are fully real and although the former has concrete existence, it is no more real for that fact (Deleuze, 1994: 208, 209). This resembles an explanation of the virtual as that which posses all the conditions for actualization but is not actual. In architectural design, this difference of actual and virtual allows to experience something still real, even if it is not actual, that is, to grasp the potential of future objective existence in the reality of the virtual. Architectural methodology uses a virtual field that represents the necessary conditions under which real experience is actualized, such that actualization and the object belong to the virtual (Deleuze and Parnet, 2007: 149). For its part, architectural conceptualization encompasses the real and defines the (virtual) conditions for actualization, indeed, executes it precisely by way of translation from one form of reality into another.

Deleuze developed the conception he encountered in Charles Peirce (who in turn borrowed it from Scotus), that being virtual is being real without necessarily being actual, where the term virtual contains another, and can elaborate in detail the techniques of architectural conceptualization. The other is particularly significant in designing an object because "no object will produce a simple and proper concept of itself and a simple and proper concept of another object unless it contains this second object essentially or virtually" (Scotus, 1987: 23). The virtual thus contains the other; and the possibility, potential, or contingency of the other is the very essence of architectural production. This production of objects of architecture is enabled by the presence of the future (and existence of the other) in the course of creation. It allows constant virtual life of the object, not only through hypothetical models, simulations, or imitations of reality, but deconstruction of presence and absence of objects and their projections, as its augmented reality.

Imperfect in "Perfection of Power"

Architectural creation is directed at the perfection of form, or the search for a kind of ideality wherein the architectural object tends towards temporary suspension in its own perfection. We find three important conceptions in Aquinas, which elaborate meticulously a methodology of designing an architectural object. First, all substances seek their "own perfection," and everything is directed towards their "final end," which is a fully realized state of existence or actuality (Aquinas, 1981). Second, aside from actualization or realization, we also find in Aquinas the idea of duration (in the sense of repetition), and that a substance cannot achieve its final end without exercising the powers it has in virtue of its substantial form. The emphasis is less on the "final end" itself than on the capacities and powers to actualize perfection. Although in architecture (self-)completion in perfection means the complete actualization of the object, its specific capacities, and powers to perform the activity of the concept, above all there must be the capacity and conditions for actualization. A further requirement is that there be an act, an activity, a movement that would transmute, transfer, or translate something from pure potential into the actual. Third, "perfection of power" (potentiae perfectionem) is denoted by virtue, but this power is exhausted by the act itself: "Virtue denotes a certain perfection of a power. Now a thing's perfection is considered chiefly in regard to its end. But the end of power is act. Wherefore power is said to be perfect, according as it is determinate to its act" (Aquinas, 1981). This means that the capacity of power is determined by the act, which can be the realization of the architectural object. If the virtual is that which possesses all the conditions for actualization, and it precedes actualization, then it has the power to transform the realities subsumed within it while maintaining the state of potential, the not yet of the act keeping it from completely actualizing. However, the problem appears due to the power of the virtual to exhaust itself, while actualization itself implies, but also thematizes the end of power.

The power of the architectural concept lies in its (infinite) intentionality towards (another) object. The concept engages the virtual in order to materialize its own absence in the future present through the virtual: that is, to materialize the actual. Thus, the virtual is an instrument of the concept, a technique and technology for the production of the future architectural object. The concept's creative power comes first from the capacity to engender, to encompass, and unify into a whole; further, it virtualizes absence through the materiality of the object; and finally, through its projections into the real object, it can direct the constitution and meaning of the object of architecture.

The concept has the capacity to accept and encompass (pre-existing) existences of the object in the perfect and imperfect way, for its materialization to project or actualize intentional ideality. Imperfection of existence only seemingly paradoxically (as in Aquinas) ensures materiality:

> "Now it is plain that the effect pre-exists virtually in the efficient cause: and although to pre-exist in the potentiality of a material cause is to pre-exist in a more imperfect way, since matter as such is imperfect, and an agent as such is perfect; still to pre-exist virtually in the efficient cause is to pre-exist not in a more imperfect, but in a more perfect way" (Aquinas, 1981).

The existences of the architectural object complicate the questions of its origin and its potential reality. First, what is the status of possible reality and is this also a kind of reality, or only a possibility? Further, what is the ontological status of the concept of presence within the object? Is it only potentially present within or does it act, producing a given reality? Possibilities always have some sort of reality of their own, although it sounds paradoxical, and contradicts Bergson. The issue is not simply the actualization of the possible, which would reduce it through action and realization, simply exhausting given potential. In the virtual, actuality and potentiality are inextricably intertwined because the virtual is an open form of potentiality that also contains the possibilities of its actualization. Deleuze's, but also Eisenman's interpretation, would be that the virtual is not mere present absence, that is, the reality of absence. It is not only Eisenman's presentness, but the possibility of always other, the actualization of the other before the actualization of the architectural object and the visualization of the possible—the creation of new potential. The possibility of maintaining potential in actualization, or against Bergson, that there is a moment when the possible is real—this is the contingency of the ideal object of architecture or the perfection grounded in Aquinas' determination. The virtual always materializes a difference—potential and actual, the real and reality, intellect and appearance. Finally, in order for difference be constructed, there must be an act, acting, patent conceptual transformation that takes one form of existence into another.

(Sur)Realism of the Virtual: Attempting the (Im)Possible

There seems to be yet a fourth state of existence of the object, one which is conceptually most important for creation and for the existence of the architectural object —the (sur)realism of the virtual. Traversing the path from potential, as the possible,

Figure 6
The Real and Reality: City Art Gallery, Neoarhitekti, Architectural competition (2010) &
Conical Cenotaph of the Sepulchre Chapel (1784), Etienne-Louis Boullée

moving from the real to actual, determining the time actualization, the concept always projects (much like the projection) a new modality of reality. Following Eisenman, we could call the (sur)realism of the virtual the absence of presence and explain it in the following fashion: 1) in the course of conceptualization, there are moments when reality of the possible as an emptiness or absence of the future object will be permanently built in; 2) after the materialization of the object it will be built into the potential of its own dematerialization. This is emptiness, own absence in reality, continuity of the object in the surreality of the virtual. This is the life of the concept through maintenance of the object as never fully actualized, and allowing that the possibility of difference between virtual and actual be once again encompassed conceptually—which is the creation of the new architectural concept.

Put another way, the absence of visibility of the future object conceptually opens a new contingency, surpassing the limits of the possible, to reveal the very specific place that will be built as virtual, but literally real, into a future projected/designed object. We also find his necessity not to see the object of a visible entity, as well as the possibility to see something invisible in the visible, in Giambattista della Porta, who systematized knowledge about the camera obscura, with advice to artists and architects how to use it. We find the idea of projection or the virtualness of the object in Porta's following fragment:

> "Before we start from the understanding that we see the image hanging in the air, we will teach how it can be done to see images of any item hanging in the air. It will be the most miraculous of miracles, without a mirror, but also without the visible object. [...]...But let us wonder... how might we see an image hanging in the air in the middle of the room, without seeing the mirror, nor the object of the visible thing, while being able to walk around, seeing the image from all sides."

When the thought about an object without a visible object possibly appears in documented form (such as a drawing or text), then the intangible abstraction of the physical object becomes at once its functional and formal ability to produce the entirely new in the project. Finally, as René Magritte explicitly demonstrated, "the object never matches its projection, just as words do not match the text they explain" (Magritte, 1929: 32—33). The identification of these differences, tensions and mismatches of projections is documented in the architectural project. Thus, we can interpret the architectural project as a process of continuous intermediation among projections. Peirce used the term interpretant, as an intermediate concept, which in his category list plays the same role as the notion "I think" in the Kantian deduction of pure concepts of understanding (Kiryushchenko). Similarly, the architectural project is the connecting of intermediate concepts and bringing together of plurality into conceptual unity. The project thus becomes an act of continuous development directed to a possible future, as Durbiano and Armando explain:

Figure 7
The Final End: Blocks 25-26: CITY PARK, central zone of New Belgrade, project by
Neoarhitekti, Architectural competition, (2006) & *Conical Cenotaph of the Sepulchre Chapel*
(1784), Etienne-Louis Boullée

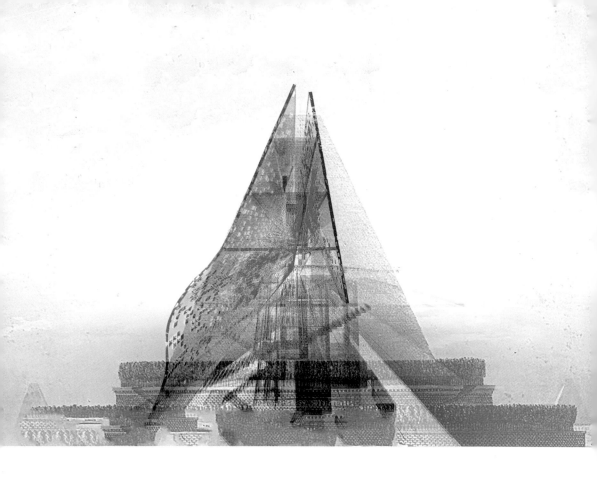

"At every point in the process there is only one perspective instituted toward a future that corresponds to the one document by the project collective: a set of intentional actions unified up to that point. Even the most radical demands can rely on this 'not yet existent future, which for this reason might still be,' as a promise that can be sustained (or left aside). In the course of the design process and considering the future of the work, all battles are virtual."

Through the movement of projection, the virtual allows the architectural concept continuity of acts and actions, ensuring its own duration into a new potential for architectural production and architectural project. Inventiveness and generating new potential is the condition of innovation in an architectural project. In a sort of parallelism and self-projection and self-establishment, the concept liberates new complex relations and conceptions of certain functions and strategies, imagining new realities of the virtual through the architectural project.

Notes

[1] "In agency, the agents themselves are no longer only the actors/authors of action; instead, they are also caught up in a system of relations that shifts the place and authority of action and modifies... In its contemporary uses, 'agency' is thus the point where the dualisms action/passion and agent/patient are erased and also where the subject/agent is defined in a new way." (Balibar, Laugier, 2014: 18)

[2] Eisenman introduces another condition to complement the relation presence/absence: "presentness": "deconstruction of the presence/absence dialectic is inadequate for architecture precisely because architecture is not two-term, but a three-term system. In architecture, there is another condition, which I call presentness, that is neither absence nor presence, form nor function, neither particular use of sign nor the crude existence of reality, but rather an excessive condition between sign and the Heideggerian notion of being"
Conference ISSUES? Concerning the Projects of Peter Eisenman. Bojanić pointing to a letter from Eisenman to Derrida in 1990. (Bojanić, Djokić, 2017: 13).

[3] Reality is something in the thing. So that in each thing several realities may be posited (Micraelius, 1203–05).

[4] "Respondeo dicendum quod virtus nominat quandam potentiae perfectionem. Uniuscuiusque autem perfectio praecipue consideratur in ordine ad suum finem. Finis autem potentiae actus est. Unde potentia dicitur esse perfecta, secundum quod determinatur ad suum actum. Sunt autem quaedam potentiae quae secundum seipsas sunt determinatae ad suos actus; sicut potentiae naturales activae. Et ideo huiusmodi potentiae naturales secundum seipsas dicuntur virtutes. Potentiae autem rationales, quae sunt propriae hominis, non sunt determinatae ad unum, sed se habent indeterminate ad multa, determinantur autem ad actus per habitus, sicut ex supradictis patet. Et ideo virtutes humanae habitus sunt" (Aquinas 1981).

[5] Bergson made a careful distinction: the possible is the opposite to and of the real, which means that possible is not "possible" as part of the real, nor is the virtual the actual, but as such posses a reality. The virtual does not have to be realized but rather actualized (Deleuze, Bergsonism, 1988: 96).

[6] Giambattista della Porta, Magiae Naturalis, sive de Miraculis Rerum Naturalium, libri IIII, (ca. 1535–1615). Taken from Maldonado, 2015.

[7] "Prima che partiamo dal ragionamento del veder l'imagine pendente nell'aria, insegnaremo come si possa fare che veggiamo le imagini pendent nell'aria di qualsivoglia cosa; il che sará cosa mirabile piu di tutte le meravigliose, principalmente senza specchio, e senza l'ogetto visibile. [...] Ma diciamolo... come si veda una imagine nell'aria in mezo una camera, che non si veda lo specchio, né l'ogetto della cosa visibile, e caminando intorno intorno vedrai l'imagine da tutte le parti." Giambattista della Porta, Magiae Naturalis, sive de Miraculis Rerum Naturalium, libri IIII, (ca. 1535–1615) (Maldonado, 2015: 9).

[8] "In ogni momento (t) del processo esiste una sola prospettiva istituita verso il futuro (T) che corrisponde a quella iscritta dal collettivo di progetto, cioè all'insieme delle azioni intenzionali che sono state unificate fino a quel punto. Anche le istanze più radicali possono contare su questo 'futuro che non c'è

ancora e quindi ci può ancora essere,' come su una promessa che si può ancora mantenere (o deviare). Durante un processo progettuale tutte le battaglie sono virtuali, se si considera il futuro dell'opera (T)" (Armando, Durbiano, 2017: 396).

References

Aquinas, T. St. (1981), *Summa theologiae, trans. Fathers of the English Dominican Province*, Westminster, Christian Classics.

Armando, A., Durbiano, G. (2017), *Teoria del progetto architettonico: dai disegni agli effetti*, Roma, Carocci.

Balibar, É., Laugier, S. (2014), *Agency*, in B. Cassin (ed.), "Dictionary of Untranslatables: A Philosophical Lexicon," trans. S. Rendall et al, New Jersey, Princeton University Press, pp. 17—24.

Baschera, M., Lichtenstein, J. (2014), *Actor* in B. Cassin (ed.), "Dictionary of Untranslatables: A Philosophical Lexicon," trans. S. Rendall et al, New Jersey, Princeton University Press, pp. 9.

Bergson, H. (1922), *Matter and Memory*, New York, Macimilian Co.

Bergson, H. (1959), *L'évolution créatrice*, Paris, Les Presses universitaires de France.

Bojanić, P. (2017) *Opening,* in P. Bojanić, V. Djokić (eds), "Peter Eisenman. In dialogue with Architects and Philosophers," Udine, Mimesis International, pp. 9—17.

Courtine, J. (2014), *Reality*, in B. Cassin (ed.), "Dictionary of Untranslatables: A Philosophical Lexicon," trans. S. Rendall et al, New Jersey, Princeton University Press, pp. 879—87.

Deleuze, G. (1988), *Bergsonism*, trans. H. Tomlinson, B. Habberjam, New York, Zone Books.

Deleuze, G. (1994), *Difference and Repetition*, trans. P. Patton, New York, Columbia University Press.

Deleuze, G., Guattari F. (1994), *What Is Philosophy?*, Columbia New York, Columbia University Press.

Deleuze, G. (2007), *What Is the Creative Act?*, in "Two Regimes of Madness, Texts and Interviews, 1975–1995," transl. A. Hodges, M. Taormina, Los Angeles, Semiotext(e), pp. 317—30.

Deleuze, G., Parnet, C. (2007), *Dialogues II*, trans. H. Tomlinson, B. Habberjam New York, Columbia University Press.

Eisenman, P. (1970), *Notes on Conceptual Architecture: Towards a Definition,* "Design Quarterly," vol. 78/79, pp. 1—5.

Eisenman, P. (2004a), *Architecture and the Problem of the Rhetorical Figure*, in (1987) "Eisenman Inside Out. Selected Writings 1963—1988," New Haven, Yale University Press, pp. 202—7.

Eisenman, P. (2004b), *Architecture as a Second Language*, in (1987) "Eisenman Inside Out. Selected Writings 1963—1988," New Haven, Yale University Press, pp. 227—33.

Eisenman, P. (2007), *Written into the Void: Selected Writings, 1990—2004*, New Haven, Yale University Press.

Eisenman, P., Roman M. (2015), *Palladio Virtuel*, New Haven, Yale University Press.

Esposito J., *Virtuality*, "Digital Encyclopedia of Charles S. Peirce." Available at: digitalpeirce.fee.unicamp.br.

Kant, I. (1998), *Critique of Pure Reason*, trans. P. Guyer, A. Wood, Cambridge, Cambridge University Press.

Kiryushchenko, V., *The Idea of Virtuality in Peirce's Semiotics and Deleuze's Transcendental Empiricism: Kantian Variations.* Available at: https://www.academia.edu/9395515/THE_IDEA_OF_VIRTUALITY_IN_PEIRCE_S_SEMIOTICS_AND_DELEUZE_S_TRANSCENDENTAL_EMPIRICISM_KANTIAN_VARIATIONS.

Magritte, R. (1929), *Les Mots et les images,* "La Révolution surréaliste," vol. 12, pp. 32–3.

Maldonado, T. (2015), *Reale e Virtuale*, Feltrinelli Editore, Milano.

Micraelius, J. (1661), *Lexicon philosophicum terminorum philosophis usitatorum*, Stetini, Mamphrasius, Höpfnerus. Available at: http://diglib.hab.de/drucke/201-29-quod/start.htm.

Pellegrino, C. (1971), *Del concetto poetico*, in G. Valletta, (ed.), "I dialoghi e le Rime di Camillo Pellegrino," Messina - Firenze, G. D'Anna, pp. 62—105.

Scotus, J. D. (1987), *Man's Natural Knowledge of God*, in "Philosophical Writings: A Selection," *trans.* A. Wolter, Indianapolis, Hackett Publishing, pp. 13—33.

Steinweg, M. (2014), *What is an Object*, in A. Hudek (ed.) "The Object," Cambridge, The MIT Press, pp. 42—4.

Vesnić, S. (2020), *Arhitektonski koncept: Objekt stvarnosti i subject iluzije (Architectural Concept: Object of Reality and Subject of Illusion)*, Novi Sad - Beograd, Akademska knjiga, IDESE.

THE POIETIC AND SYMBOLIC PLACE OF THE PROJECT IN THE CONTEMPORARY ARCHITECTURAL SITUATION

Pierre Caye

Pierre Caye, a former fellow of the Ecole normale supérieure de la rue d'Ulm and director of Research at the at the Centre Jean Pepin of the CNRS (Centre Nationale de la Recherche scientifique) in France, devotes a large part of his research to the relationship between art, technology, and production. He is the author of several works, including *Empire and Decor*, *Le vitruvianisme et la question de la technique* (1999), *Morale et Chaos, Principes d'un agir sans fondement* (2008), *Critique de la destruction créatrice, Production et humanisme* (2015), *Comme un Nouvel Atlas, D'un état meilleur que la puissance* (2017) and most recently *Durer: Elément pour la transformation du système productif* (2020).

I will make three preliminary remarks on the situation of the project.

I will begin with Alberti's (1966) definition of the project: conceiving of the entire work in the mind and in advance (*praescribere in mente ac animo*), in minute detail (*ex omni parte*), by means of lines and angles (*lineis et angulis*), without material inscription (*seclusa materia*), i.e., in the abstract, until rumination, as Le Corbusier has it—Alberti prefers constant thought (*iterum et iterum*)—makes the project plump from the architect's mental studio like a ripe fruit. The modernist movement was later to add an idealist dimension in that the project is the foremost tool driving progress, emancipation, and transformation in society—what Argan referred to in the title of one of his essays as *Progetto e destino*, project and destiny. For Alberti, the project was a mental technological tool used to design artifacts; in the modernist movement, it became a historical, political, and social agent.

The project is a conception that has been increasingly neglected by contemporary theory and in which society no longer recognizes an architectural function. Let me be clear: there is no architecture without a project, for obvious practical and legal reasons. Building permits require a basic, then a detailed preliminary design. The project is still a definite presence in everyday architectural production. Yet contemporary architecture no longer places its poietic and symbolic power in the project, unlike the modernist movement or Renaissance architecture; it is no longer the site where architecture is identified by its discourse; it is becoming a secondary task, undergoing automatization in agencies.

Some might say it matters little, as long as the project remains at the heart of the everyday reality of architecture. But precisely *because* the project appears ancillary and marginal from the point of view of the values that institute architecture on the social stage, it is readily automatized, subcontracted to artificial intelligence, CAD, and machines, to the point of further degrading its symbolic value in a sort of vicious circle. The more the project is symbolically degraded, the more it is automatized; the more it is automatized, the less the architect is called on to recognize themselves in it and invest their energy in it.

Bringing the project back into the conversation today certainly implies taking the measure of the notion in the contemporary episteme. I'm not here to teach you your trade, I'm not the best placed to do that, nor will I suggest such and such more or less new protocol for conceiving of architectural projects. I simply want to think along with you about what *projecting* means today, intellectually and symbolically.

Contemporary architectural discourse makes ever more frequent reference to fuzzy logic, randomness, chaos theory, deconstruction, networks, and even rhizomes—a linguistic repertoire borrowed from contemporary philosophy, epistemology, and social sciences. These new discourses are thought to sign the death of the project and the reason or productive intelligence it makes manifest. These discourses claim to liquidate the project and take over its role because the project is seen as a straitjacket inhibiting the potentialities of architecture fostered by computing and new materials. The discourses claim to be freeing architecture from itself, its past, and the old rules and patterns that, the argument goes, weigh it down and stop it developing in new directions. As such, these new discourses set out to critique architecture and the architectural tradition in a revolutionary way, as an internal critique denouncing architecture's isolation and inward gaze, of which the project is held to be symptomatic, along with its lack of reactivity to social movements, new technologies, and societal trends, and its splendid isolation in its own, one-track, disciplinary and corporatist logic. It is now castigated for something that Nietzsche (1889) held to be proof of its grandeur—its sovereign distance:

> "Now it is plain that the effect pre-exists virtually in the efficient cause: and although to pre-exist in the potentiality of a material cause is to pre-exist in a more imperfect way, since matter as such is imperfect, and an agent as such is perfect; still to pre-exist virtually in the efficient cause is to pre-exist not in a more imperfect, but in a more perfect way" (Aquinas).

Reacting to this, Georges Bataille (1929: 117), himself a great reader of Nietzsche, deemed architecture "the expression of order and authority" and compared great monuments to embankments, "pitting the logic of majesty and authority against all the unquiet elements"; the human order is, in origin, as one with the architectural order, which is merely its development. Hence, he concludes, monumental productions are currently the true masters worldwide: his 1929 text refers to "architectural penitentiary guards." This is all linked to the project, the principle of reason, to what Heidegger was much later to call the *Gestell* (Enframing).

Today, however, the true masters are the financial networks, not the planning engineers of the inter-war period, and architecture itself is increasingly caught up in logics of real estate promotion. The shift from architecture to networks is clearly a fundamental revolution in logics of domination.

To adapt to these new logics of domination by networks, what is increasingly promoted today is an open, flexible, ductile, reactive architecture capable of blending into society's multiform praxis. The idea is that architecture and society must set each other free. A noble idea, the opposite of what Bataille says: for Bataille, architecture is the expression by which man alienates his own freedom by means of his will to power, the foremost instrument of man's self-alienation by the superego. So, turn this relationship on its head. But in the process of mutual liberation, there is an implicit order to be followed: first of all society must be freed from architectural domination, what Bataille calls its " penitentiary guards," from the rationality of the project and its abstract logics of territorial control, before architecture—once society has been freed from architecture and thanks to its newfound freedom—is in turn freed from its own will to power that alienates it and renders it sterile; it is set free from its self-alienation and self-restriction in relation to what it can do, in relation to the virtual power of liberation and utopia it bears within itself. Thus, the argument goes, architecture in the contemporary world is able to return to its avant-garde role in transforming society, as the modernist movement called for in its day.

Yet in my opinion, this type of critique remains somewhat too idealistic. By which I mean that it forgets that architecture is a social art not only because it, more than most other art forms, speaks to the community, but also—and this is often overlooked—because it is an art that is commissioned and contracted as well as project managed, and as such it remains strongly subjected to the economic, technological, and political exteriority expressed by what I am calling the constructive apparatus—the full range of stakeholders in construction, from building firms and the public works industry, engineering consultancies, promoters, banks with their real estate interests, the real estate divisions at major companies, and so on who have a part to play in construction, financing it, dictating terms, and naturally seeking to exploit it and subject it to their own exploitative ends; architecture is not liberated if it is not first liberated in relation to the system of production that determines it. And I would argue that the architectural project's duty is to free architecture from being subjected to the system of production. Which, let me note in passing, was no less true in the Renaissance.

I would like to return to this noble idea of mutual liberation, which I share, though my take on it is somewhat different: there is no liberation without mutual liberation—we can only set ourselves free by freeing each other, that is, by liberating, through our own liberation, that which alienates us from its own alienation: Marx's great teaching. The dialectic of freedom, a virtuous circle, liberty generating liberty.

Simply, before liberating society from architectural domination to liberate the potentialities of architecture (as in the new discourse), we must first liberate architecture from society (Nietzsche is right). By society I mean, very pragmatically, the economic and social organization in which architecture finds its place. In other words, the constructive apparatus and the system of production that subjugates it, with the hope that once liberated, architecture will in turn liberate society from its subjection to the system of production, i.e., play its part in ensuring that the system of production no longer involves the total engagement of men or the enframing of the world. That is my own Utopia.

An internal critique is therefore not enough to drive architecture forward, enrich its logics of conception, and deepen the understanding of its forms; we must also be able to influence and transform the commission and the constructive apparatus that dictates it. I considered that the "post-modern" or "contemporary" type of discourse, i.e., references to fuzzy logics, randomness, chaos theory, deconstruction, networks, and even rhizomes contribute rather, doubtless by some cunning of reason, to furthering architecture's submission to the commission and the building industry far more than it frees architecture from its chains. Let me argue, somewhat polemically, that the so-called "contemporary" discourse in architecture weakens the project contractor compared to the contracting authority and the constructive apparatus. Or, to put it another equally polemical way, we cannot liberate society by alienating or subjecting the arts to its regulatory or organic discourses, however new and flattering they may be. And this is how the project as a symbolic form, not merely as a technological tool, holds its value, because it was an instrument of liberation by its very origin.

A good critique of architecture can only be simultaneously internal and external: the discipline can only move, open up, and feed on the wealth of the countless social praxes that run through it if it remains in turn equal to influencing and modifying the exteriority of the commission. It is pointless challenging architecture's dogmatic dimension if in the end it is still subjected to the equally dogmatic bodies of knowledge of the engineer, sociologist, and economist, or even the local councilor or real estate promoter. This shines a light on the risk of architecture losing its identity and its mission, which for me is the gravest threat to its capacity for social transformation. And this is where the notion of the project still has much to teach us.

Yet today we cannot start out by placing the project on the table and postulating its *a priori* existence. Our situation in relation to the project differs radically from the Renaissance, which I would dare define as the point of origin for modern architecture precisely insofar as the Renaissance forged the project's theoretical and practical tools. In the Renaissance, the question of the project imposed itself by its very newness and its promise of mastering reality. The project heralded the birth of a genuine method of design and technological production that had no earlier equivalent in the history of reason. The texts of Antiquity did indeed provide for some of the project's tools, but it was Renaissance architects and theorists such as Alberti, Filarete, the Sangallo family, Fra Giocondo, Raphael, Palladio, and Barbaro, among others, who set out how to use it, succeeding in linking the various tools together to form a complex, operational mental machine. The architectural project, insofar as it enriches the modes of rationality and influences modern technology, is the most characteristic symbolic form of Renaissance art. In the early 20th century, the modernist movement, for its part, rediscovered the original sense of the project, its inventive dimension, lost by the academicism of the Paris *Ecole des Beaux-Arts* and the techniques of architectural composition it taught in the nineteenth century.

It is less easy to identify the architectural project in the situation of contemporary rationality and its tools. This is why the project no longer imposes itself *a priori*; rather, a path must be drawn to justify it, which furthermore can only contribute to an improved understanding of its operativity. Today, other forms of logic seem to impose themselves as the models of reason. First we are seeing a sophistication of traditional techniques of reasoning: systems of formal logic, which extend far beyond the architectural project in terms of rational precision (if not in imaginative power). We are also witnessing the emergence of new, non-linear approaches to rationality—fuzzy logics, complex systems, chaos theories. And finally, the project seems to be a victim of its own success. Projects are everywhere, not only in business life, but also in everyday life: if everything is a project, then the risk is that the concept itself dissolves into banal ineffectiveness. In these conditions, in which its identity is becoming disoriented, it is understandable that the notion of the architectural project is in turn becoming more flexible and fluctuating. This is why it is difficult to begin the process of thinking about architecture with the project, though it remains the fundamental operator within the discipline. I have preferred to give a negative demonstration, as it were, of the blind alleys of certain discourses that tend to consign the project to the dustbin of history.

The architectural project is a mental operation that allows us not only to plan and organize the building works, but also to unify the conception of the work itself. The architectural project's incomparable strength—what it does better than any other artistic or technological practice—is its capacity to dilate time and space by means of architecture to take the fields of immanence and transience in the networks of the productive system and create hiatuses, fissures, islands, shelters, differential loci, which correspond to deconstruction in the philosophical sense much better than the architectural one, since the aim is indeed to be able to inhabit the *reverse* of the structure. The architectural project gives man a genuine power to shift gear, to change the regime by which time and space are dispensed, an interstitial power in both meanings of the term: in the sense that it creates interstices in the continuous fabric of economic and social interactions, and also in the sense that the power is fragile, always verging on inefficacy, a power to downshift rather than to intensify.

To protect ourselves against the alienation that the system of production subjects us to and against total engagement, we must cultivate our sense of time and space. I do not know, for instance, how it is possible to talk about sustainable development without a sense of duration. The first thing to do to guarantee duration for economic development is to conquer, or reconquer, a sense of duration, which also means reconquering a sense of space and territory.

The idea is not to reduce distances or to cultivate instantaneity as suggested by new information and communication technologies, but to *dilate* space and time. I would even go so far as to say that the more we give ourselves the technological means to reduce distances and waiting times, the more important it is to preserve space, presence, and duration. The dilation of time and space does not consist in re-lengthening that which has been cut short or braking that which has been sped up. The aim is not to return to the days of the stage coach and the conquest of the wide open spaces of the American West, when the map of the world was still full of vast blank spaces and unknown lands. The aim is to take the process of acceleration and reduction and to create an intensity in our relationship to time and space—an intensity that cannot be obtained by merely reducing space and accelerating time. Architecture is a body of knowledge and a practice that allows us to dilate undifferentiated, linear spaces, and, by means of this spatial dilation, to generate duration.

References
Alberti, L.B. (1966), *L'Architettura [De re aedificatoria]*, I, 1. In G. Orlandi et P. Portoghesi (eds), Milan, Il Polifilo, pp. 19—21.
Bataille, G. (1929), *Architecture*, "Documents," vol. 2, p. 117.
Nietzsche, F. (1889), *Götzen-Dämmerung oder wie man mit dem Hammer philosophiert*, § Streifzüge eines Unzeitgemäßen, XI, Leipzig, C. G. Nauman.

DIAGRAMS BEYOND THE AVANT-GARDE.
Several Reasons Why Diagrams Are (Still) Worth Making in Architecture
Andrea Alberto Dutto

Andrea Alberto Dutto is a research and teaching associate at the Department of Architectural Theory at the Faculty of Architecture of the RWTH Aachen University. In 2017 he completed his PhD at the Politecnico di Torino in cotutelle with the RWTH Aachen University. His research focuses on catalogs, handbooks, and maps oriented to architectural design.

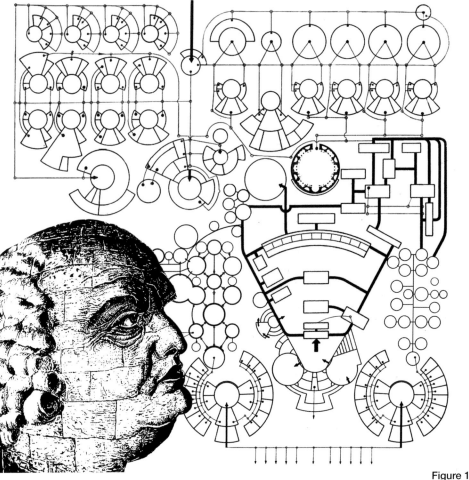

Figure 1
A. A. Dutto, Diagrams Beyond the Avant-Garde, 2021.

A widespread trend in architecture is the generation of statements with immediate effects in the form of artifacts (e.g., spoons, buildings, or cities). This haste tends to hide a whole series of intermediate stages that lie between the mind of the architect and its outcomes (namely the artifacts themselves). This kind of attitude is well exemplified in the Renaissance. At that time, the architectural treatise displayed buildings by leaving everything else (i.e., materials, details, …) to a later phase, and hopefully to be managed by someone else than the architect (Merrill, 2017). In contemporary architecture, things have not changed much. This is due to the aggravating circumstance in which—since the Renaissance—several revolutions have taken place over the last two centuries. Such revolutions have shown their effects precisely in the intermediate sector that lies between the architects' minds and their built artifacts. It is this intermediate sector that architects have come to share more and more with bureaucrats and other technicians.

Nevertheless, not everything that was a result of the Renaissance is actually outdated or wrong. Simply put, along with the Renaissance, another kind of attitude emerged, which has now reached a dignified status. This attitude has been exemplified, for instance, in handbooks published from the mid-18th century onwards, which follow the encyclopedic trend of the Enlightenment. These handbooks overturn the deductive procedure of the Renaissance treatises, insofar as they display the primacy of techniques over ideas and form-making desires. Indeed, based on the intent to be more radical, it could be claimed that handbooks portray the building only as a hypothetical outcome of the architectural praxis. Therefore, handbooks clearly state that there might be a building only after a concertation between technicians from different disciplines. According to this attitude, architects can produce certain effects in the building process only if they master specific techniques and "skills." Somehow, their "ideas" can be okay, but this only matters to them and no one else, unfortunately. What matters most is how they will be able to advance their technical "skills" throughout the negotiation with other technicians. This essay focuses on one of these technical "skills."

I

This introductory remark brings us to the subject of this essay, namely, the diagram. I do not believe it is necessary to go further in introducing it. Anyone who has a minimum of familiarity with contemporary architecture knows that with the beginning of the second millennium, "diagram architecture" emerged as a real trend (Garcia, 2010; Ito, 1996). Nevertheless, after a peak of popularity that lasted about two decades, such an approach is now ideologically sterile. It is curious to observe, for instance, that in the atlas "Architettura del Novecento—Teorie, Scuole, Eventi" (2012), edited by A. Ferlenga and M. Biraghi, the item "diagram" is missing. How is it possible to see no trace of a diagram in hundreds of entries and a thousand pages? Evidently, lemmas such as "digital architecture," "composition," and "program" are considered more significant than "diagram." However, although this is just a local example, it would be interesting to extend this investigation to other atlases and dictionaries if these were not increasingly rare, or rather not too distant from extinction, as nobody reads this kind of publication any longer.

II

We can make two hypotheses about the rapid extinction of diagram architecture. The first hypothesis is that—like all avant-garde stuff—at first it was celebrated and then shortly after buried and eventually forgotten. The absolutely novel character with which a mixed group of scholars and architects have hastened to enhance the potential of the diagram is, in fact, the son of an avant-garde ideology that refuses to see the diagram as product of an historical process that was concerned with architecture as a discipline (in the context of this essay, "avant-garde" coincides with Peter Bürger's "Neo-Avant-Garde" from 2010). Actually, the overall mainstream avant-garde hurried to see in the diagram an epistemological break from the past due to an encounter with the sciences (Pai, 2002) or, rather, art (Eisenman, 1999). Nevertheless, it would be rare to find at least one author who considers the diagram simply as an evolution of the conventional techniques of architectural representation without looking outwards.

The second hypothesis concerns the excessive attribution of architectural expressiveness to the diagram. To sever any link of continuity with the previous architectural typologies, the diagram is sometimes employed as a powerful generator of new shapes, which are deliberately strange and absurd enough to contrast with traditional buildings. Such tactics are for the boorish avant-garde an "if-then" situation: if the pre-diagrammatic architecture was about repetition (think of building typologies), then the diagrammatic one will be about difference. ... If pre-diagrammatic architecture expressed a conjunction between institutions and forms, then the diagrammatic one will be about disjunction… and so on and so forth.

More generally, diagram architecture was seemingly born under a banner proclaiming the urgency for architects to maintain hegemony in the creative process; all this was done at a time when architecture faced a crisis triggered by the spread of computer graphics. As with other tools of representation in architecture, the diagram was infused with the power to shorten the distance between architects and buildings by completely omitting what stands in-between (or rather, by simulating an in-between as a virtual, non-existent thing).

This is, for example, very evident in Peter Eisenman's claim that "the diagram acts as an agency which focuses on the relationship between an authorial subject, an architectural object and a receiving subject; it is the strata that exists between them" (Eisenman, 1999: 35). The three "items" that he mentions are, in fact, one: the author himself, though being subdivided into the three sub-entities of his mind, his architectural ideas, and an (imaginary) receiving subject, is still Peter Eisenman himself.

III

However, by rejecting the season of diagram architecture tout court, one runs the risk of throwing the baby out with the bath water. There is, in fact, the risk of confusing an avant-garde phenomenon (here "diagram architecture") with an ordinary phenomenology of the diagram as a tool. To avoid this incident, I propose two possible research orientations. The first concerns the diagram as a technique of representation, the genealogy of which dates back to the systems of architectural notation that began to reach an early maturity from the beginning of the 19th century (see Dutto, 2018). To this end, I propose that we acknowledge the architectural diagram as a system of notation capable of producing an effect that can be verified in the practice of architectural design. The second orientation of research concerns instead the diagram as an epistemological device for evaluating typological repertoires in light of massive extra-disciplinary influences of both a material (e.g., technological devices or building materials) and immaterial nature (e.g., actions or procedures). Translated into philosophical terms, these two provisional research orientations highlight, on the one hand, a technological focus and, on the other hand, an ontological one.

IV

Before going forward, I would like to briefly explain why a corpus of handbooks (rather than journals or other kinds of publications) is to some extent useful for the purpose of this argument. As I said at the beginning, handbooks replace the simplified author-building process with a more complex phenomenology populated by different techniques and technicians who participate in the building process. Until the early 20th century, there was no trace of diagrams in handbooks related to building design and construction. It is reasonable to think that up until that moment, there was no need to produce diagrams, as the building types were sufficiently repetitive, and it was unnecessary to employ an alternative notation system to that of plan/section drawing. If we leaf through the voluminous Daniele Donghi's "Manuale dell'architetto" (1905–35), we will find diagrams in the sections of the publication dedicated to the contributions of non-architectural disciplines (i.e., hydraulic, electric, etc.). To this extent, Huyming Pai is right when he writes that diagrams made in the domain of non-architectural scientific disciplines anticipate architectural ones.

However, what is difficult to verify is the hypothesis that architectural diagrams—which would appear almost half a century later—were derived from (or had something to do with) such extra-architectural domains. We must not forget that, simultaneously with handbooks, academic publications addressing architectural design in the domain of the Ecole des Beaux-Arts employed notation systems based on simple signs (i.e., graphs made with straight lines and circles) that were essentially proto-architectural-diagrams

(Palma, 2011). Such notation systems influenced the subsequent diagram trend that occurred in architecture between the 1930s and the 1950s, although the rhetoric of academic terminology survived in a more simplified or essential way. For instance, we find this kind of phenomenon well exemplified in a sector of publications that, in Italy, is acknowledged as "Caratteri distributivi degli edifici" (Eng. Distributional Features of Buildings; Viviani, 1964). What these publications inherit from academic composition is a diagrammatic mindset that is not attributable either to chance or to stylistic choices. Simply put, the use of diagrams in architecture arose when typological repertoires of the mid-19th century became useless in relation to increasingly complex programs. Unlike plans, which reflect the wall consistency of buildings, diagrams renounce this figurative correspondence and translate the building into abstract figures. Such abandonment of traditional repertoires represents the price to be paid by architecture to maintain its legitimacy within the professional framework that operates in the building field. The diagram presents itself as a technological achievement (or, more modestly, a bulwark of survival) of architects in the increasingly struggle-to-build domain.

<u>V</u>

Claiming that the diagram is a technology should not seem strange in the current scenario in which we see technology exemplified with particular entities such as unicorns and "supercazzole," a funny Italian word that corresponds indirectly with the English word "gobbledygook" (Ferraris, 2018). According to a recent philosophical argument developed by Maurizio Ferraris, technology would be placed in an intermediate space between ontology and epistemology, that is, between what exists and what we know about what exists. This space would be populated by "schematisms without concept" (Ferraris, 2018: 7) or agents of unconscious connection between reality and knowledge. For example, the diagrams that architecture students produce instinctively and privately (immediately after, getting rid of them) would be part of this domain. This is certainly due to a widespread prejudice, according to which the rendering of the building prevails over all those materials and tools employed in the intermediate stage of architecture making. Among these "waste" materials, the diagram is somehow considered as an excessively clumsy and embryonic expression of the building, and therefore as something to avoid spending time and effort upon.

In this sense, Ferraris's formulation, according to which technology differs from ontology, is confirmed: the diagram is a technology because it works even in the absence of the building; we can produce diagrams of buildings, events, and other entities that may not even exist. On the contrary, however, Ferraris's dissociation between technology and epistemology is less convincing. Indeed, it is difficult to consider the diagram as a purely instinctive drawing that can be produced in the absence of technical knowledge. Actually, if diagrams look unintelligible (or like nothing more than scribbles that communicate nothing), it is because they are made in the absence of technical knowledge about diagram-making. In this sense, I would hardly call them diagrams. The same goes for the "supercazzola" (or "gobbledygook"): has the reader ever tried to produce it without any technical knowledge about it? If so, they would have noticed that the first attempt was sufficiently embarrassing and would have emitted a guttural sound or an improvised sequence of words that had almost nothing in common with the hieratic emptiness of, for instance, Ugo Tognazzi's "supercazzola" in the film "Amici miei" (1975). This is because even the "supercazzola," as the diagram, is a matter of technical knowledge.

VI

Hence, if the diagram is not an instinctive creation, what is its epistemological background? To this question, those who have boasted the title of supporters of diagram architecture offer no useful answer. For instance, Eisenman claims that the diagram is the product of sculptural actions such as cutting, translating, and rotating (1999) that are typically related to conceptual art. Others, such as Pai (2002), believe that the diagram is an instrument of dialogue with other disciplines with an essentially exorcising function of so-called disciplinary autonomy (where autonomy basically entails the possibility for architects to hold both questions and their answers). As stated in §II, for almost all diagram architecture supporters, the diagram stands for the possibility of solving all the problems of architecture at the same time, with the same optimism that the pioneers of International Style conferred on the machine. But this excess of optimism soon clearly fails. This is how the avant-garde works (and fails).

It should be noted that the exit from this impasse is crucial not only to recover the diagram, but also to evaluate the legacy of the avant-garde. This exit implies an antithetical position compared to the avant-garde itself for at least two reasons. On the one hand, it is necessary to demonstrate that the diagram is not an absolute novelty; rather, it develops in continuity with previous systems of notation (see §VII), which constitutes its epistemological background. On the other hand, it is necessary to deny that the diagram is an all-encompassing device. Therefore, it can face some specific problems, but certainly not all the problems of architectural design.

More generally, this means also accepting, with a certain disenchantment, that the operational field of the diagram is that of ordinary design practice and not just a banner of the avant-garde.

VII

Among the publications of the 1930s and 1950s that deal with the main types of public and commercial buildings (as seen in §IV), it is not uncommon to come across handbooks accompanied by a large number of diagrams, the so-called "distributional diagrams" showing how rooms, furniture, and devices are placed into buildings. These handbooks are not broadly known these days because they remained in a shadow casted by the critique of vulgar functionalism, which simplistically dismissed them with comic definitions such as "bubble diagrams" or "decorated diagrams" (Herdeg, 1985). Upon careful observation (and less vitiated by prejudices), "distributional diagrams" present some features that contrast with the hypothesis that sees them as architectural scribbles.

If we take as an example the handbook by Ruggero Cortelletti, entitled "Elementi di composizione degli edifici civili" (1936), we can see at work a logic of composition of simple elements into complex arrangements. Simple elements are represented through laconic signs, like straight lines, circles, or other regular geometric figures. Such signs are then arranged according to axis configurations (more precisely, the handbook provides a set of 43 axis configurations) in continuity with the way traditional composition was developed at the Ecole des Beaux-Arts (Egbert, 1980). However, Cortelletti's composition is not nostalgic of its academic forerunner. Indeed, it is interesting to note how Cortelletti applies the compositional technique on a basin of building typologies that is completely detached from any academic ancestor. Instead of palaces and churches, Cortelletti deals with buildings such as bus stations, car washes, and slaughterhouses. In this sense, his attitude can be provisionally defined as "utilitarian composition." In fact, it is widely known that academic composition envisaged compliance with a rigorous hierarchy among building types (based on the concept of "character"), at the apex of which were the most representative building programs. After a century, with authors such as Cortelletti, the same techniques were applied not only to stately homes or churches, but also to much less representative buildings. The diagram thus emerged from the dissociation of a previous notation system (the academic composition)—both from a repertoire of plastic forms (building typologies) and from a specific system of (aristocratic) values. The purely utilitarian use of the rules of composition reveals their versatility as freed from metaphysical rhetoric.

VIII

Obviously, academic composition is not the only reference for the production of diagrams. In the first half of the 20th century, various diagrammatic expressions coexisted. It is needless to recall how Durand's modular grids are reflected in the structural diagrams of prefabricated buildings, just as proto-industrial factory layouts are reflected in urban layouts. Beyond individual techniques, what needs to be observed is that almost all of these diagrammatic expressions describe both material and immaterial components of public institutions. The elements that make up these diagrams are not just architectural spaces, rooms, or halls. To these are often added categories of objects that do not necessarily meet spatial criteria, such as subjects (e.g., children, parents, or animals) and actions (e.g., reading, eating, or exchanging). On the one hand, these non-spatial items emphasize the disjunction between diagram and building (see §IV); on the other hand, they provide social objects with a presence, namely a simplified sign (i.e., circle, line, or square) within the diagram. From this point of view, the diagram appears not only as a prosaic functionalist tool, aimed at transforming functional instances into built forms, but also as an attempt to delve into the depths of institutions and dissect their components, dividing them into families and, finally, reproducing the structure of their empirical and conceptual connections. In fact, this operation frees the diagrams from the issue of a priori schemes, specifically a correspondence between facts (building layouts) and concepts (institutions or building types).

The multiplicity of diagrammatic forms that can result from the same institution shows that there is no a priori scheme: the diagram always proves to be dissociated from a specific subject. In this sense, it is interesting to recognize a convergence between diagrammatic thought and some positions of contemporary philosophy that attempt to counter Kantian "correlationism." Among these, in particular, the Object-Oriented Ontology is worth mentioning, although the reader will have to excuse me if I avoid going into philosophical arguments. After almost a century, experimentation on the architectural diagram remains absolutely topical not only from the point of view of its making, but above all because of its employment to verify how institutions turn themselves into matters of architecture. It is scandalous how some programs of institutions (especially public ones) survive today in the total disinterest (on the side of scholars) in verifying their actual existential possibility in contemporary society. Perhaps this is also why diagrams are (still) worth making in architecture.

IX

Therefore, it is important to underline the potential of the diagram as a tool that evaluates institutions, facts, and attitudes. To this extent, it is essential to remember the work already done by scholars such as Thomas A. Markus (1993) or Anthony Froshaug (1959), from which the diagram emerges as an analytical tool aimed at dissecting buildings into their spatial components. In particular, Froshaug proposes a visual methodology based on the use of graphs, which allows him to evaluate the building plan in relation to its complexity. He employs diagrams to unmask the complex plastic forms through which avant-garde architecture claims to present itself as the bearer of a rupture from the past. Then, he shows how ordinary—or somehow traditional—spatial organizations feature many avant-garde buildings, such as Le Corbusier's house in La Plata (Frosghaug, 1959). Thus, rather than being revolutionary, at a closer look, avant-garde outcomes appear to be totally reconciled with the state of affairs they (apparently) pretend to struggle with. On the contrary, the diagrammatic analysis of some ordinary—and notoriously resistant to avant-garde plastic expression—spontaneous building types can sometimes reveal surprising spatial complexities.

Diagrams reveal that architectural forms can greatly deviate from the meaning their author-architect intended them to hold. To this extent, it is useful to recall the concept of "fantastic," with which Roger Caillois intended to show how an artwork is able to produce a meaning for the observer that is totally dissonant with the one declared by its author (Caillois, 1965). Perhaps this kind of "fantastic" is something that diagrams are able to reveal as well. According to their technical functioning, diagrams eradicate the prejudice for which a building (or a part of it) can ultimately be reflected in an (ultimately) true meaning, which is intentionally provided by an author (Armando and Durbiano, 2009). More generally, we could argue that thinking diagrammatically is also a good way to save time from the pointless search for the (ultimate) truth in architecture.

X

In conclusion, I would like to briefly resume the main argument of this essay to avoid some possible misunderstandings. First, I would like to clarify that the choice of referring to a sector of old handbooks has no ideological (or taste-based) reasons and does not imply any nostalgia or sympathy. The reason is purely operational: handbooks provide a sufficiently coherent and rich corpus to advance some epistemological hypotheses on different modes of diagrammatic representation in architectural design. The second clarification concerns the substantially negative summary of the so-called "diagram architecture" avant-garde. To this end, I would like to clarify that this is not an evaluation that I extend to the works of the individual authors that intellectually supported this avant-garde trend. What I wanted to point out is that an excessive attribution of meanings to the diagram has resulted in a rapid decay of the diagram itself. Taken as the banner of the avant-garde, the diagram quickly carried out its mission of finally being swept away along with the debris that accumulated in the avalanche of residue from previous and subsequent avant-garde developments. Incidentally, I would like to emphasize that this essay intends to present itself as a contribution to a broader archaeological process in the debris of the architectural avant-garde, which promises to be long and tiring, but nonetheless promising.

Finally, it should be noted that the excess of schematism with which I outlined the story of diagram architecture does not in any way exclude the experiences that followed and that still concern the activity of architects and scholars in relation to diagram-making (Fedorchenko, 2019; Gasperoni and Gleiter, 2019; Stapenhorst, 2016). I think it is clear that the diagram no longer constitutes a defined theoretical core but has merged into other discourses, including ecology, digitalism, and parametricism, to name but a few. However, I leave the burden of analyzing this diaspora to others. In any case, the survival of the diagram in contemporary architectural discourse also constitutes the hope that there is still someone willing to seriously measure themselves with this theme, to listen to the different positions, and to retrace its evolution.

References

Armando, A., Durbiano, G. (2009), *Davanti ai valori degli altri*, in A. De Rossi (ed.), Grande Scala: Architettura politica forma, Trento, ListLab, pp. 27–58.

Biraghi, M., Ferlenga, A. (eds.), (2012), *Architettura del Novecento*, Torino, Einaudi.

Bürger, P. (2010), *Avant-Garde and Neo-Avant-Garde*, "New Literary History," v. 41, n. 4, pp. 695–715.

Caillois, R. (1965), *Au Coeur du Fantastique*, Paris, Gallimard.

Cortelletti, R. (1936), *Elementi di composizione degli edifici civili*, Milano, Hoepli.

Dutto, A. A. (2018), *The Legacy of Handbooks: The Paradigm of Distribution in Architectural Design*, Bergamo, Tecnograph.

Egbert, D. (1980), *The Beaux-Arts Tradition in French Architecture*, Princeton, Princeton University Press.

Eisenman, P. (1999), *Diagram Diaries*, New York, Thames & Hudson.

Fedorchenko, M. (2019), *The Tools of Mediation: Extending the Diagrammatic Project*, in V. Cavedagna, A.A. Dutto (eds.), *Schema. Verso un dizionario filosofico-architettonico*, Torino, Philosophy Kitchen, pp. 145–69.

Ferraris, M. (2018), *Intorno Agli Unicorni: Supercazzole, Ornitorinchi e Ircocervi*, Bologna, Il Mulino.

Froshaug, A. (1959), *Visual Methodology*, "Quarterly Bulletin of the Hochschule für Gestaltung, Ulm," v. 4.

Gasperoni, L., Gleiter, J. (2019), *Architektur und Diagramm ein theoretisches Experiment*, Berlin, Technische Universität Berlin.

Garcia, M. (ed.), (2010), *The Diagrams of Architecture*, Chichester, Wiley.

Herdeg, K. (1985), *The Decorated Diagram: Harvard Architecture and the Failure of the Bauhaus Legacy*, Cambridge, MIT Press.

Ito, T. (1996), *Diagram Architecture*, "El Croquis," v. 77, pp. 18–24.

Markus, T. A. (1993), *Buildings & Power: Freedom and Control in the Origin of Modern Building Types*, London; New York, Routledge.

Merrill, E. (2017), *The Professione di Architetto in Renaissance Italy*, "Journal of the Society of Architectural Historians," v. 76, n. 1, pp. 13–35.

Pai, H. (2002), *The Portfolio and the Diagram: Architecture*, Discourse, and Modernity in America, Cambridge, MIT Press.

Palma, R. (2011), *Il programma: spazio del testo e figure del progetto*, G. Motta, R. Palma, A. Pizzigoni (eds.), *La nuova griglia politecnica: architettura e macchina di progetto*, Milano, Franco Angeli, pp. 189–221.

Stapenhorst, C. (2016), *Concept: A Dialogic Instrument in Architectural Design*, Berlin, Jovis.

Viviani, R. (1964), *L' insegnamento di caratteri distributivi degli edifici a Firenze: metodi, ricerche, contributi*, Firenze, Libreria ed. Fiorentina.

DOCUMENTS, MONUMENTS, LINEAMENTS.
On Pre-existing Elements of Innovation in Construction Drawing
Klaus Platzgummer

Klaus Platzgummer holds a Master's in Architecture from the ETH Zürich (2015) and a Master's with distinction in History and Critical Thinking in Architecture from the Architectural Association (2016). His dissertation at the AA examined encyclopaedic orderings of architectural knowledge and won the Graduate School Prize for Writing (2017). Klaus is currently a Teaching and Research associate at the Department of Architectural Theory, TU Berlin and a Tutor for History and Theory Studies at AA. He was a visiting lecturer at the Technion in Israel in 2019.

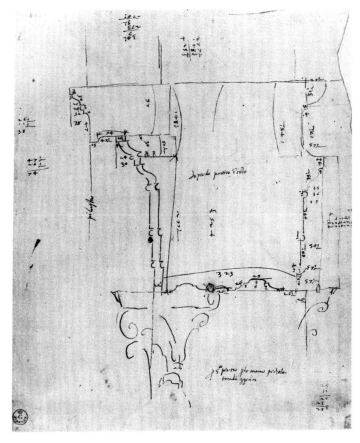

Figure 1
Antonio da Sangallo the Younger, Rome, St. Peter, Working drawing with measurements in one hundredth of a piede, shows in section their reduced entablature (1519 or later). Source: Christoph L. Frommel, Nicholas Adams (eds.), The Architectural Drawings of Antonio da Sangallo The Younger. Vol. II (New York: MIT Press, 2000), 293

Documents

In his book *Die Schrift: Hat Schreiben Zukunft? (Does Writing Have a Future?)* (1987), the philosopher Vilém Flusser (1920–91) expands a model for the historicity of the cultural technique of writing. Flusser points out that over the long history of writing, two forms have emerged: Inschriften and Aufschriften; that is, writing *into* surfaces and writing *onto* surfaces. He summarises *Inschriften* as "monumental" and *Aufschriften* as "documentary."[1]

While the creation of writings *into* surfaces is a laborious, slow, and thoughtful process (e.g., inscriptions *into* stone), the application of characters with pen and ink *onto* paper is a hectic one. The "fact that the gesture of writing is both hectic [...] and faltering at the same time strikes back at the writer's consciousness. It structures [her or his] 'historical consciousness.'"[2] It gives "insight into the structure of the lineally oriented thinking (and acting). Namely, in the structure of thinking (and acting) that unrolls along a time that, coming from the past, hurries towards the future, passing through the present without staying there."[3] Flusser even goes so far as to assert that "critical thinking"[4] can be found in the dialectic between hectic writing down and thinking. The decisive factor in Flusser's model is ultimately the *materiality* of the surface being written into or onto, which significantly determines the speed of writing and thus the relationship between the writer and the medium.

Perhaps it seems obscure to discuss the issue of *innovation* by focusing on the materiality of the surfaces on which humankind deploys its cultural technique of writing. However, according to anthropologist André Leroi-Gourhan (1911–86), how humanity deals with the materiality of the environment is not a side issue when it comes to the question of innovation— quite the contrary. It is important for understanding innovation. In his *Milieu et Techniques* (1945), Leroi-Gourhan argues that "création *ex nihilo*" or "l'invention pure" *(the pure invention)* is fundamentally impossible. According to him, creations or inventions are always conditioned by 'éléments préexistants' *(pre-existing elements)* and these are to be found "dans le matériel ou les traditions du groupe" *(in the material or the traditions of groups)*.[5] He claims even that these two pre-existing elements are at the origin of all innovation: "à l'origine de toute innovation."[6]

In *Le Geste et la Parole* (1964), Leroi-Gourhan demonstrates the role of materials and traditions by means of countless examples. From the first animated clocks and automatons in the Middle Ages to the invention of photography in the 19th century, technical progress does not arise from nowhere but is an entanglement of "material expression" and a "favorable environment for innovation."[7] It is argued here that such entanglements can also be found in architectural practices.

Monuments

The technique of construction drawing has for centuries involved the application of signs *onto* a specific material: paper. However, this was not always the case. Anticipated by the drawing techniques of the Cathedral huts,[8] modern construction drawing on paper or parchment—as a composito of geometric figures, numerical measurement chains, and written annotations—had its genesis most probably in the circles of Antonio Sangallo the Younger (1484–1546) (Fig. 1).[9] Prior to this, in the Middle Ages until approximately the 13th century, the relationship between the acts of drawing and building was rather different. Construction drawings were usually monumental and inextricably interwoven with the craftsmanship of the building. On construction sites, master builders worked with geometric figures, applied with stencils into the stone, and used the four basic arithmetic operations to determine the overall proportion of buildings. An impressive example of this can be seen in the drawings in the cathedral of Soissons, dating from the middle of the 13th century, where the builders applied blind arcades and tracery windows at a ratio of one to one. Here, construction drawing's decisive surfaces were not sheets of paper but stone floors and walls on site, with these drawings growing alongside the construction process itself. Such drawings become buildings, just as the building constitutes the drawing.

The widespread use of drawings on paper (or parchment) since the Renaissance led eventually to a fundamental reorganization of construction sites. It became unnecessary for sites to be constantly supervised by master builders, not least because construction drawings on paper could be produced offsite and used to communicate with the workers at the construction site. These drawings were also no longer dependent on the "slowness" of the construction process. The process of drawing had been radically separated from that of building, such that the historicity of construction drawing became independent of the historioity of the construction site.

Regarding the cultural technique of writing, Vilém Flusser characterizes Inschriften (i.e., writing *into* a surface) as monumental. This is not because of the sheer size of the writing; rather, Inschriften are monumental because to engrave into wax or to chisel into stone demands "prudence and contemplation." This also applies to a certain extent to the medieval construction drawing process because carving life-size construction drawings into floors and walls was laborious.[10] However, drawing in stone also involved a thoughtfulness that combined with a basic religious attitude. Just as paper has determined the historical consciousness of architects since the Renaissance, in previous centuries, stone did the same. These traces by medieval master builders *into* stone did not form a hectic or even "critical" consciousness but a historical consciousness that was contemplative.

Lineaments

For decades, architects have made recourse to a device—the computer—for producing construction drawings. These digital drawings do not follow the logic of either Inschriften or Aufschriften. Rather, they reflect the cultural technique of *Vorschriften*[11]—prescripts. A computer operates with algorithms, which are simply rules for a calculation process following a (sometimes) repetitive scheme. Per definition, graphics appear on a screen *a posteriori* to an algorithmic operation.

In analogy to the material basis of drawings (i.e., stone, parchment, or paper), the materiality of computers likewise constitutes the historicity of drawings. Indeed, the historical transition from paper to digital drawings is not as simple as Mark Wigley, for example, would have us believe. In his essay *Black Screens: The Architect's Vision in a Digital Age*, he states that, with the advent of computers, paper has been replaced by a "black screen."[12] However, the materiality of digital drawings is not a flat "black screen"; it is a mechanism of silicon chips, magnetic hard disks, copper cables, and liquid crystal displays. With the advent of computers, simple surfaces have been transformed into deep and multi-layered ones, which explains why digital drawings follow their own logic (i.e., of Vorschriften).

The permanent presence of digital drawings is not graphical; it is merely a voltage difference on a magnetic hard disk. The presence of drawings on a screen is only the "automated presence"[13] of those voltage differences: 60 times per second. In this sense, digital drawings are predominantly non-graphical, or imperceptible. The computer is, however, able to represent non-graphical digital drawings as perceptible ones; that is, as graphical images on a screen. A computer's cables, graphics card, random-access memory, and central processing unit serve to mediate between the non-graphical and the graphical.

It is ironic that half a millennium ago, Leon Battista Alberti (1404–1472) was at a similar point in history as we are now: he already had a conception in mind of drawings that were partly non-graphical. In the preface to his treatise *De re Aedificatoria*, Alberti introduces the concept of "lineaments," writing that a "building is a form of body, which like any other consists of lineaments (*lineamenta*) and matter (*materia*)."[14]

Thus, he radically divides buildings into two parts. While lineaments are the "product of thought," matter derives from nature.[15] For Alberti, a building is, on the one hand, a lineament or scheme in the mind of the architect, and on the other, simply matter.

In the first book of his *De re Aedificatoria*, Alberti specifies the initial definition by saying that the

> "function and duty of lineaments [is] to *prescribe* an appropriate place, exact numbers, a proper scale, and a graceful order for whole buildings and for each of their constituent parts, so that the whole form and appearance of the building may depend on the lineaments alone. Nor do lineaments have anything to do with material."[16]

Having said that, one should by no means succumb to the often-postulated fallacy that lineaments equal drawings, are graphical, and therefore are a material and physical image. If lineaments are images at all, they are mental images and purely meta-physical.[17] Lineaments are prescriptive (i.e, Vorschriften) and in this sense, a scheme *a priori* to both drawings and building.

Thinking in lineaments is not restricted to their conception in Alberti's *De re Aedificatoria*. Rather, thinking in lineaments is a modern *tradition* of architectural thought, so internalized

Klaus Platzgummer – Documents, Monuments, Lineaments.
on Pre-existing Elements of Innovation in Construction Drawing

that architects almost forget that they are always confronted with lineaments when drawing. During the 20th century, this completely internalised tradition became entangled with the materiality of complex electronic sign carriers; that is, silicon chips, magnetic hard disks, copper cables, and liquid crystal displays. According to André Leroi-Gourhan, such entanglements of *traditions* with the *material* expressions of a time are pre-existing elements of innovation. Like all innovations, the cultural technique of digital drawings is not a pure invention. Far from being creations *ex nihilo*, today's digital construction drawings are inextricably interwoven with the long history of architectural lineaments.

Notes

[1] Flusser, V. *Die Schrift. Hat Schreiben Zukunft?* (Göttingen: Immatrix Publications, 1987), p. 21.

[2] Ibid., p. 23.

[3] Ibid.

[4] Ibid.

[5] Leroi-Gourhan, A. (1973), *Milieu et techniques.* (Paris: Éditions Albin Michel), pp. 387—88.

[6] Ibid., p. 388.

[7] Ibid., *Gesture and Speech* (Cambridge: MIT Press, 1993), pp. 183, 214, 233; see also Mario Carpo (2001), *Architecture in the Age of Printing, Orality, Writing, Typography, and Printed Images in the History of Architectural Theory.* (Cambridge: MIT Press), p. 119.

[8] Böker, J. (2014) *Architektur der Gotik—Gothic Architecture.* Salzburg: Anton Pustet, pp. 15—28.

[9] Ackermann, J. S. (1954) *Architectural Practice in the Italian Renaissance,* "Journal of the Society of Architectural Historians" 13, no. 3 (October): pp. 3—11.

[10] It is plausible to apply this model for the historicity of the technique of writing also to drawing practices. Indeed, it is Flusser himself who argued that "the writer is not a painter, he is a draughtsman. ... The writer is a drafter, draughtsman, a designer, and a semiologist." See Vilém Flusser, Die Schrift. Hat Schreiben Zukunft? (Göttingen: Immatrix Publications, 1987), pp.

21—22.

[11] Flusser, V. (1987) Die Schrift. Hat Schreiben Zukunft? (Göttingen: Immatrix Publications), p. 57.

[12] Wigley, M. (2017), *Black Screen; The Architect's Vision in a Digital Age,* in "When is the Digital in Architecture?", ed. Andrew Goodhouse (Montréal: Canadian Centre for Architecture, 2017), pp. 177—192.

[13] May, J. (2019), *Signal. Image. Architecture. (Everything is already an Image),* New York: Columbia University Press, pp. 91—104.

[14] Alberti, L. B. (1988), *On the Art of Building in Ten Books,* ed. Joseph Rykwert, Neil Leach, Robert Tavernor. Boston: MIT Press, 5; original Latin wording added by the author.

[15] Ibid.

[16] Ibid., p. 7; emphasis by the author.

[17] Mitchell, W. J. T. (1984), *What Is an Image?,* New Literary History 15, no. 3 (Spring 1984): pp. 504—507.

References

Ackermann, J. S. (1954), *Architectural Practice in the Italian Renaissance,* "Journal of the Society of Architectural Historians," vol. 13, n. 3, pp. 3—11.

Alberti, L. B. (1988), *On the Art of Building in Ten Books,* ed. Joseph Rykwert, Neil Leach, Robert Tavernor, Boston, MIT Press.

Böker, J. (2014), *Architektur der Gotik – Gothic Architecture,* Salzburg, Anton Pustet.

Carpo, M. (2001), *Architecture in the Age of Printing, Orality, Writing, Typography, and Printed Images in the History of Architectural Theory,* Cambridge, MIT Press.

Flusser, V. (1987), *Die Schrift. Hat Schreiben Zukunft?,* Göttingen, Immatrix Publications.

Leroi-Gourhan, A. (1973), *Milieu et techniques,* Paris, Éditions Albin Michel.

Leroi-Gourhan, A. (1993), *Gesture and Speech,* Cambridge, MIT Press.

Wigley, M. (2017), *Black Screen: The Architect's Vision in a Digital Age,* "When is the Digital in Architecture?," ed. by Andrew Goodhouse, Montréal, Canadian Centre for Architecture, pp. 177—192.

May, J. (2019), *Signal. Image. Architecture. Everything is already an Image,* New York, Columbia University Press,.

Mitchell, W. J. T. (1984) *What Is an Image?,* "New Literary History," vol. 15, n. 3, pp. 504—7.

ON THE TEMPORALITY OF THE PROJECT
Petar Bojanić

Peter Bojanić is a principal research fellow at the Institute for Philosophy and Social Theory of the University of Belgrade. He received his PhD in 2003 from the EHESS (Paris) and the University of Paris X. Bojanić is director of the Center for Advanced Studies of the University of Rijeka. He teaches philosophy of architecture at the University of Belgrade, and has authored numerous texts on the relation between philosophy and architecture, as well as a new edition of *Peter Eisenman. In Dialogue with Architects and Philosophers*. Currently he is writing a book on the project and projective acts.

Presently, I will elaborate on a passage from Henri Bergson's 1902-03 lectures about how English is learned, and how to acquire its best expression (pronunciation). However, before we get to Bergson, I would like to offer a few of my own thoughts to strengthen the connection between time (specifically, the future), action, and the community. Imagine, if you will, how much conversation, back and forth, chatter, etc. needs to take place among organizers, participants, representatives of various authorities for a short summer school at, say, the Politecnico di Torino.[1] At some point, before it started, there was a clear intention (let us call it "empty intention"[2]) that the school take place. Then, while it was happening, we were participating in it, talking within it and about it (when it had become "(ful)filled intention" or just intention), the summer school had ceased to exist in the future or to exist merely as a project to be or project to be realized. In taking place, the school certainly had a new modality. Unclear ideas, intentions, conceptions (concepts[3]) of the summer school in Politecnico Torino (the space, location), formulated and constructed over the course of the previous year or the previous several months, through various communal acts, as a complicated project (with a document, budget, money, order, work plan, schedule, timing), all had to come together in the course of a few days. They had to take place by holding us (the organizers, the students, the guest lecturers) together as a group with a given task. The future (the school now being actualized and objectivized) had in one way or another replaced the concept and project. A group of people, together, had designed and organized the transmission of a series of amorphous mental entities into our current communal social acts and facts. The future must conform to the present. I do not need to list all the consequences of this future that took place, but certainly the school as a social fact or repertoire of social facts had eliminated the time of execution of the project and design of this very school.

"Eliminated time" actually represents the erasure of temporality in the project, a temporality only possible within the project—this is what I am above all interested to show.[4] Let me formulate my claim in reverse: when the project is no longer—there is no longer any future. The project ensures the future. Or, to achieve complete circularity, let me introduce a third element: without the future, a group or a "we" cannot possibly exist.

When it appears that the project is taking place, we will all together (in the days the school was taking place) assess whether the project corresponds to the concept that preceded it, which is to say, whether the project was executed better than thought (as in the saying "it went better than I expected," or when the project realized surpassed the concept, what was "in the head," "the idea," or "on paper," the comparison of the expected and what remained unbuilt). Or whether the project has fallen apart. What does a failed project mean? Does not the meaning of the word "project" (to throw something forward, to pitch) already imply that every project is necessarily failed? The very possibility of comparing what was taking place then with other summer schools or some idea of an ideal, imagined (then, or previously) summer school implicitly opens the possibility for constructing a next project and the future as such. Thus, as soon as it appears that a project has been executed[5] and ceases to exist, a new project or slew of projects appears on the horizon. If several protocols, such as "possibility," "horizon,"[6] and "imagination" ("as if") are in some way "mingled" and "entwined," would that be enough to show that the basic modus of project temporality—the future, what is yet to come (avenir in French) or what is to follow—has finally been revealed?[7] If "the future" is revealed within an imaginary distance between the concept and project, between two words or notions always difficult to differentiate, does then this modality of time have special status in the "time-space" relation? How much future is there necessarily in space? Better still, is future more connected to space than is, for example, the past?

I would now like to systematize a few difficulties by constructing several conditions that refer to the revealing of the future and temporary nature of the project. I would like to provisionally insist on a weakness found in certain languages spoken by a great number of people that makes the future difficult to linguistically stabilize and document: German and English do not have a future tense, using instead auxiliary verbs, respectively, "werden" (to become), "will"/"be going to."

The first condition refers to the pronoun "we." Whence "we" and how is it possible? "We" who produce certain social acts as part of a project (residents of a city, for example, who pass by each other, live side by side, tolerate one another, etc.[8]) also construct its following, its new projects.[9] 'We' is always what is left over from a project just completed and what is always altered and constituted anew ("new" or "sudden" is always both possible and impossible). The future is implicitly present in each expression of a given state that is addressed to some other or others (individuals): if I promise something to someone, there is an assumption of time needed to make good on the promise.[10] Further, every address to another is simultaneously the expectation of a reaction and reciprocity, also always temporally conditioned (between my saying "hello" and your responding "hello" there is an interval; between my Viber message, and your response, there is a period in which you are perhaps answering or in turn asking a question of someone else). "Give me time" or "take your time" or "I will buy time" can confirm the future as an interval in which various actions are to be performed. Reticence to answer or address someone else is a kind of negative social act. Finally, the still complicated and ill-defined position of a head or leader in a democracy opens the act of ordering (or consulting, suggesting, advising) to future time and thus producing inequality. Alexandre Kojève gives a very simple example of some of these issues, in which the authority of the project creator (the subject) is incidental compared to the authority of the project itself: "Let us consider a familiar example. A band of kids gather to play. One of these kids proposes to go and steal apples from the orchard next door. Immediately, by doing so, he casts himself in the role of the band's leader. He became this leader because he saw *further* (*plus loin*) than the others, because it was he alone who thought out a *project*, while the others did not manage to get beyond the level of immediate facts" (Kojève, 2014: 63; and 2004: 74).

For a group to potentially remain together, confirm its own "we-mode" (for two to remain together, since love is above all continuously projected), and preserve its 'co-presence' (such as to meet and work together the following year in Torino), various project operations (co-regulations) have to be introduced: correcting mistakes in the production of social acts, exclusion of the undisciplined, repetition, forecasting, differentiation of the possible from the impossible, insistence anew, insistence on the new, amendment, etc.

The second condition also refers to the pronouns "we" or "us," referring to an important connection of the future with space (co-presence or co-present implies "the local structure of we-space itself") (Krueger, 2010: 4). It is as if the future is primarily that form of time that allows and ensures the connection between time in general and space. The simple fact of my passing time unfolding inseparably from my body extending in space can be entirely simultaneous with the simple fact of your passing time unfolding in your body extending in space. Two temporalities and two spatialities that do not intermingle are always recognized in the present. However, physical (and not only physical[11]) co-present contact always introduces the aspect of future: orientation and location (and dislocation, a term by Peter Eisenman). Based on this, my existence in the future is directly dependent on the future I could occupy along with others. The architectural protocol does not necessarily appear with the invention of space, but only with the introduction of "our" time (or "our" future) into space.

Petar Bojanić - On the Temporality of the Project

The various problems that occur in the course of our common or simultaneous penetration as a group into a given location and its duration there, its co-existence or common being in a single place, all demand a necessary reconstruction of the connection between architecture and philosophy (or sociology).[12] The first task or epistemological operation would consist of constructing an architectural terminology that meticulously follows the repertoire of various gestures (steps, moments, points, sequences) made in the course of a communal taking of space (from concept and project to object and the material). How do we name the various gestures and provide an order of notions that would correspond to the archaeology of philosophical and historical notions? Parallel to this, a new reading of philosophical texts from an architectural perspective allows for correcting their logic and establishing new connections between the future (time) and space. Here is an example. At the same time that Bergson thematizes time in his seminars (although it is equally important how he even enters the abstract problem of time), Georg Simmel publishes his 1903 text "Über räumliche Projektionen sozialer Formen."[13] I would like to unreservedly insist that the idea of a project, or perhaps a sketch of any future theory of the project, has been constructed at this very time within an imaginary exchange between Bergson and Simmel. Simmel's title could be a translation and addition to a well-known expression from Kant, which also requires intervention if we introduce the dimension of time, that is, the future. Simmel calls the transfer or shift of social forms "spatial projection." If we pull apart this phrase, we have social forms launched from somewhere or projected into space. Casting social forms into space is actually a temporal operation that relies on social forms maintaining themselves or existing only in space (these social forms are actually constructions protecting the relations among people, what connects them and their or our "we"). However, by combining this protocol with a 1908 sentence by Simmel, written in the style of John Searle ("The boundary is not a special fact with sociological consequences, but a sociological fact that forms spatiality itself") (Simmel, 1992: 697), it becomes clear that social acts in fact establish space. Space is always already social space, constituted in time to come. The project (or projection, design) actually brings future time to space. Only in this way is the construction of the social complete. Agents or subjects occupy or make space by projecting their mutual relations. Simmel cites Kant's sentence from "Paralogisms" several times ("Criticism of the fourth paralogism of transcendental psychology"; the always relevant passage on the difference between idealism and realism). Speaking of space as representation:

> "This perception thus represents (staying for now only with outer intuitions) something real in space. For first, perception is the representation of a reality, just as space is the representation of a mere possibility of coexistence."
>
> *Diese Wahrnehmung stellt also, (damit wir diesmal nur bei äusseren*

Anschauungen bleiben) etwas Wirkliches im Raume vor. Denn erstlich ist Wahrnehmung die Vorstellung einer Wirklichkeit, so wie Raum die Vorstellung einer blossen Möglichkeit des Beisammenseins. (Kant, 1999: 428 [1781: 374]).

Space is really a representation of mere possibility of coexistence. The phrase can also be rendered into English as "possibility of being together." Only in this one place does Kant use this word, so difficult to translate, *Beisammenseins* —"being next to one another." The social is here only implicit, but the phrase provides a primer for Simmel's suggestion that space is always ready to accept any future projection.

The third condition—which is implicitly the first necessary condition to give the future form—refers to the connection between the concept and expression. Thus, prior to the condition in which the group constitutes the project in the future in order to sustain itself in the present (which is a fundamental characteristic of strategy—"having a project"), and prior to the second condition in which social forms penetrate into space all at once, constituting it, there is a complicated attempt to conceptualize the concept through expression and expressivity. In the introductory session of his second seminar on December 5, 1902, Bergson differentiates relative and absolute knowledge. English pronunciation provides him (whose mother was English) with an example. After concluding that his English is completely contaminated by French and "in service to French" (*en fonction du français*), Bergson says:

"What would it take to have absolute knowledge? It would be necessary to be transported to England, live among the English, living an English life, immersed in the flow of English pronunciation … Relative knowledge means knowing from outside of what one is learning; relative knowledge of English expressions is having knowledge outside England, being and residing in France. It means knowing English in service of French elements and expressions. On the other hand, absolute knowledge of English expressions is knowing not from the outside, but from within. In order to have such absolute knowledge of expressions, I must not stay at home, I must go to England. I can then learn to use not my home expressions, but those foreign, know them in themselves, as the philosophers say."

Que faudrait-il pour en avoir une connaissance absolue? Il faudrait me transporter en Angleterre, il faudrait vivre avec des Anglais, vivre de la vie anglaise, il faudrait me plonger dans le courant de la prononciation anglaise; (...) Connaitre relativement c'est connaître du dehors, c'est être en dehors de ce qu'on apprend; connaître relativement la prononciation de l'anglais, c'est la connaître étant hors de l'Angleterre, étant en France et restante en France; c'est connaître l'anglais en function

*d'éléments de prononciation française. Au contraire, connaître absolu-
ment cette prononciation, c'est la connaître non pas du dehors, mais du
dedans. Pour connaître cette prononciation absolument, il ne faut pas
que je reste chez moi, il faut que j'aille en Angleterre; je connais alors
la prononciation non plus de chez moi, mais chez elle, en soi, comme
dissent les philosophes.* (Bergson, 2016: 18—19)

This is a magical passage from a man who was well-nigh bilingual, yet insisted on a specific difference that concerns a few crucial notions that frame any
possible knowledge about time. Let me list them here, provisionally:

a) precision (a register we would today easily confuse for perfection, yet
Bergson ascribed the invention of precision of articulation and demonstration
to the Greek genius[15]), which is in harmony with others and concerns socialization or the social (Bergson uses the phrase *"la vie sociale"*) (Bergson, 2019:
134—135). It includes a locality that surpasses people who live in a given location. Bergson differentiates England, life with the English, and English life;

b) concept (since Bergson's seminars are really about the construction
of the concept, such as the concept of knowledge of expression ("absolute
knowledge of expression" (*connaître cette prononciation absolument*);

c) "active expression" (the phrase is mine) since the concept for Bergson
is "an invitation to action" (*une invitation à agir*) or "above all a suggestion of
possible action" (*avant tout une suggestion d'une action possible*) (Bergson,
2016: 64), meaning c1) action, and c2) expression (the imperative is to express
oneself absolutely—to express the concept). To know—to know absolutely—
means to express oneself absolutely or correctly.

Why is the concept (*"le concept"* or *"la pensée conceptuelle,"* words that
Bergson uses interchangeably) (Bergson, 2019: 125) (May 2, 1902)[16] important
for Bergson, and why is the theory of the concept constructed by Bergson
really an introduction into an imaginary never-written study of the project?[17]
Time and duration are what cannot be expressed through concepts (*par des
concepts*).[18] But time as future begins with naming, with language and expression of what is initially present in the mind (*à l'esprit*).

"I am saying that it (the noun, substantive) first refers to the individual.
When I say 'man' or 'table,' it is in the singular, individual form that the concept
presents itself to the mind."

(*Je dis qu'il (le nom, le substantif) exprime d'abord l'individuel. Quand je dis:
l'homme, la table, c'est une conception individuelle, un concept d'individu que
se présente d'abord à l'esprit.*) (Bergson, 2019: 126) (May 2,1902).

If time as such cannot be rendered or expressed in language ("there is an interval that remains unexpressed" (*il y a un intervalle qui reste inexprimé*)), language as well as the expression of everything else begins in the future tense.
Action, as the actual beginning of the project (and action is in opposition to

perception, according to Bergson [2016: 70]), "throws time back outside"[19] and is regulated by the precision and rigor of expression in uttering the concept.[20]

> "Among else, man is a speaking being, a social being, and will assign words to concepts. Being much more malleable than any corporeal approach he takes, the word will also render the concept much more malleable and flexible. Man will make use of the word not only to speak to others, but to speak to himself."
>
> *L'homme est, en outre, un être qui parle, un être sociable, et ce concept il va le designer par un mot, et ce mot étant un signe beaucoup plus maniable que ne le serait l'attitude corporelle prise par lui, ce mot va render le concept beaucoup plus maniable, aussi plus mobilizable. Il se servira du mot non seulement pour parler aux autres, mais pour se parler à lui-même.* (Bergson, 2016: 72)

The production of concepts is an entirely artificial, human thing, as is the project. "The concept has its origin in action and is above all an instrument for action" (*concept a son origine dans l'action et il est avant tout un instrument d'action*) ("a concept expresses an action" (*un concept exprime une action*)) (Bergson, 2016: 73). Action creates concepts and concepts draw on action. The second operation marks the birth of the project.

Bergson offers no further explanation of "speaking to himself" (*pour se parler à lui-même*), despite this being a substantive aspect of speech addressed to others. It is thus possible to speak of a further construction or speculation about a project that is individual or mine alone. In any case, the idea that it is possible to speak to oneself is deduced from speech addressed to others and implying their response. Speaking to others is to invite them to action, or better still, joint action. Several possibilities follow from this: first, that I cannot express on another's behalf (I can help and complete someone's words or sentences, I can translate, but never replace another in "expressing a concept"). Second, precise expression implies retaining those who hear me (as well as those who have yet to hear me) in the given space, preserving our common use of the space. Third, expressing the concept would be equal to expressing one's own concept or one's self—expressing oneself is expressing one's concept. This means gaining time in anticipation of others' responses, which is common construction of projects and the future.[21] Fourth, good expression is necessarily compulsive and pressing (*Zeitnot*, urgency, priority, prevention, etc.).[22]

> "All concepts have, more or less, a practical goal, and all concepts are our questions addressed to reality, from a subjective standpoint, regarding the attitude we should adopt towards it and it towards us. A concept is a rubric, a class into which we enter an object. Finding the right class

for each object, asking ot it whether it goes here or there, ultimately means asking it what it is in relation to us, what we can make of it."
(*Tout concept a, plus ou moins, une destination pratique, tout concept est une question posée par nous à la réalité, au point de vue relative, à l'attitude que nous devons prendre vis-à-vis d'elle ou qu'elle prend vis-à-vis de nous; un concept c'est une rubrique, une classe dans laquelle nous faisons rentrer un objet. Chercher dans quelle classe un objet peut rentrer, lui demander s'il est ceci ou cela, c'est au fond lui demander ce qu'il est par rapport à nous, ce que nous pourrions faire de lui*). (Bergson, 2016: 73)

Notes

[1] The present paper grew out of a lecture given at the Innovation in Practice Summer School, Torino, in September 2019. The author would like to thank Giovanni Durbiano and Alessandro Armando for their invitation and hospitality, as well as Valeria, Elena, Andrea, and Edoardo for organizing the school. In particular, I am grateful to the participating students and my co-presenter Snežana Vesnić—conversations we had were very useful in providing specific terminology, and went a long way to giving this text its ultimate form.

[2] Husserl speaks of an intentionally empty horizon (*intentionaler Leer-horizont*), an absence to be filled (*eine ausfüllende Leere*). (Husserl, 1966: 6) Cf. Losoncz 2017.

[3] In speaking of the "*concept*" when lecturing about time, Bergson neglected to make use of something that might more precisely explain his intention—the "empty concept," which has a history from Kant to Sartre. As opposed to the "authentic" concept, the "empty concept" refers to something fictitious that has no corresponding "reality." In the commentary of his translation of Aristotle's "Peri Ermenias," Boethius recognizes the existence of empty concepts. Alain de Libera translates Boethius' "*intellectus*" as "*concept*," because in Boethius "*conceptio*" and "*conceptus*" are synonymous with "*intellectus*." "Boethius was apparently the first to recognize that there is such a thing as empty concept, i.e., intellections that have no corresponding real subject, such as centaurs and chimeras or ones invented by poets." (*Or Boèce est, évidemment, le premier à reconnaître qu'il y a des concepts vides, i.e., des intellections qui ne correspondent pas à une réalité sujet, comme celles que les poètes ont façonnées, centaures ou chimères*) (Libera, 1990: 418).

[4] Divine creation, the various acts of Adonai in the course of creating everything, only partially satisfy the criteria to be named project or the product of a project. When he thinks (conceptualizes) or simply says, Adonai has already created. It is as if there were no process of creation or time of execution of the project.

[5] English is wonderfully helpful with the word execute: where other European languages use some variation of 'realized' for the operation of bringing something to fruition, English more commonly uses a word meaning to kill, to remove from existence.

[6] These two words speak to the constitutive primacy of the future and evoke the phenomenological hermeneutic method.

[7] Does the future arrive or follows and moves ahead? How can we describe what has yet to happen? Does one wait for the future, or is it constructed and anticipated? Projection and design is an artificial operation of preparation for what is to come thus reducing the uncertainty of "what has yet to arrive."

[8] In Hebrew, making time has the same root with the invited one, with hospitality. The invitation produces the future.

[9] For example, within this group working together on the notion of the future, I have entirely different projects and plans with Giovanni Durbiano, Alessandro Armando, Snežana Vesnic, Edoardo Fregonese, Joerg Gleiter, etc. Maurizio Ferraris wrote to me a few days prior my arrival in Torino, saying "We must meet when you arrive. I have many projects to share with you" (*j'ai beacoup de projects à partager*). Is there such a thing as an unsharable project that would still keep the characteristics of the project?

[10] Interestingly, when constructing his argument on the difference between performative and constative, John Austin never speaks of time implied in any successful performative act. If I promise to replace your bike tire, is there not an implied agreement of deadline by when I will do so? A promise necessarily introduces time.

[11] Does Skype (Viber, WhatsApp, or Signal) co-present mean "present" and does it mean common space? Also, does telepathy contain a future moment or an announcement of future time?

[12] This reconstruction should be constantly thematized in order to compare and harmonize two different productions of knowledge. Take, for example, the question of the 'Architecture Biennale 2020' curator, Hashim Sarkis: "How will we live together?" It is a remake of the seminar held by Roland Barthes in 1976/77, "Comment vivre ensemble?"

[13] "The Spatial Projection of Social Forms" is first published in *Zeitschrift fⓧr Sozialwissenschaft*, 6, 5, 1903, 287–302. Reprint: Simmel, 1995. Along with some other writing, it will be incorporated into a chapter of his *Sociology* where he thematizes the notion of space.

[14] A version of this passage appears in Chevalier, 1959: 6.

[15] "Should I wish to arrive at perfection, I would have to continue indefinitely, into infinity – when I might reach perfect reproduction – but this could never truly take place." (*et si je veux arriver à la perfection, il faudra que je continue sans fin, à l'infini – j'obtiendrai la reproduction parfait -, mais elle ne sera jamais véritablement réalisée.*) (Bergson, 2016: 88, 90, 30) The perfect, which is good and gone, is not the same as the realized. The project substantively resists the complete or finished, which as such definitely belongs to the past; the project is ceaseless.

[16] The following academic year, Bergson says the following: "the concept, which is to say, the general idea, simple, abstract" (*le concept, c'est-à-dire l'idée générale, simple, abstraite*) (Bergson 2016: 69).

[17] What philosophers call the concept, says Bergson, "that is, the idea, the representation, that which can be in its entirety intellectually manipulated" (*c'est-à-dire l'idée, la représentation, en tant qu'elle a été préparée entiérement pour la manipulation intellectuelle*) occurs in three ways or through three operations. The origin of this manipulation lies in "the faculty of the intellect par excellence" (*la faculté intellectuelle par excellence*) or "ability to form concepts and think in concepts" (*faculté de former des concepts et de penser par concepts*) (Bergson, 2016: 56, 60—61).

[18] "The conclusion is this: if there is something that cannot be expressed through concepts, if there is something defiant of all symbolic representation, it is the object we will be speaking of this year – time. We will be exploring different theories of time and duration." (*La conclusion est celle-ci: s'il y a quelque chose qui ne puisse pas s'exprimer par des concepts, s'il y a quelque chose qui soit réfractaire à toute espèce de représentation symbolique, c'est precisément l'objet dont nous allons parler cette année, c'est le temps, c'est la durée, don't nous allons examiner les différentes théories*) (Bergson 2016: 77).

[19] "*L'harmonie, comme le projet rejette le temps au dehors*" ("Harmony like project, throws time back into the outside") (Bataille, 1973: 70; Bataille, 1988: 56).

[20] If we take precision as our guide, we must necessarily consider as inexistent anything that is not expressible with perfect clarity, not to mention that which is not expressible at all" (*Là où on tient à la précision avant tout, on est amené necessairement à considérer comme inexistant ce qui n'est pas exprimable avec une précision parfaite, à plus forte raison ce qui n'est pas exprimable du tout*) (Bergson, 2016: 91). Analyzing Parmenides' poem on pages 94 and 95, Bergson insists that what cannot be expressed is not real, although he is aware that "becoming" (*devenir*) is always difficult to express. It is remarkable that Deleuze lifted this idea many years later.

[21] How does a turning signal work in traffic? The conception or set of conceptions about the functioning of the turning light in traffic, recognizing traffic rules, car use technique, as well as holding various concepts about movement in space (left, right, forward, backwards), all draw us into the operation of movement. I have the intention to turn left, which I signal thus projecting in time my future left turn. Signaling (singular or plural) is an address to others, it is a call for us to jointly consider my intention. By their joining into this consideration, it becomes a spatial projection of (one or more) social forms or social facts.

[22] "Question: you were a boxer? Tadao Ando: it was a question of survival. I had to earn money for my grandmother who raised me in a working-class neighborhood in Osaka. There was a boxing

club across the street. I thought I could win. I had a trial and went professional. Box consists of being forced to fight someone. There is no pulling back once you are in the ring, this space designed for fighting. You can count only on yourself. Compulsively, the gestures become automatic. Now, on a project, I act as if in the ring." (Enjalbert, 2017: 41).

References
Bataille, G. (1973), "L'expèrience intèrieure", in *Oevres complètes*, vol. 5, Paris Gallimard, pp. 7—181 [Bataille, G. (1988), "Inner Experience," trans. L. A. Boldt, New York, SUNY Press].
Bergson, H. (2016), *Histoire de l'idée de temps. Cours au Collège de France 1902—1903*, Paris, PUF.
Bergson, H. (2019), *L'dée de temps. Cours au Collège de France 1901-1902*, Paris, PUF.
Chevalier, J. (1959), *Entretiens avec Bergson*, Paris, Plon.
Enjalbert, C. (2017), *Entretien avec Tadao Ando*, "Philosophie magazine," vol. 114, pp. 39—43.
Husserl, E. (1966), *Analysen zur passive Synthesis* (1918-1926), XI, 6, Den Haag, Martinus Nijhoff.
Losoncz, M. (2017), *Phenomenologies of Empty Intentionality*, "Filozofska istraživanja," vol. 37, n. 3, pp. 529—544.
Libera, A. de (1999), *L'art des généralités: théories de l'abstraction*, Paris, Aubier.
Kant, I. (1999), *Critique of Pure Reason*, trans. P. Guyer, A. Wood, Cambridge University Press, Cambridge.
Kojève, A. (2004), *La notion de l'Autorité*, Paris, Gallimard [Kojève, A. (2014), "The Notion of Authority," trans. H. Weslati, Verso Books, London].
Krueger, J. (2011), *Extended Cognition and the Space of Social Interaction*, "Consciousness and Cognition," vol. 20, n. 3, pp. 643—57.
Simmel, G. (1992), *Soziologie: Untersuchungen über die Formen der Vergesellschaftung*, in *Gesamtausgabe*, vol. 11, Frankfurt am Main, Suhrkamp.
Simmel, G. (1995), *Aufsätze und Abhandlungen 1901—1908*, in *Gesamtausgabe*, vol. 7/1, Frankfurt am Main, Suhrkamp.

NARRATING INNOVATION.
Some Stories in the Voice of Practitioners
Federico Cesareo and Valeria Federighi

Federico Cesareo holds a PhD from Politecnico di Torino and is one of the editors of *Ardeth*, an architectural scientific journal that focuses on the power of the project. He is a member of LabOnt Arch (the interdepartmental Center for Ontology of the University of Turin) and he has been part of the working group of "Pratiche di ordinaria innovazione," a research project of the Alumni Association of Politecnico di Torino on architectural design forms of innovation.

Valeria Federighi is an architect and assistant professor at Politecnico di Torino. Her research work focuses on analyzing mechanisms of innovation in architecture as expanding practice. She is on the editorial board of the journal *Ardeth* and she is part of the China Room research group. She is the author of *The Informal Stance: Representations of Architectural Design and Informal Settlements* (AR+D Publishing, 2018) and co-editor of *The Eyes of the City: Architecture and Urban Space after Artificial Intelligence* (Hatje Cantz, 2021).

The relationship between the world and the words we use to represent it is a widely debated issue among linguists, language philosophers, and semiologists (Austin, 1974; Eco, 1979; Searle, 2009). Less debated and less studied is the relationship between the models that can be produced from that relationship and their analytical possibilities in the study of specific disciplines focused on the performativity of actions that are carried out through words (Leonardi, 1976; Sbisà, Weigand, 1994). If in the title of his most famous work Austin asked "How to do things with words?" here we ask ourselves what can we say about the things we know through words: that is, what happens when we want to know things, starting from the words that have been used to represent them? This working perspective can be found in rather ordinary research activities such as the interpretation of the results of qualitative interviews: How do we know what is the degree of correspondence between what is said and the event or action that is told?

In the course of a research carried out on the concept of innovation in architectural practice,[1] this very question was addressed: after 32 interviews with architects and architecture professionals, 75 tales of innovation were collected. Predictably enough, these were stories that did not describe the world from an objective or adequate point of view, but from a markedly subjective and situated one: each of those stories is the result of an attempt on the narrator's part, to retell experienced events from a perspective of innovation. In agreement with Bruner (1987; 1991) we propose that the actions told by the interviewees were part of a narrative process that evaluated as correct a number of choices; these were not correct in absolute terms—or, they could not be considered so *a priori*, but only through the assumption of a specific perspective on the world that, in this specific case, was concerned with the achievement of some form of innovation.

From this point of view, by providing mechanisms for the production of social and cultural meanings from a clearly situated point of view, narration acts as a connector between reality and the individual's agency. Despite the momentary equivalence between different actions that are possible at a specific moment in practice, the action that is carried out subsequently acquires a value that is dictated by the need to legitimize every choice made, through the construction of a generating principle that (in our case) is capable of producing innovation. Therefore, in the retrospective accounts of the designers, even those actions which at the time were carried out somewhat casually, as it happens in day-to-day practice, later became choices with a strong finalistic value.

While each tale of innovation retained its own uniqueness, from this perspective the 75 tales began to reveal a similar narrative structure. Specifically, each design process was narrated according to a sequence of three actions: (I) the representation of a state of ordinary practice; (II) the introduction of an event or irruption (e.g., the economic crisis, the pandemic, the purchase of a property, the revelation of a problem, etc.); and (III) the presentation of a moment of invention able to produce effects on the initial state of ordinary practice. This structure finds a strong analogy with Gerald Prince's (1982) model of the "minimal story," according to which every narrative is composed of a sequential organization consisting of (I) initial state, (II) event, and (III) final state. According to Prince's model, the narrative is the result of two relations between these states: (a) a causality between the second and third state, and (b) a thematic correspondence between the first and third states.

Although the stories had profound differences, the possibility of describing the sample through Prince's model thus revealed a narratological comparability. For the research, what this meant is that it was possible to assess how innovation in architectural design practice was expressed through the narrative structure used by practitioners, and not in spite of it. However, a flattening of all the stories within a single narrative model prevented the capture of their mutual differences: to be able to commensurate the stories with each other, it was necessary to be able to produce descriptions through a finite set of cross-sectional variables. Among the various narrative models that could be found, one in particular seemed particularly flexible in being able to accommodate the heterogeneity of the stories collected. This is the model developed by Guido Ferraro in his book *Theories of Narration* (2015). Starting from a reworking of the famous models of Propp (1928), Lévi-Strauss (1963), Greimas (1968), and Bremond (1973), the proposal of the Italian semiologist allows us to describe multimodal forms of expression of narration through the use of three variables corresponding to as many planes of signification.

Firstly, all narratives deal with the real. In other words, they talk about objects, events, and actions that we have, or can have, experience of in real life. In the case of this research, this clearly translates into a series of obvious physical entities, such as the building or built space, but also project documents, approvals, regulations, protests, negotiations, etc. As a result, there is a series of entities that are not only physical-technical, but also that have to do with the social context within which the design is developed. In this sense, even intangible entities such as a design promise are part of this level of signification on the basis of their belonging to a regime of social action (Searle, 2009: 85–95). In our research, therefore, the level of reality describes a socio-technical context within which actions and events take place that can be experienced through a series of effects that the project manages to engender. From this point of view, the raising or lowering of the economic value of an area as an effect of a project also falls within this level of socio-technical reality.

It is then possible to identify a second level of signification determined by the distance between the entities that populate the level of reality and the meaning that can be attributed to them. This level of symbolic elements acts according to mechanisms of substitution between a signifier and a meaning in the form of "X stands for Y": in the design of a bank, for example, the glass façade may symbolize the transparency of the bank, its luminosity, or even its fragility, depending on the system of values that are associated on this level of signification by the narrator and its narrative. Aside from the extent to which a project is capable of producing effects, the extent of each of those effects of the project can thus be measured on a level of symbolic reference (i.e., on the level of meanings that are attributed to that experienceable effect). However, this is not an absolute level of signification, but a relative one: the attribution of meanings is produced on the basis of the cultural context in which the effects of the first level of signification are assessed. In *Mythologies*, Lévi-Strauss (1964) analyzes some myths of the Matako population of the Amazon, showing how the meanings they associate are far different from those associated by someone who does not belong to the same cultural context. The distance between the values of different cultural groups is not only spatial, but also temporal. A famous example is the case of the Eiffel Tower: at the time of its approval, most Parisians considered it a "monstrous piece" (Planat, 1886); today, the same community associates to the same tangible effect (i.e., the same metal structure) a very different set of values and meanings, such as the ideals of romanticism and progress, while also considering it a symbol of Paris and France (Orsenne, 2017).

The third level of signification concerns what Ferraro, drawing from Greimas and Fontanille (1991), calls the pathemic component. This is a component of desire, or intention, to undertake a series of future-oriented actions, on the basis of the recognition of a difference in potential between the present state and the future. In the former a lack or damage is recognized, which determines an attribution of meaning that configures the future state as more desirable than the present one. This produces an intention (at the level of the individual or of the community) that assumes the appearance of a "narrative program," which refers to a situated, inner, and projectual reality that attributes meanings to events within a particular perspective of action. This means that it is possible to trace an intentional root within narratives (both generally speaking, and in narratives told by designers) that makes it possible to assess the degree of association produced by the narrative program. This is an intentionality that, in the case of our research, cannot be thought of as anything but decentralized and distributed, as it is directly proportional to the associations that the project was able to construct: the stronger the desire or intentionality (at the level of social reality), the more numerous its associations can be said to be.

Through this narrative model, the three levels of signification were parameterized for each of the 75 tales collected. This is certainly a qualitative assessment, but it has the merit of clearly parameterizing the stories that were collected. This made it easy to identify the components that allowed certain types of design events to be described as innovative by the architects and professionals interviewed. In an attempt to report the measurements of the three levels of signification, we produced a diagram in the form of a triangle on which we positioned each tale of innovation (Fig. 1).

Each of the three corners represents the maximum value of one of the three planes of signification. Vice versa, the points furthest from these vertices (which lie on the lines joining the other two corners) represent their minimum values. The axis culminating with vertex R represents the reference to reality, that is, the quantity of effects on the level of socio-technical reality that were said to have been produced by the project within each story; we can call this variable the *effectiveness* of the project. The S vertex, on the other hand, identifies the symbolic level on which the project's meanings lie; or, rather, it assesses the extent of the meanings that are associated with the effects produced by the project. This variable allows us to measure the *values* of the project. Finally, the axis identified by the vertex P orders the pathemic-intentional component traceable in the stories. This is a measurement of the extent of the network of associations that led to the effects as measured on the first level, and we can call it the project's *associations*. For each of these three axes, we will report the synthesis of a paradigmatic tale to make each of the measured parameters clearer:

Tale 1

In 2012, a real estate developer buys a historic building at auction, located in the center of Torino, that was partially rebuilt after World War II. The operator asked the studio of architect 1 to develop a proposal for redevelopment of the building, but the project clashed with the urban regulatory plan (the PRG) that prevented

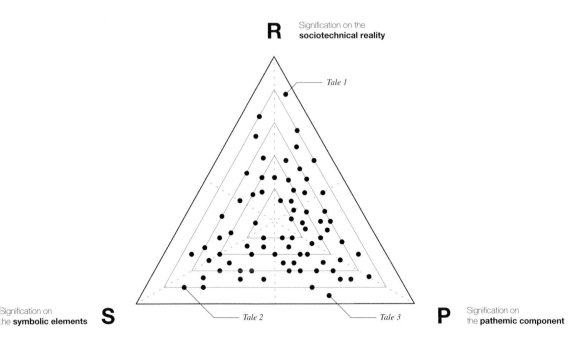

Figure 1
Diagram of the innovation stories ordered along the three narrative axes

altering the volume of post-war reconstructions. The architect drew up a project that complied with the regulatory requirements, but that was rather banal, and submitted it to the technical office. At the same time, however, he contacted the *Soprintendenza* and stressed the limitations of setting this project as precedent. He convinced the institution to let him develop a different design that would not comply with standing regulations but would solve many problems and take into account the public space of the adjacent piazza. The Soprintendenza, thus convinced, rejected the first "banal" design which had been meanwhile approved by the technical office, and, in addition to authorizing an alteration to the original volume, went so far as to approve an urban planning variant to the PRG in agreement with the technical office.

As presented, this first tale does not introduce a particularly clear or important value system; the tale seems to focus on the relationships that led to the approval of the project, but although the role of the network of associations produced is not to be underestimated, its extent does not seem particularly more significant than that of any other planning processes (the city technical office, the design studio, the building protection authority). What is stressed in this tale, on the other hand, is the project's efficacy: the effects that the project, in its different configurations, documents, and exchanges, was able to produce. Through its utter banality, the design manages to get itself rejected and to create a consensus regarding the need for a remodeling of the volume; in addition to the foreseeable effects produced by the construction of the new volume, the project stimulates a planning variant that will in turn have repercussions on a series of other projects and on their effects.

Tale 2

The architects are contacted by a client who wants to turn a dilapidated shelter on their mountain property into a shed to keep firewood dry. As local law didn't allow demolition and successive reconstruction, the architects decided to keep the existing perforated brick wall, cap it with a concrete beam, and use it to reveal the stratification of previous modes of habitation. The renovated brick wall becomes a spatial *dispositif*, with the sides facing the public street articulating into a bench that locals and visitors alike can colonize, and the sides facing the property opening up to reveal the shed's core function.

Beyond the not particularly extensive socio-technical effects, and the intended associations allowed by the added public function of the bench, this tale is particularly interesting from the point of view of innovation in design practice for the way it is able to construct a narrative around it. Such a narrative builds on a system of values that are particularly relevant in the contemporary cultural context, and have to do with a geography of small Italian settlements that are at risk of either depopulation or, alternatively, over-exploitation, and the push to find new ways of constructing a sense of community through the design of space. In this sense, therefore, the values introduced by the tale greatly transcend the effects and associations produced.

Tale 3

In April 2020, faced with the uncontrolled expansion of the pandemic, the World Health Organization set up a desk to provide technical support for the transformation of existing hospitals or facilities around the world into Covid treatment centers, through the drafting of technical reports for spaces and flows in emergency support structures. As coordinator, the interviewed architect organizes an international infrastructure of research institutions and professionals with highly specialized expertise. Due to a necessary speed of response time, architect 3 introduces a protocol of action that directs the delivery of specific documents defined *a priori* on the basis of the time available. Thus, instead of having timeframes that can be extended due to the emergence of specific circumstances and needs, for the new protocol, it is precisely the delivery time of the deliverables that determines which interactions can be undertaken and which subjects can be involved.

As in the previous tale, we notice a rather limited extension of the socio-technical effects told: technical reports are mentioned, that we can imagine impacting actions and flows passing through the emergency support structures. More relevant are certainly the meanings that pass through this narrative: we are dealing with transnational humanitarian values in response to a pandemic emergency. However, the aspect that seems most relevant on a project innovation level is the network of associations that is presented: the protocol project makes it possible to speed up response times between individuals and organizations, but above all to clearly establish a series of relationships that, depending on the needs and availability of time, is capable of extending itself by involving increasingly specialized skills located on a global scale.

In light of the analyses carried out on the sample of 75 tales, it seems possible to affirm that the model we have derived from Ferraro's allows us to discretize stories of project innovation on the basis of the three parameters we have identified: effectiveness, values, and project associations. This measurement does not attempt to eliminate or look beyond the narrative, but considers it as the prerequisite for comparability between the tales. It is precisely at the level of the narrative that it was possible to trace the three levels of signification that led to as many parameters. The evaluations carried out through this model have allowed us to quantify those factors of a given story of design practice that have produced innovation at the level of the tale that can be told. Were they the effects it produced on a level of socio-technical reality? Or the meanings that its effects introduced? Or was it the construction of the network of associations that led to the effects?

This seems to imply that in order to be told as innovative, an architectural project must be able to produce a vast quantity of effects, that it must be able to attribute to them important meanings for a given community of reference, or that it must be able to construct an extensive network of associations between the entities that take part in the design process. In fact, as we can also see in the three tales we have just reported, despite the possible preponderance of one of these aspects, the stories of innovation in architectural practice always seem to be produced through a combination (however partial) of all three of these parameters. The numerically limited sample of tales available does not allow for reliable information on the distribution of stories along the three axes. The objective is to understand, by applying this method to a larger sample, whether it is possible to determine a hierarchy between these parameters that is capable of outlining a (narrative) genesis for innovation in the design practice.

The 75 tales of innovation that we collected speak of entities, events, and actions that happened in the past. This is different from the action of the designer who, in order to legitimize her design and increase its associations, constructs narratives of things that do not yet exist and that project a potential future. From this point of view, design sociologist Storni (2009), starting from the Latourian difference between thing and object, distinguishes between an action that refer-

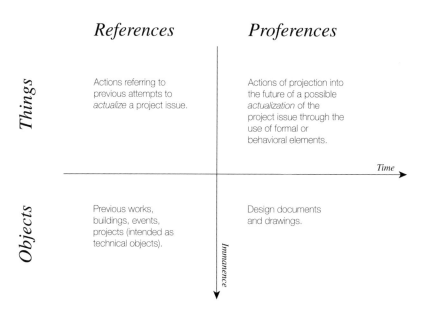

References　　　　　　　*Proferences*

Things

Actions referring to previous attempts to *actualize* a project issue.

Actions of projection into the future of a possible *actualization* of the project issue through the use of formal or behavioral elements.

Time

Objects

Previous works, buildings, events, projects (intended as technical objects).

Design documents and drawings.

Immanence

Figure 2
Minimum ontology of architectural design practice

ences something that exists or has existed (re-ference) and one that references something that has not existed yet (pro-ference).

The mechanism of narrative production that underscores our tales of innovation is clearly a reference; the same mechanism, though, can be found in some project interactions. This is particularly evident within those interactions that accompany the presentation of a design proposal through graphic documents. Although such documents clearly envision a condition that exists in the future, designers tend to produce narratives that work in the past, that is, they produce narratives that refer to the moment of the production of the document: through a mechanism that is reminiscent of Prince's minimal story, they tell the story of how they reached that specific configuration that is represented in the document. A specific reference to the design document is told, or to the story of its production (1 - we wanted to install parquet, but 2 - they asked for fire certification, therefore 3 - we chose gres instead), although that document is clearly a proference as it speaks of something that is not yet in the world.

This means that in every design narrative we can observe a combined action of the three levels that we borrowed from Ferrero's model: every design narrative speaks of entities that are experimented with on a level of sociotechnical reality (R), to which specific symbolic meanings are associated (S) through mechanisms of increasing desirability (P) of the projected configuration, as opposed to the current/actual configuration. The difference from the stories that we analyzed is in the filter that was applied to those events, in the perspective from which the correctedness of past choices is evaluated (as Bruner suggests). If the common factor of the 75 stories is to be found in the achievement of innovation, the perspective in projective design narratives may depend on other factors: other effects to be achieved, other systems of value, other instances and associations to be included and satisfied (normative systems, interests of different groups, networking, etc.). Each design narrative can find its place in a triangular diagram such as the one we proposed before: this operation makes explicit the three levels of signification of a specific design narrative. This leads to operate simulations, or tests, of design narratives in order to find which level is narratively predominant within a specific context of legitimation. In turn, this can lead to the construction of patterns of strategies that can allow practitioners to increase the performativity of their design-as-narrative.

Notes
[1] We wish to thank the Alumni Association of Politecnico di Torino that provided funding for the research, and sociologist Francesca Silvia Carosio, whose experience and fieldwork was fundamental in structuring and conducting the interviews.

References:
Austin, J. L. (1962), *How to do things with words,* Cambridge (MA), Harvard University Press.
Boradkar, P., Gutkind, L. (2016), "Designing Narrative, Narrating Design," *Innovation: The journal of the Industrial Designers Society of America*, 35(4), pp. 14–16.
Bremond, C. (1973), *Logique du récit*. Paris, Seuil.
Bruner, J. (1987), "Life as Narrative," *Social Research*, 54(1), 11–32. The New School.
Bruner, J. (1991), "The Narrative Construction of Reality," *Critical Inquiry*, 18(1), pp. 1–21.
Bulkens, M. G., Minca, C., Muzaini, H. B. (2015), "Storytelling as Method in Spatial Planning." *European Planning Studies*, 23(11), pp. 2,310–26.
Eco, U. (1979), *Lector in fabula: La cooperazione interpretativa nei testi narrativi*, Milano, Bompiani.
Edgell, R. A., Moustafellos, J. (2017), "Toward an Architectural Theory of Innovation: Explicating Design, Networks, and Microprocesses," *Journal of Creativity and Business Innovation*, 3, pp. 5–34.
Ferraro, G. (2015), *Teorie della narrazione: Dai racconti tradizionali all'odierno storytelling*, Roma, Carocci.
Ferraro, G., Santangelo, A. (eds.) (2017), *Narrazione e realtà: Il senso degli eventi*, Canterano, Aracne.
Greimas, A. J. (1969), *La semantica strutturale*, Milano, Rizzoli.
Greimas, A. J., Fontanille, J. (1991), *Semiotique des passions: Des etats de choses aux etats d'ame*, Paris, Editions du Soleil.
Latour, B. (2000), *Pandora's hope: Essays on the reality of science studies*, Cambridge (MA), Harvard University Press.
Latour, B. (2013), *An inquiry into modes of existence: An anthropology of the moderns*, Cambridge, Harvard University Press.
Leonardi, P. (1976), "Introduzione: Searle, la filosofia del linguaggio e la linguistica contemporanea," in J. Searle, *Atti linguistici: Saggi di filosofia del linguaggio*, Torino, Bollati Boringhieri, pp. 7-18.
Lévi-Strauss, C. (1963), *Structural anthropology*, New York, Basic Books.
Orsenne, C. (2017), *La Tour Eiffel: Un phare universel*, Paris, Massin Charles.
Planat, P. (1886), *La construction moderne: Journal hebdomadaire illustré; art, théorie appliquée, pratique, génie civil, industries du bâtiment*, Paris, Impr. F. Leve.
Prince, G. (1982), *Narratology: The form and functioning of narrative*, Berlin, Mouton.
Propp, V. J. (1966), *Morfologia della fiaba*, Torino, Einaudi.
Sbisà, M., (1994), "Language and Dialogue in the Framework of the Analytic Philosophy of Ordinary Language," in E. Weigand, *Concepts of dialogue. Considered from the perspective of different disciplines*, Berlin-Boston, De Gruyter, pp. 159–70.
Searle, J. R. (2009), *Atti linguistici: Saggi di filosofia del linguaggio*, Torino, Bollati Boringhieri.
Storni, C. (2009), "Sulla nascita degli arte-fatti," *E/C rivista dell'Associazione Italiana di studi semiotici*, 3/4, pp. 225–38.

ARCHITECTURE & TERMINOLOGY
Petar Bojanić and Snežana Vesnić

Dictionary

A.

Absence /ˈabs(ə)ns/, *n*. **1**. Absence is not a void. Absence is not being present. Not being present could be understood as being past or future. If something is absent it is not here. Can something be absent in architecture if it is not present somewhere else?

C.

Composition /kɒmpəˈzɪʃ(ə)n/, *n*. **1**. A creative work (a creative mo ntage). The nature of the constituents of a mixture.

Concept /ˈkɒnsɛpt/, *n*. **1**. Having an idea of what the ideal object could be in the future, considering what it already was; a beginning of a designing process which is being manifested in a design after the real object is made. **2**. To inividually make sense/comprehension of reality perceived by putting things in relation/motion; instrument of action. **3**. More than/comes after, an idea, idea (elements + me) + intuition. **4**. Something conceived in the mind, but already structured in some way, yet not well defined. **5**. A series of processes that organise the ideas for a project. **6**. A container for a grasped phenomenon.

D.

Design /dɪˈzʌɪn/, *v*. **1**. A chain of actions which has no begginig and ending; it is an action that object demands and without which it would not exist. **2**. Process of translating and transforming projections. **3**. Process of thinking or creating, after an idea, before or after an object. **4**. The research used for the conception of a project. **5**. The process of creation of an object. **6**. A scheme that is marked down.

Desire /dɪˈzʌɪə/, *n*. **1**. An initiator – actuator; the core of a concept which is free from any boundaries; on its way leading a concept to a project, desire is always slipping away - in a moment it gets fulfilled it disappears. **2**. The irrational impulse that might become an obsession if not satisfied.

Disappearance /dɪsəˈpɪərəns/, *n*. **1**. Act or fact of disappearing, a ceasing to appear or exist in one or another type of context.

Diversity /dʌɪˈvəːsɪti,dɪˈvəːsɪti/, *n*. **1**. The coexistence of di- fferent types of things or people. in the same "whole".

F.

Figure-form /ˈfɪgə - fɔːm/ , **1**. The structure of an object that is always present but not always seen (The Schema).

Figure-image /ˈfɪgə -ˈɪm.ɪdʒ/, **1**. Something that belongs to the order of the visible as an outline (The theme).

Figure-matrix /ˈfɪgə - ˈmeɪtrɪks/, **1**. The object that creates reality, which is never seeable or explainable (The archetype).

Foam /fəʊm/, *n*. **1**. (Peter Sloterdijk in: Spheres) amorphological metaphor for formation of non-integrative inner worlds, microspheres (bubbles) in the context of modern world and architecture of immunity. „When everything has become the center, there is no longer any valid center."

Frame /freɪm/ *n*. an action which emphasizes a particular elements of a composition.

I.

Innovation /ɪnəˈveɪʃ(ə)n/ *n*. **1**. To arrange the existing in a non-existent way, to organize relations between existing elements in a way nobody else already has. **2**. Innovation is (re)arranging known elements in different ways / new relations. **3**. A new way of thinking of a notion. **4**. To re-create something new from something already existing **5**. A process of finding better and more efficient way to achieve somthing. For example, improving a project. **6**. Taking something that exists and turn it into something new.

Immunize /ˈɪmjʊnʌɪz/ *v*. **1**. To provide stable existence by strenghtening processes and substance inside and so controlling the effect of outside.

M.

Method /ˈmɛθəd/ *n*. **1**. A way of thinking and approaching to expression of a concept. **2**. Tool for projecting. **3**. A modus operandi, a way of thinking about something. **4**. A specific procedure for accomplish or approach something **5**. A procedure to develop a project. A systematic procedure, following a particular tecnique. **6.** Manner of doing something in a specific way.

Medium /ˈmiːdɪəm/ *n.* **1.** A tool for communication, a position in the middle or between other things, an intermediate agency.

Montage
/mɒnˈtɑːʒ, ˈmɒntɑːʒ/ *n.* **1.** Determination of a whole, a method of producing a composite whole from elements in space and time, a technique to compose by assembling, overlaying, and overlapping many different materials or elements collected from different sources **2.** Operation of assembling different pieces, generating a new ''whole''.

Movement /ˈmuːvm(ə)nt/ *n.* **1.** The act of motion, physical displacement in space.

O.

Object /ˈɒbdʒɛkt/ *n.* **1.** Something passive which demands an action, but is not capable to produce an action by itself. **2.** Discovered only on the outside, the end. **3.** A material or immaterial result of a project. **4.** The material form of a project. **5.** Something existent in the real world and that can be perceived by the senses. **6.** Is a thing put before the mind or sight.

P.

Perception /pəˈsɛpʃ(ə)n/ *n.* **1.** A way of collecting external impulses; creating an image in mind - the ideal object, that coressponds with the real object which is being perceived. **2.** What there is on the outside according to the inside. **3.** An ability to "catch" something. **4.** What we experience as stimulus from our surroundings **5.** The ability to feel, to react to the physical world; awareness given by the five senses. **6.** Is the act of grasping a phenomenon which can result in a concept.

Programme /ˈprəʊɡram/ *n.* **1.** A scenario which assumes actions in a design. **2.** A set of bound activities in a project or realized in object. **3.** A group of actions caused by architectural space in a space. **4.** A systematic process. **5.** A series of actions that are necessaries to achieve a result, usually referred to a program working on a computer. A series of activities located in the same building. **6.** A written proclamation of actions in a systemized way.

Protective islands /prəˈtɛktɪv/ /ˈʌɪləndz/ **1.** regulated on the inside, co-dependendent yet insulated, no personal/direct exchange but mimetic infiltration of norms, media, symbols etc.

Project /ˈprɒdʒɛkt/ *n.* **1.** A product of the projection. **2.** A result of design process with others. **3.** A thought or group of thoughts shared with someone **4.** A Program that is to be followed to create something **5.** An individual or collective effort in order to achieve a particular and well defined aim, in a methodic and structured way. **6.** The process of realizing a projection.

Projection /prəˈdʒɛkʃ(ə)n/ *n.* **1.** Expressing ideal object (personal) so it becomes a social object. **2.** Representation; presentation of a similar image. **3.** An action of a transmutation. **4.** A forecast of a future situation or a possible outcome **5.** A visualisation of the future. An estimated outcome of the project, based on one or multiple studies. **6.** An image that is put before something.

R.

Rhythm /ˈri-thəm/ *n.* **1.** A strong, regular, repeated pattern of movement or sound. A measured flow.

S.

Sphere /sfɪə/ *n.* **1.** (Peter Sloterdijk in: Spheres) space of coexistence. Sphere as an expression of the human need for community and of love. The world as a macro-sphere that consists of many fragmented but contiguous spheres (foams). "Act of solidarity is an act of sphere formation, that is to say the creation of an interior".

T.

Technology /tɛkˈnɒlədʒi/ *n.* **1.** A tool for transforming an ideal object into real object. **2.** Cooperative mechanisms that support the architectural program. **3.** A tool of production. **4.** The sum of knowledge applied to science. **5.** The application of scientific knowledge for practical purposes and for research. The result is some kind of ''machinery''. **6.** What enables a technique to be applied systematically.

Petar Bojanić and Snežana Vesnić –
Architecture & Terminology

Comparison of definitions

„We perceive objects and conceptualize them with our own method."*

person A	person B
Perception is a way of collecting external impulses; creating an image in mind - the ideal object, that coressponds with the real object which is being perceived.	**Perception** is what there is on the outside according to the inside.
Object is something passive which demands an action, but is no capable to produce an action by itself.	**Object** is discovered only on the outside, the end.
Concept is having an idea of what the ideal object could be in the future, considering what it already was; a beginning of a designing process which is being manifested in a design after the real object is made.	**Concept** is to inividually make sense/comprehension of reality perceived by putting things in relation/motion. Instrument of action.
Method is a way of thinking and approaching to expression of a concept.	**Method** is a tool for projecting.

Substitution of the original sentence

„We perceive objects and conceptualize them with our own method."*

We collect impulses which creats an image of an ideal object of something passive that demands action and get an idea of an ideal what the object could be in the future which is the beginning of a design process with our own way of thinking and expression of it.	We discover only the outside of which is according to the inside and make sense out of reality perceived by putting things in relation which gives us an instrument of action with our own tool forprojection.

*This sentence is arbitrarily chosen.

As the first and most important institution, language institutionalizes all institutions, gives them power to become disciplines and produce knowledge. Precision of linguistic expression shows capability and strength, as well as the particularity of profession. In architectural theory and practice, language explains processes of architectural design, while in architectural philosophy it reveals conceptualization and thematization. Finally, linguistic systematization is a necessary condition of education.

Comprising various notions, the design process allows for the generation and development of connections among them. Moreover, diagrams of these connections can be translated into design processes, in turn determining the form of the architectural project and object. Today, the idea of architectural

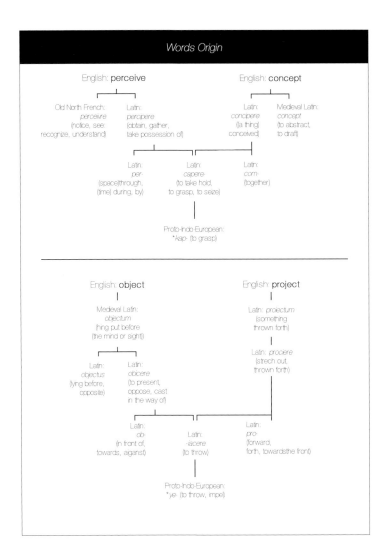

Words Origin

English: perceive

- Old North French: *perceivre* (notice, see; recognize, understand)
- Latin: *percipere* (obtain, gather, take possession of)
  - Latin: *per-* (space)through, (time) during, by)
  - Latin: *capere-* (to take hold, to grasp, to seize)

English: concept

- Latin: *concipere* ((a thing) conceived)
- Medieval Latin: *concept* (to abstract, to draft)
  - Latin: *com-* (together)

Proto-Indo-European: **kap-* (to grasp)

English: object

- Medieval Latin: *obiectum* (thing put before (the mind or sight))
  - Latin: *obiectus* (lying before, opposite)
  - Latin: *obicere* (to present, oppose, cast in the way of)
    - Latin: *ob-* (in front of, towards, against)
    - Latin: *-iacere* (to throw)

English: project

- Latin: *proiectum* (something thrown forth)
- Latin: *prociere* (strech out, thrown forth)
  - Latin: *pro-* (forward, forth, towardsthe front)

Proto-Indo-European: **ye-* (to throw, impel)

terminology's systematization has as its goal proficiency within the field and its practice, as well as the definition and explanation of architectural creation, production, and communication. Clearly, the architect's actions are fluid and continuously draw on other disciplines. A precise reconstruction of 'originally' architectural terms used by architects is necessary for their autonomy and to ensure the freedom to transgress disciplinary borders. Further, problematizing language in architectural theory and practice also destabilizes given design processes, allowing for new connections, contingencies, and inspiration.

Our intention is to examine the potential of the architectural concept for the entirely 'novel' in architectural design, as well as establish processes of the architectural project, while naming all acts, agents, gestures, instruments,

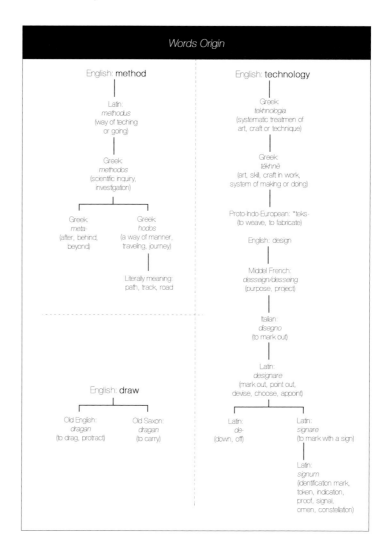

Words Origin

English: method

Latin:
methodus
(way of teching
or going)

Greek
methodos
(scientific inquiry,
investigation)

Greek:
meta-
(after, behind,
beyond)

Greek:
hodos
(a way of manner,
traveling, journey)

Literally meaning:
path, track, road

English: draw

Old English:
dragan
(to drag, protract)

Old Saxon:
dragan
(to carry)

English: technology

Greek:
tekhnologia
(systematic treatmen of
art, craft or technique)

Greek:
tékhnē
(art, skil, craft in work,
system of making or doing)

Proto-Indo-European: *teks-
(to weave, to fabricate)

English: design

Middel French:
desseign/desseing
(purpose, project)

Italian:
disegno
(to mark out)

Latin:
designare
(mark out, point out,
devise, choose, appoint)

Latin:
de-
(down, off)

Latin:
signare
(to mark with a sign)

Latin:
signum
(identification mark,
token, indication,
proof, signal,
omen, constellation)

elements the project makes use of. Thematizing notions allows for the reconstruction of the architectural project, using words as a corporeal or poetic moment to imagine new concepts. Drawing on previous thematizations of interaction of the drawing, model, textual analysis, which have all developed the discipline, the idea of the project is to use text as a direct design technique, to better guide conceptual creation.

The main focus of the workshop is to render architectural conceptualization visible, that is, expressing, naming, and explaining the architectural concept in an architectural form. In the course of this (de)constructing the project, students will attempt to establish, mark, and reveal architectural terms. By placing them into an appropriately formed matrix (idea, concept, conception, design, project,

Petar Bojanić and Snežana Vesnić -
Architecture & Terminology

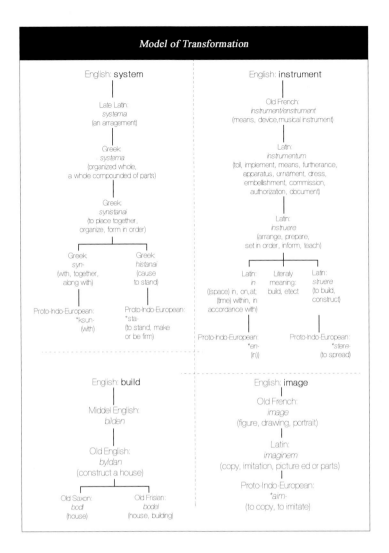

Model of Transformation

English: system

Late Latin:
systema
(an arragement)

Greek
systema
(organized whole,
a whole compounded of parts)

Greek
synistanai
(to place together,
organize, form in order)

Greek
syn-
(with, together,
along with)

Greek
histanai
(cause
to stand)

Proto-Indo-European:
ksun-
(with)

Proto-Indo-European:
sta-
(to stand, make
or be firm)

English: instrument

Old French:
instrument/enstrument
(means, device, musical instrument)

Latin:
instrumentum
(toll, implement, means, furtherance,
apparatus, ornament, dress,
embellishment, commission,
authorization, document)

Latin:
instruere
(arrange, prepare,
set in order, inform, teach)

Latin:
in
((space) in, on, at;
(time) within, in
accordance with)

Literally
meaning:
build, erect

Latin:
struere
(to build,
construct)

Proto-Indo-European:
en-
(in))

Proto-Indo-European:
stere-
(to spread)

English: build

Middel English:
bilden

Old English:
byldan
(construct a house)

Old Saxon:
bodl
(house)

Old Frisian:
bodel
(house, building)

English: image

Old French:
image
(figure, drawing, portrait)

Latin:
imaginem
(copy, imitation, picture ed or parts)

Proto-Indo-European:
aim-
(to copy, to imitate)

architectural project, platform, *dispositif*, arena…), they will indicate and explain the connections between the architectural concept and project. The instrument for this purpose is the text: it is at once the object of work, and the tool for destabilizing any possible architectural methodology.

Introducing the philosophical text (concept) into the architectural project creates the virtual, a reality in which it is possible to see the creation or definition of conceptual content. By sequencing and framing architectural gestures, acts, analyses, experiments, we will simulate the conceptualization and thematization of an architectural project. We will deconstruct the design process by introducing philosophical concepts into the project.

Ivana Lakić

Having focused on Sloterdijk's Spheres, what was brought to my attention are his thoughts on world's decentralization, alienation, and formation of contiguous fragmented inner worlds, intersecting and overlapping but non-integrative bubbles—a foam. When matter foams it gains fertility. A sphere is an interior in solidarity. System is immunized = stable existence provided by strengthening processes and substance inside and so controlling the effect of the outside. Islands were detected according to the position of the greenery and in relation to the existing structure. The pulsating giardini is followed by the old structure as a place for meeting and performing, leading to third phase, a tower, technological- and IT-oriented hub. Strengthening position of the old by providing an annex is how the island is immunized. One by one, courtyards come to life. Can islands act as impenetrable, agitating foams and still make a space of coexistence?

Ueli Saluz

Two Regimes of Madness, Texts and Interviews 1975—1995
Gilles Deleuze (1925—1995), edited by David Lapoujade, translated by
Ames Hodges and Mike Taormina

What is the Creative Act?

The idea behind my animation was to symbolically represent Gille Deleuze's idea of "creative activity." He says that a creative act is always an invention of something. This something is different in every discipline. Every discipline has some specific boundaries and all of them share the greater boundary of space-time. He describes the act as very solitary which means not completely because he quantifies it. So here are the symbols I used in the animation: the outer box represents space-time; the inner boxes represent disciplines (different colors for each discipline); the oscillating spheres represent creative activities (same color than the discipline because Deluze says an idea in cinema will always be cinematographic); the lines represent the communication between the disciplines and space-time. (The color is always in-between the two communicators because they have to speak a language that is understandable to both.)

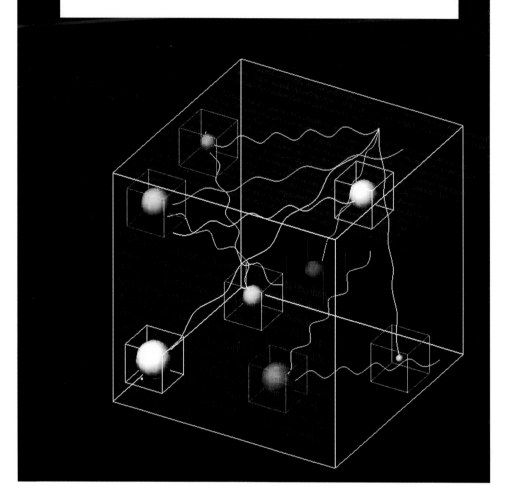

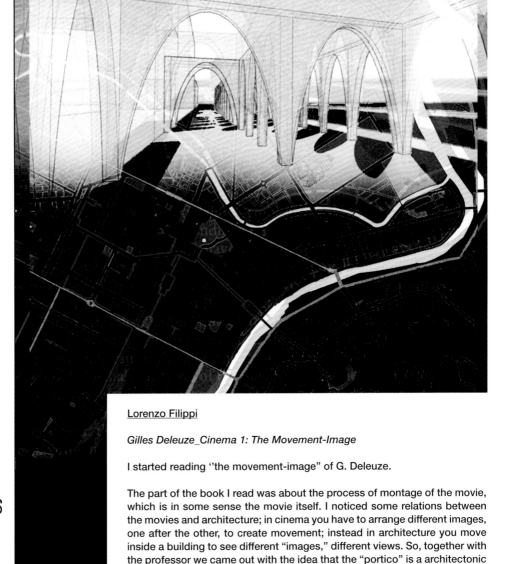

<u>Lorenzo Filippi</u>

Gilles Deleuze_Cinema 1: The Movement-Image

I started reading ''the movement-image'' of G. Deleuze.

The part of the book I read was about the process of montage of the movie, which is in some sense the movie itself. I noticed some relations between the movies and architecture; in cinema you have to arrange different images, one after the other, to create movement; instead in architecture you move inside a building to see different "images," different views. So, together with the professor we came out with the idea that the "portico" is a architectonic element that gives the idea of movement. And in the end I tried to use this element in the new part of the city to create this "movement" and create new connections with the rest of the city.

Đorđe Bulajić

Gilles Deleuze_Cinema 1: The Movement-Image

Montage as an experimental research methodology

In the first book of Gilles Deleuze's philosophical diptych, entitled "Cinema 1: The Movement-Image", in which Deleuze, regarding Bergson's theses on movement, classifies the ways of perceiving and producing a film from 1895 to 1985, montage is defined as a "composition, the assemblage [agencement] of movement images as constituting an indirect image of time." Following the direction of thought of Bergson, Deleuze, and Soviet film director and film theorist, Sergei Eisenstein, this experimental project aims to deconstruct the text by French sociologist and philosopher Jean Baudrillard by establishing the new methodological apparatus based on the principles of montage technique. By using a diagram as a representational tool, this research tends to establish a connection between three different mediums—text, a video, and an image.

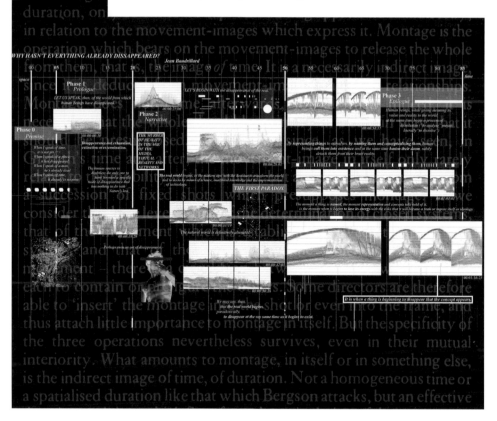

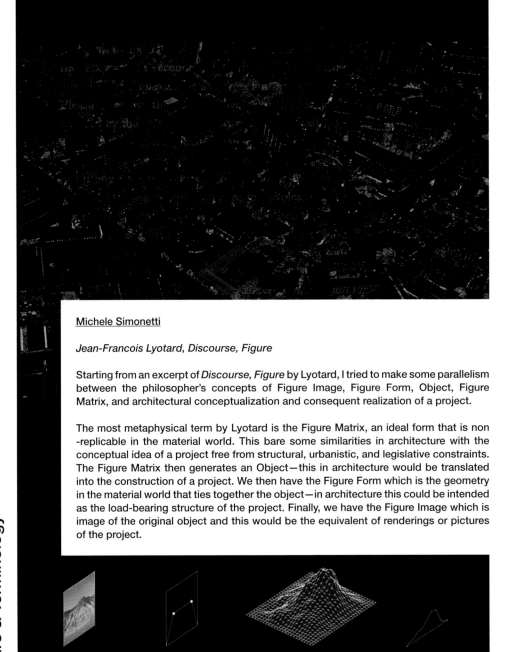

Michele Simonetti

Jean-Francois Lyotard, Discourse, Figure

Starting from an excerpt of *Discourse, Figure* by Lyotard, I tried to make some parallelism between the philosopher's concepts of Figure Image, Figure Form, Object, Figure Matrix, and architectural conceptualization and consequent realization of a project.

The most metaphysical term by Lyotard is the Figure Matrix, an ideal form that is non-replicable in the material world. This bare some similarities in architecture with the conceptual idea of a project free from structural, urbanistic, and legislative constraints. The Figure Matrix then generates an Object—this in architecture would be translated into the construction of a project. We then have the Figure Form which is the geometry in the material world that ties together the object—in architecture this could be intended as the load-bearing structure of the project. Finally, we have the Figure Image which is image of the original object and this would be the equivalent of renderings or pictures of the project.

FIGURE-IMAGE   FIGURE-FORM   OBJECT   FIGURE-MATRIX

Desire's Complicity with the Figural

Katarina Ognjenović

Jean-Francois Lyotard, Discourse, Figure

Reading the given text, the term *desire* was analyzed through the architectural paradigm. "The fulfillment of desire, or wish-fulfillment (Wunscherfullung), holds in itself the absence of the object".

What does an absence of the object mean? By deconstructing the layers of time, we are being confronted by unchanged particles of Desire, which is a starting point for creating an architectural object that—with its movement and lightness—disappears in its own time projection. Architecture never exists for itself, but for desire's constitution. An aim is to create a space where desires are being created without being fulfilled. Far from being oriented towards a specific object, desire can only be attained at a point where one does not seek or perceive something as an object any more than one perceives oneself as a subject.

DISCOURSE, FIGURE

Innovation from the Practice. A Perspectival Fragment
Alessandro Armando and Giovanni Durbiano

The article tries to define the range of possibilities for innovation in architectural design. Through a concrete example of design practice conducted in the real world, a method to produce maps aimed at identifying effective design strategies is proposed. Mapping strategies is possible by betting on the instability of the project, which can be divided into two fields. The first is meant as process instability, due to the continuing possibility that the result of the project must be modified and adapted to the conditions of negotiation and decision during its process. The second is meant as product instability, linked to the limited duration in time of the effects of a project, after it has been completed. Considering that the process instability corresponds to a mobility of the final objective, which depends both on external and internal conditions of the process, the case studied allows us to enter the folds of a segment of the design evolution process, to bring out the relationships of concatenation that link between the adjustments undergone by the drawings, to shape the chains of deviations and to observe how the project progressively consolidates.

Unpacking Architectural Design Practice *in the Folds* of Decision-Making Processes. An Innovative Mapping Tool
Elena Todella

The kind of complexity of decision-making processes of urban and architectural transformations is often accounted as a linear process of subsequent steps and decisions, from the project to its execution. Since projects rarely move forward without detours to buildings, how is it possible instead to take account of their diversions, as constituent elements of the decision-making process? By shifting the attention from the products of architecture—as buildings—to the processes of project production and negotiation, this paper traces a taxonomy of multiple entities with different ontologies that interact in a multi-sited and large-scale process. In this sense, a mapping tool is proposed to investigate—from the inside—what architects do and how projects operate in an ongoing decision-making process, in projecting decisions that would have not otherwise been possible to witness without being in the folds of the process.

Innovation Trajectories. Retracing the History of Area-Based Initiatives
Caterina Quaglio

In the diffusion of area-based initiatives in Europe, a strong emphasis was placed on innovation as both a prerequisite and a result of the work carried out by professionals. However, even when innovation in design and other professional practices has occurred, it has rarely been the result of voluntary and planned actions. Research conducted today allows us to bring to the fore not only the contextualization of innovative practices in a wider *collective*, but also to question how they spread over the long run through formal and informal processes. Drawing on the history of three area-based programs developed between the 1980s and 2000s, this text aims to interrogate the actual conditions and modalities of innovation in design practices and their impacts in different professional and institutional contexts. In particular, the relationship between individual learning and collective capitalization is investigated as a fundamental dimension in order to assess the potential of innovative design practices to overcome the specific contingencies of a project.

Design Echoes. Four Stories of Projects that Resonate with Urban Rules
Caterina Barioglio and Daniele Campobenedetto

The effects of architecture extend beyond their localization. The anthropic modification of the spatial environment produces echoes in terms of urban rules, technical requirements, cultural shifts, and behaviors that travel beyond the place in which the modification occurs. While these effects of built and unbuilt projects are part of the outcomes of design, they are hardly considered part of the design process. In most cases, they just occur. How, and through which tools, could these non-local effects of design be recognized? More generally, is it possible to consider localized design as a means of representing and addressing general and comprehensive issues? In this visual essay, we attempt to face these questions, exploring the relationship between architectural projects and urban rules as a way of tackling the theme of design echoes.

Experiencing the Possible. The Design of Open Devices for Modification of Marginal Contexts
Gianfranco Orsenigo

Today the project has to face *complexity* and *uncertainty*. Complex because we witness multiple and conflicting needs, responsibilities, knowledge, and problems. Uncertain due to lack of resources, changing political intentions, and hesitant time of realization. *Inactivity* seems to be an inevitable condition, particularly in marginal contexts. From the architectural perspective to shack this state, it seems necessary to see the design process as an "ecology of practices" (Stangers 2005). An attitude capable of overcoming the traditional public-private system and developing an attitude to deal with contingency. A posture to cluster projects, policies, spaces, and skills creatively. Through a self-reflexive critique of two research experiences, I try to empirically explore how architectural design can equip itself to become a key stage of transformations involving marginal territories. The reflection shares intermediate outcomes related to a *method* and open *documents*.

Potential. Defining, Decoding, and Assessing the Potential in Existing Buildings
Elena Guidetti

The concept of *potential* emerges as crucial in the current preservation debate. Within the field of adaptive reuse, this research aims to define, decode, and assess the *transformative potential* in existing buildings through a post-functional perspective. The theoretical objective is to add this novel concept to the preservation theory in evaluating existing buildings. The task is to express the *transformative potential* as a relationship between dimensional features and materials in a diachronic and trans-scalar perspective, outlining a pattern within existing features and adaptive reuse interventions.

Developing Images into Voices of Concern.
Some Notes on Using Networked-Images and Participatory Setting for Inquiring into Public Issues
Donato Ricci

The essay tries to unfold the specificities of a design approach to repurposing online images to study, inquire, and intervene in urban issues. The scope is to extend and further the role of large image corpora visualizations beyond pure analytical or critical purposes. To this extent, the 'DEPT.' project is described. A series of visual artifacts—data- and media- visualizations, catalogs, tableaux, and scores were conceived during the project to progressively bring online images to public and participatory settings. The contribution details needs, intellectual frameworks, methodological choices, and visual artifacts conceived in the project to transform networked-images into shared and collective expressions of the issues under inquiry.

INNOVATION FROM THE PRACTICE.
A Perspectival Fragment
Alessandro Armando and Giovanni Durbiano

Alessandro Armando, architect, is Associate Professor of Architectural and Urban Design at the Politecnico di Torino, from which he holds a PhD in Architecture and Building Design. His current research activity focuses mainly on the theory of the architectural project. He is founder and member of the editorial board of *Ardeth* (Architectural Design Theory) magazine. In his professional practice as an architect, he is a partner of the DAR Architettura office, with M. Di Robilant and G. Durbiano.

Giovanni Durbiano is Full Professor of Architectural and Urban Design at the Politecnico di Torino, from which he holds a PhD in History of Architecture and Urban Planning. Since 2017, he has been president of ProArch, the Scientific Society of Italian Architectural Design Professors. Since 2021, he has been a member of GEV committee for the evaluation of Italian academic research in the architectural field. In 2017, with Alessandro Armando he founded the academic journal *Ardeth* (Architectural Design Theory).

Innovation Viewed From Practical Experience:
A Perspectival Fragment

The concept of innovation, however it is to be understood, presupposes the possibility of acquiring something (knowledge or skills) permanently. The "something" of innovation must be new (*novum*) and stabilized. Of course, stabilization allows innovation to be variously integrated into technical systems, very quickly becoming a functioning part of a larger whole. Thus, good innovation soon loses its particular *novum* character in favor of an established effect on reality in general.

Architectural design has a very specific problem in dealing with innovation, as it is characterized by at least two forms of instability. Projects are unstable both during their development process and once they are finished. In the first case we are dealing with process instability, i.e., the everlasting possibility that the final project may have to be modified and adapted to the conditions of negotiation and decision-making that have changed during its course. This characteristic would be unthinkable for most projects involving objects produced in the industrial sector: if we are designing a new car model, it is very unlikely (though not impossible) that we will end up with a bus, or a tractor. In architectural design, however, this is exactly what happens: the dynamic instability of the process leads to the design of something that was initially intended to be a "car-building" and that turns out to be a "tractor-building." In the second case we are dealing with product instability, i.e., the limited duration in time of the effects of a project after it has been completed. While the patented design of a chair can be preserved for many decades, be resold at a high price, and determine the production of chairs even a century after it has been drawn up, an approved architectural project must be built immediately, otherwise, given the continuous alteration of the physical and social world on which it acts, it risks remaining on paper forever.

The instability of architectural projects is not only a flaw and a limitation, but also a positive characteristic that should be exploited strategically. *Process instability* corresponds to the mobility of the final goal, which depends on conditions that are both external and internal to the process. To use a metaphor, it is as if the architectural project were an archery contest with a moving target, whose movements depend also (but not only) on the archer. It is clear that, in such a case, a stable improvement in one's ability to hit the moving target (i.e., *innovate*) would correspond to a different advancement compared to simple refinement of one's aim. *Product instability*, on the other hand, corresponds to the progressive erosion of the overall conditions that make it possible to carry out the project: it is as if having hit the mark opens a gap that must be crossed before it closes again. For example, once a project is approved and contracted out, there are time limits and deadlines that must be met. Improving the ability to "cross the gap" thus means being more efficient in implementation, thanks to skills that often go beyond the architect's role and involve other disciplines, such as technical, operational, and economic/financial skills.

Consequently, in the context of architectural projects, possible innovations are confronted with the instability of both the process and the product of the project, increasing in one case the effectiveness of the on-going project work and in the other the efficiency of its implementation. While innovation that addresses the dynamic process of instability may concern the work of architects from within, innovation that addresses the posthumous instability of the product is mostly external, for reasons that are easy to understand: a project that has been delivered, approved, and contracted out is in the hands of others (those who execute it, or the conditions that make it executable) and, even when the direction of the work is entrusted to the architects, they play a role of guarantee and supervision in the context of an already existing project. In this short text we will therefore deal with innovation in the architectural project starting from the question of its dynamic instability and, drawing on practical experience, we will try to suggest a more general—tactical and strategic—description of innovation. The practical experience of the restoration of a historical building, being an extraordinary case in its presuppositions (the wing is inside a monumental

Alessandro Armando and Giovanni Durbiano -
Innovation from the Practice. A Perspectival Fragment

complex), but the object of ordinary practice (i.e., subject to all the prescriptions and demands of any public intervention), appears particularly suitable for this exercise. In fact, the case has nothing innovative about it in itself, but having experienced it from the inside, we can recognize and show the ways in which the project was modified in the course of successive exchanges and passages. Entering into the depths of the project action and describing a segment of the project evolution process analytically can allow one to observe how the project progressively consolidates and where it is possible to introduce elements of innovation. The hypothesis we propose is that innovation may lie both in the instrumental invention of maps that better anticipate the interweavings we will attempt to illustrate, and in the clinical attitude towards similar situations, in the form of a handbook not of solutions but of problems to prepare for, as happens in military strategy manuals that set out recurrent critical situations.

Innovation drawn from professional practice is not the only way to raise the issue of project innovation: it would be misleading to reduce the question of architectural design to its (albeit crucial) conjugation as a professional practice. Architectural projects are much more than, and quite different from, what architectural firms, large and small, do. They are continuously produced and exchanged in public administrations, used by groups of citizens, promoted by activists, discussed and elaborated by various kinds of communities—even those that are not locally delimited—and on many different scales: from the corners of a struggling neighborhood to the whole horizon of the Critical Zone.

The problem of innovation in architectural design, therefore, also involves the capacity to construct grand scenarios, to identify the most relevant problems affecting material space, and to formulate responses through the transformation of that space—that is, by inventing an architecture for a better world, rather than focusing on the best ways to create an architecture *per se*. But this is not the case here, and it would be neither relevant nor appropriate for us to attempt a general proposition on this level. Instead, let us start from a particular circumstance, namely a fragment of a process in which we are currently involved as commissioned architects. At the moment of writing this text, the project action is in progress and we do not know how it will end: we are therefore attempting an analytical operation on the present and on a very recent past, with the aim of defining the shape of our action towards the future.

In short, the story goes as follows: we won a tender issued by the Piedmont Region for the technical and economic feasibility, final and executive project of the restoration and conservation of the wing of the 19th-century stables of the Clock Tower, part of the Mandria Castle in Venaria Reale (To). So far, the group of professionals involved in the operation (Isolarchitetti Srl, Sintecna Srl, MCM Ingegneria Srl, Nicola Restauri Srl, Dr. A. Ferrarotti, Eng. J. Toniolo, Fondazione Fitzcarraldo) has worked on the so-called "Technical-Economic feasibility project" phase between December 2020 and April 2021.

In this stage, together with the clients, we worked out at least three main versions of the final scenario. It is important here to distinguish between "project" and "final scenario," as the former term refers to the overall trajectory leading from the first project to the completed construction, while the latter indicates the spatial configuration that is set as the finish line. The final scenario is the moving target towards which our project (like the art of archery) aims its arrows.

The mobility of the target corresponds to the changes to which the scenario is repeatedly subjected, both in its general layout and in the increasingly precise definitions of its building components, destinations, technical installations, and fittings. Most of the time, the project documents represent an uncertain version of the final scenario—at different scales and according to different themes and analyses. They rarely explicitly state the intermediate stages, limiting themselves to defining the sequence of construction operations and the parts to be demolished and built. Our attempt will be to bring out the chain relations linking the many adjustments undergone by these projects, and to draw these chains of deviations from the documents that have been placed on our tables so far. We see this as an attempt at innovation, which seeks to integrate the traditional project of the final states—organized into frameworks and set up as stable "projects," progressively ordered from the preliminary to the executive—with the tracing of the intermediate stages, i.e., the succession of exchanges, between one stable framework and another. In order to clarify this hidden dimension of the project, between one explicit scenario and the next, we will arrange the intermediate working documents in a single arena, so as to trace the exchanges and adjustments that have produced effects on the project and ultimately on the future shape of the space.

Instructions on how to read the map

This attempt to outline the project action is constructed, for the sake of clarity, by reducing the project's infinite transformation process—resulting from a countless series of exchanges, constraints, and decisions—to a finite number of documents and steps. The process that led from the application project to the formalization of the technical and economic feasibility project document is divided into three scenarios (the tender project, an intermediate formalization, and the delivered feasibility project). These three scenarios are represented with an exploded axonometric drawing of the project site, trying to make the individual parts of the project comparable during their design changes. Between the three scenarios, which establish a stable state of the project, there are two arenas where, through the evidence of sets and brief descriptions (found in the notes), we tried to show the chain of associations between the project documents and the sequences of contingent convergences that determined the consolidation, or the discarding, of the different project hypotheses.

Scenario 01: The tender project

In the perspective of action that we have traversed and carried out so far, the future horizon was completely opaque at first, slowly becoming clearer as attempts were made to launch the final scenarios forward, generating a cascade of reactions and course corrections. The first launch certainly corresponds to the proposal presented in the tender, but it is more of a reasonable example of how we would like to proceed than a reliable result. After all, the tender is used to identify the group of those who will be able to carry out the project, not a definite solution: the commission judges the contestants based on their curricula and the general quality of the proposed approach, rather than any anticipated solution. Clients expect to have to deal with architects who are also capable of negotiating and adapting to many variables, which are not yet foreseeable, but which will certainly complicate the process along the way. In short, we are not the only ones who cannot see the future clearly, and we know that we will have to use our projects and scenarios to shape a complex set of circumstances, constraints, and accidents of which no one has a clear idea yet. For these reasons, the first scenario inferred from the tender proposal serves mainly to set in order the questions that we had to unravel as we went along.

Arena 01/02

Building on the tender proposal, which was evidently appreciated by the commission that evaluated it, we initiated discussions with the commissioning administration and with the conservation bodies, and at the same time we studied the characteristics of the building we had to design, through photographs taken during the inspections, historical investigations, and more in-depth measurements. The existing drawings and those produced by us (technical drawings, specific measurements of key points, sketches, notes on reports, etc.) had different lives and effects. Sometimes they consolidated their power by associating themselves with other documents; sometimes their action was interrupted by clear-cut decisions or by clashing with certain constraints; sometimes, if they failed to link up with other demands that emerged during the course of the project, so they floated alone until they left the scene.

Scenario 02: The project in an intermediate formalization

In the period from January to April, exchanges continued between the group's architects, between the architects and the clients, and with the conservation bodies. Each exchange came with dossiers containing drawings of the proposed solutions, but also calculations or historical maps to support the proposals. In each exchange, the solution put forward was related to new requirements and modified accordingly. The form of the exchange was free and the project had an exploratory character: it wandered blindly among distributional inventions, vocations of use, and technical solutions, in search of a hypothesis that, by bringing all the requirements together, could finally be stabilized. In this Scenario 02, the different solutions put forward in the dossiers produced for the discussions are instrumentally merged into a single representation.

Arena 02/03

In view of the delivery of the technical and economic feasibility project, which must be contractually agreed by a certain date, it was necessary to reach a conclusion and make all the useful choices to define the most effective project hypothesis. There was no longer any time for openings and explorations: choices were made on the basis of what was already on the table. Technical drawings began to replace sketches, and triggered checks on the conformity of spaces. If some aspect of the project went beyond the perimeter defined by the call for tenders (if, for example, the costs of the intervention exceeded the budget), it was necessary to quickly go back to the design hypothesis and modify some parts of it.

Scenario 03: The technical and economic feasibility project

Project documents are prescribed by law, in order to identify the project object in all its components, and to make it a contractual product that may be approved by the client. The contents of the project were dissected into different documents, responding to particular purposes. The project drawings were distinguished between those concerning demolitions (to be assessed by the Superintendency) and those concerning new constructions (which require verification that the new spaces comply with current regulations). Each work was described in the performance specifications. Each cost was analyzed according to a standardized price list. Every possible technical, economic, legal, and cadastral problem was anticipated and formalized. This Project set a status that, unlike the project in the second scenario, defined one solution and one solution only. At the moment of its approval, the feasibility project became an institutional object: a document capable of generating effects on the world, even independently of the intentions of its authors.

Alessandro Armando and Giovanni Durbiano - Innovation from the Practice. A Perspectival Fragment

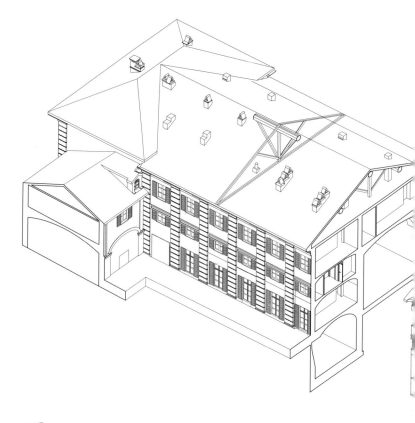

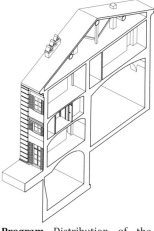

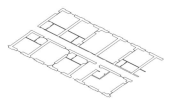

First-floor distribution Central corridor distributing the bedrooms on the first floor.

Program Distribution of the main functions: restaurant room in the north-west halls of the ground floor; kitchen, rooms, and services in the south-east halls of the ground floor and in the mezzanine area; hotel on the first floor and possibly in the attic.

Roof Urgent renovation of the roof, now at risk of collapsing.

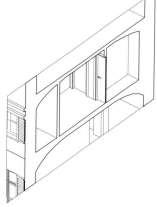

Mezzanine floor Slightly lowering of the mezzanine floor in order to reach a sufficient height to meet the code requirements.

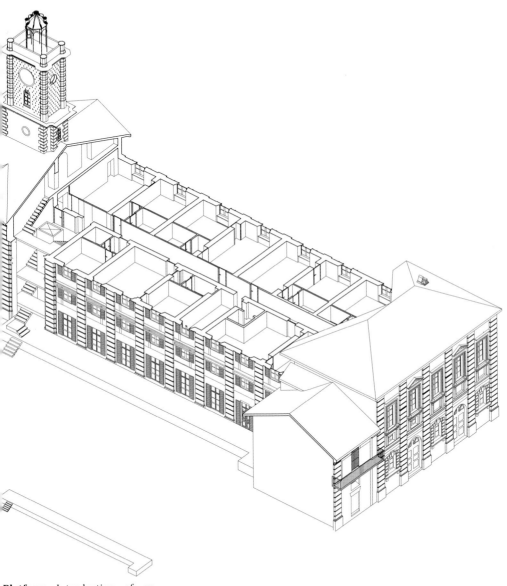

Platform Introduction of an external platform overlooking the courtyard at the same level of the rooms of the south-east lounges.

DESIGN – EXAPTATION

Alessandro Armando and Giovanni Durbiano -
Innovation from the Practice. A Perspectival Fragment

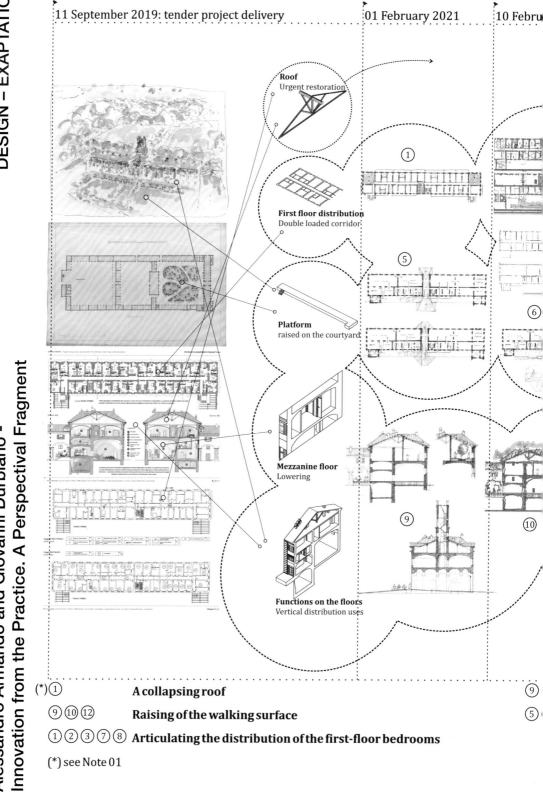

11 September 2019: tender project delivery

01 February 2021

10 Febru

Roof
Urgent restoration

①

First floor distribution
Double loaded corridor

⑤

Platform
raised on the courtyard

⑥

Mezzanine floor
Lowering

⑨

⑩

Functions on the floors
Vertical distribution uses

(*)①   **A collapsing roof**   ⑨

⑨⑩⑫   **Raising of the walking surface**   ⑤

①②③⑦⑧   **Articulating the distribution of the first-floor bedrooms**

(*) see Note 01

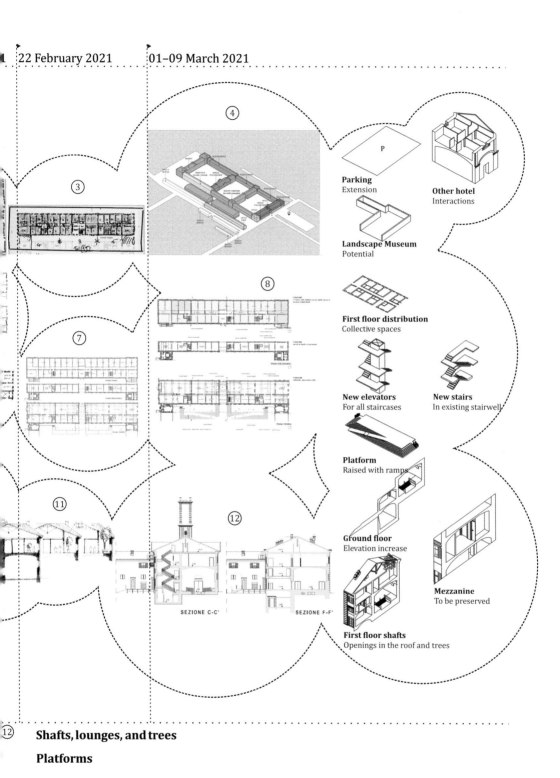

④

③

⑦

⑧

⑪

⑫

Parking
Extension

Other hotel
Interactions

Landscape Museum
Potential

First floor distribution
Collective spaces

New elevators
For all staircases

New stairs
In existing stairwell

Platform
Raised with ramps

Ground floor
Elevation increase

Mezzanine
To be preserved

First floor shafts
Openings in the roof and trees

SEZIONE C-C'   SEZIONE F-F'

⑫ **Shafts, lounges, and trees**

Platforms

Alessandro Armando and Giovanni Durbiano -
Innovation from the Practice. A Perspectival Fragment

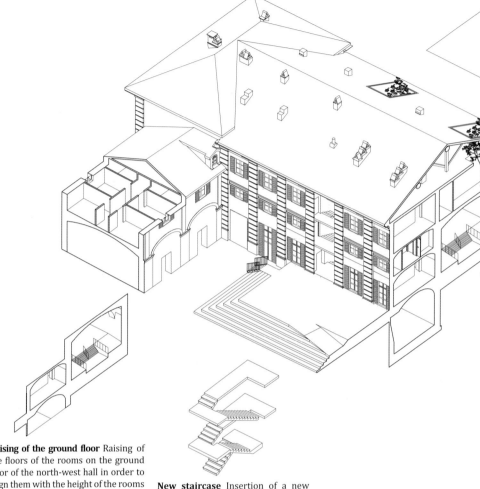

Raising of the ground floor Raising of the floors of the rooms on the ground floor of the north-west hall in order to align them with the height of the rooms of the south-east hall. This work would prompt the need to build ramps in the entrance facing the garden.

New staircase Insertion of a new staircase, symmetrical to the entrance axis.

Other hotel In order to avoid a single standard for the rooms in the main body of the building, a second array of hotel rooms might be designed with the consequent possibility of varying the range of hotel rooms in the project.

Cavaedium first-floor On the first floor, an open cavaedium could be obtained, which allows tall trees to be planted.

Mezzanine Demolition has been vetoed by the Preservation Authority .

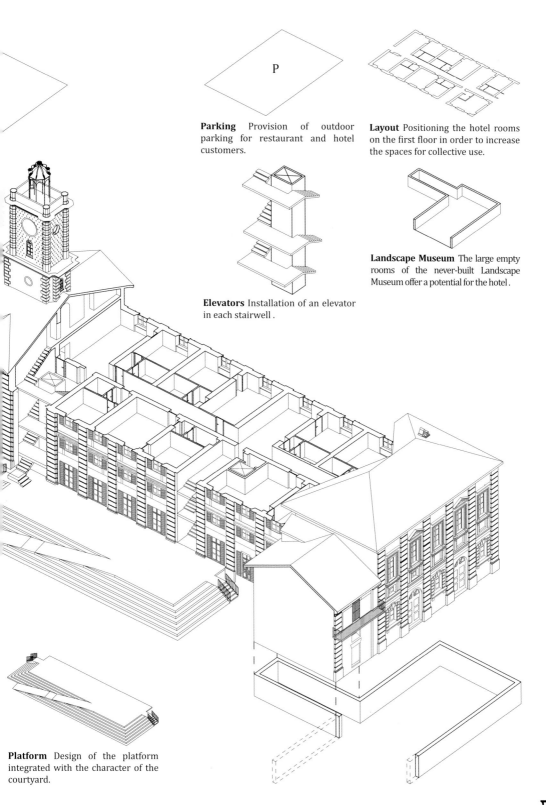

Parking Provision of outdoor parking for restaurant and hotel customers.

Layout Positioning the hotel rooms on the first floor in order to increase the spaces for collective use.

Elevators Installation of an elevator in each stairwell .

Landscape Museum The large empty rooms of the never-built Landscape Museum offer a potential for the hotel .

Platform Design of the platform integrated with the character of the courtyard.

Alessandro Armando and Giovanni Durbiano -
Innovation from the Practice. A Perspectival Fragment

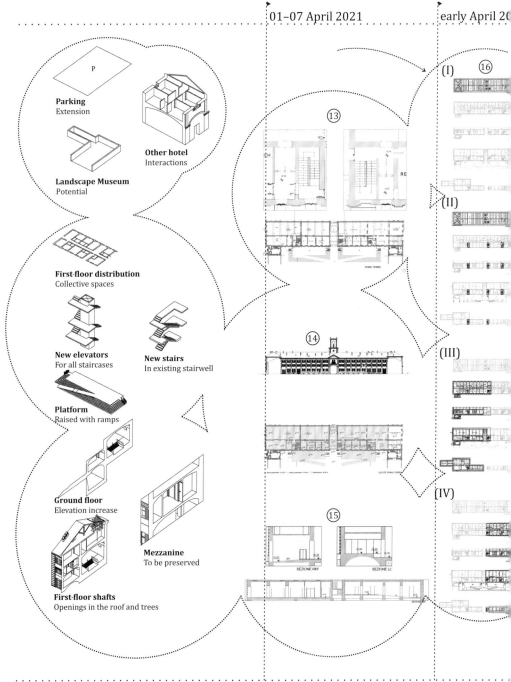

01–07 April 2021   early April 20

Parking
Extension

Other hotel
Interactions

Landscape Museum
Potential

First-floor distribution
Collective spaces

New elevators
For all staircases

New stairs
In existing stairwell

Platform
Raised with ramps

Ground floor
Elevation increase

Mezzanine
To be preserved

First-floor shafts
Openings in the roof and trees

(*) (14) (15) (21)   **Lowering of the walking surface**

(18) (20)   **Articulating the distribution of the first-floor bedrooms**

(17) (21)   **End of the shafts hypothesis**

(*) see Note 02

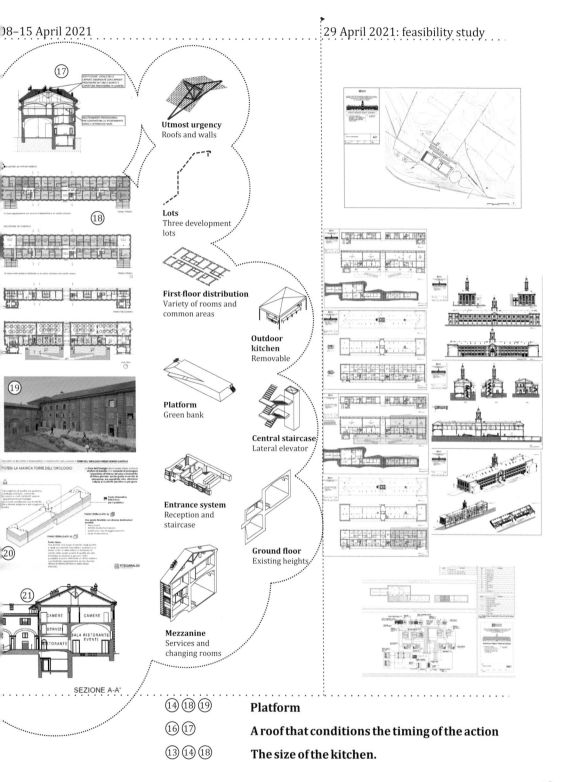

Utmost urgency
Roofs and walls

Lots
Three development lots

First-floor distribution
Variety of rooms and common areas

Outdoor kitchen
Removable

Platform
Green bank

Central staircase
Lateral elevator

Entrance system
Reception and staircase

Ground floor
Existing heights

Mezzanine
Services and changing rooms

⑭ ⑱ ⑲   **Platform**

⑯ ⑰   **A roof that conditions the timing of the action**

⑬ ⑭ ⑱   **The size of the kitchen.**

Alessandro Armando and Giovanni Durbiano -
Innovation from the Practice. A Perspectival Fragment

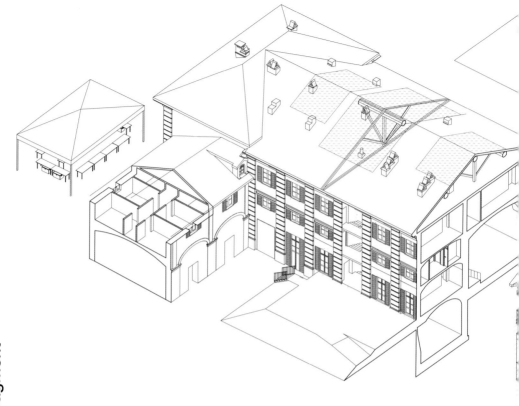

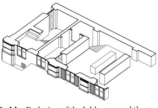

Lobby Redesign of the lobby around the main staircase.

External kitchen Redesign of the kitchen spaces to give the opportunity of using a removable external structure to accommodate catering.

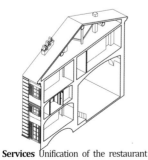

Services Unification of the restaurant service areas on the mezzanine floor.

Platform Redesign of the platform to integrate the square geometry to the courtyard's shape.

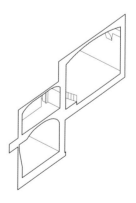

Ground floor Getting rid of the hypothesis of raising the floor of the rooms on the north-west halls and return to the original floor level, with the following introduction of a system of internal ramps.

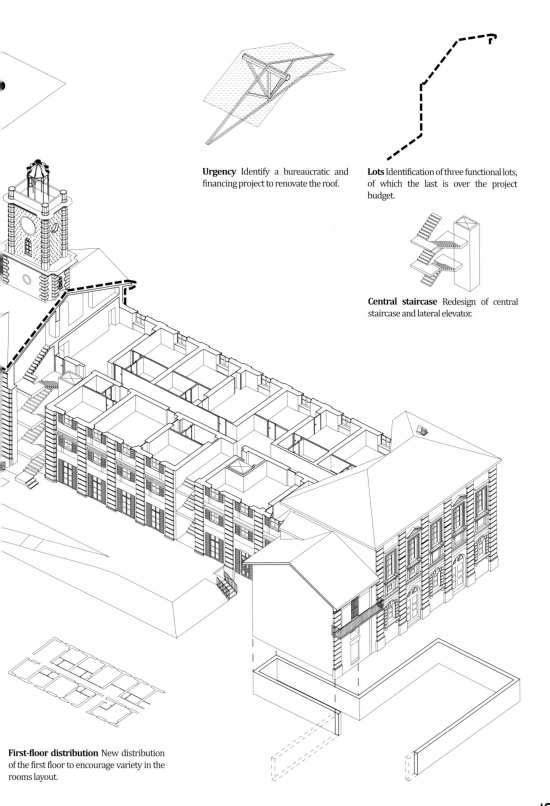

Urgency Identify a bureaucratic and financing project to renovate the roof.

Lots Identification of three functional lots, of which the last is over the project budget.

Central staircase Redesign of central staircase and lateral elevator.

First-floor distribution New distribution of the first floor to encourage variety in the rooms layout.

Notes

Note 1. Association paths and project evolution in the 01/02 arena

9, 10, 12 *Raising the floor level.* Given the different height between the former stables in the north-west wing and the service areas in the south-east wing, the project, from the outset, envisaged raising the floor level of all the halls in the north-west wing, so as to ensure a comfortable coplanar distribution for the restaurant and the events space; to channel all the ducts in the floating floor; and to reduce the distance from the tall windows of the halls. This solution was consistent with and supported the hypothesis of a platform facing the courtyard, and remained unchanged almost until the delivery of the feasibility project.

1, 2, 3, 7, 8 *Layout of the distribution of rooms on the first floor.* After examining the comb-shaped typology of the first floor, it was evident that it was designed to accommodate the hotel rooms requested in the invitation to tender, and therefore to use the central wing of the existing building as a distribution corridor. However, the articulation and character of these spaces changed several times during the course of the project. In the tender project, they were presented in a rigid form (a linear corridor and rooms that were largely the same), then in a more articulated form (a corridor with lounges in correspondence with the skylights on the roof, and larger rooms).

9,10,11,12 *Air shafts, lounges, and trees.* Triggered by the hypotheses drawn up to articulate the spaces on the first floor, the shapes of the rooms were deformed and expanded, involving the attic and roof level. Different solutions were devised: cold areas inside the room; areas that break through the attic to reach the system of three-dimensional trusses above; areas lit from above by opening up air shafts. The awareness of being set in one of the main national parks promoted a naturalistic strategy that even encouraged the introduction of low-trunk trees in the air shafts.

5, 6, 8 *Platform.* In order to allow for an overall coplanarity of the area dedicated to dining and events, and to avoid demolishing the attics of the south-eastern wing (covering valuable cellar rooms), the proposal to raise the floor level of the rooms of the former stables was confirmed by the design of a platform over the courtyard and placed at the same height, where one could eat or sit outside over-looking the courtyard. The shape of the platform changed during the course of the project in terms of size, access to services in the courtyard, and the more or less temporary or natural character required by the Superintendency, but its supporting function for outdoor activities did not change.

0 *A collapsing roof.* One of the main reasons why the client decided to take action on the building (and consequently launch the tender) was the extreme deterioration of its roofs, which are beginning to give way in several places and risk collapsing under winter loads. Given this assumption, the tender project stated that consolidation work would be carried out as a matter of urgency. The solution, considered to be of an eminently technical-statistical nature, was delegated to the competent professional, and did not, at this stage, interact with the other project documents.

Note 2. Associative paths and project evolution in the arena 02/03

14, 15, 21 *Lowering of the walking surface.* Shortly before the technical and economic feasibility project was delivered, the client requested that the floor not be raised, so as not to lose the space taken up by the connecting ramps between the rooms and the entrance hall. This invalidated one of the most binding choices of the project route, but it did not change the legitimacy of the associated platform solution.

18, 20 *Articulation of the distribution of rooms on the first floor.* The studies to differentiate the shape of the hotel rooms from those of the neighboring hotel, currently under construction, intersected with the hypotheses for the location of the restaurant's services. The need to introduce elevators to provide access to the services on the mezzanine floors promoted an extension of their route to the first floor, allowing for a condominial distribution (in groups of rooms around each of the three elevators) of the room floor. The two hypotheses—the single corridor model and the condominium model – were promoted to design alternatives, as required by the feasibility project.

17, 21 *Discarding of air shafts.* Following the rejection of the Superintendency, the idea of open-ing shafts in the roof was discarded. The idea of extending the rooms towards the attic was also discarded, as it would require urgent work on the trusses and the distribution of the rooms, which would not have fit in with the project schedule. The solution was no longer presented in the feasibility project.

14, 18, 19 *Platform*. The design of the shape of the platform changed according to the requests of the Superintendency (or what the client believed the latter would require). In the feasibility project, it was indicated that this was still a provisional form, which, without being tied to other elements, might be modified in the subsequent phases of the project.

16, 17 *A roof that sets the pace.* The static consolidation of the roofs, which was increasingly necessary given the heavy storms during the project phase, led the Administration to request an autonomous executive intervention, according to a procedure of "paramount urgency." The calculation of the intervention costs and the consideration of the need to articulate the project intervention in more or less urgent time phases led to breaking it down into three different functional lots. The last of these was placed outside the initially foreseen budget conditions.

13, 14, 18 *Kitchen size.* Because of the difficulty of defining the quality and quantity of the restaurant's clientele, which depend on a series of largely unpredictable factors, studies on the size of the kitchen have a degree of uncertainty that long prevented the project from becoming stable. Only the hypothesis of adopting an outdoor kitchen, placed in a mobile and temporary structure (a tent in the garden immediately outside the courtyard) unblocked the project's deadlock and made it possible to size the indoor kitchen and consequently all the remaining rooms in the restaurant.

UNPACKING ARCHITECTURAL DESIGN PRACTICE *IN THE FOLDS* OF DECISION-MAKING PROCESSES.
An Innovative Mapping Tool
Elena Todella

Elena Todella is an architect and a post-Doc research fellow at Politecnico di Torino. She holds a PhD in "Architecture. History and Project." Her research activities concern complex urban and architectural transformation processes—followed from the inside—in their decisions, negotiations, design practices, by focusing on both architectural design and decision-making levels. From 2016 to 2018 she was part of the "Masterplan Team" of Politecnico and from 2020 she has been involved in an excellence project about the Sustainable Development Goal 11.

Architectural design theory, in the last few decades, has been characterized by some important paradigm changes. Indeed, starting in the 1980s, the architectural design process became the object of empirical attention primarily through traditional sociological or anthropological approaches linked to the analysis of the workplace context (Blau, 1984) or professional practice in engineering and architecture (Henderson, 1991; Cuff, 1992). Then, in the last decade, a new wave of interest in practice in the social sciences has emerged (Schatzki et al, 2001). Specifically, such interest has been drawn to architectural and engineering professions (Houdart and Minato, 2009; Yaneva, 2009; Jacobs and Merriman, 2011), with reference to several participants in the architectural design project through ethnographies and "thick descriptions" (Geertz, 1973). We can refer to this trend as an "ethnographic turn in architecture" (Yaneva, 2017).

These studies shifted attention from the products of architecture—as buildings and places—to the processes of project conception and modification. As a result, architecture is understood as a collective process of negotiation between human and non-human entities (Yaneva, 2017)—then as sociotechnical systems—as ethnographic methods and tools are used within architectural research (in the form of participant observation, interviews, and conversations). Investigating the architects' practices—that is, what they do on a daily basis—aims at assigning priority to the pragmatic content of their actions, rather than their theories and ideologies (Callon, 1996; Yaneva, 2005 and 2017). In tracing ethnographically as models, projects, and designs are produced, negotiated, and disseminated, these "new ethnographers" (Yaneva, 2017) aim to follow the design production and the architects as professionals in the act of a practice. From this perspective, the operative dimension of the architectural design process is understood and investigated as the place in which the real is modeled in material entities (i.e., as drawings, models, and artifacts in general).

These perspectives, which connect the application of Science and Technology Studies (STS) and Actor-Network Theory (ANT) to architecture, can be linked to the "ecology of practices" (Stengers, 2005 and 2010; Yaneva, 2017; Frichot, 2017), a concept that, starting from a claim of legitimacy in the science field (Stengers, 2005 and 2010), implies the possibility of knowledge of reality. This reality is not investigated from an intelligible point of view, but by focusing on how we experience it and interact with it (Stengers, 2005). This makes it possible, for instance, to consider practices precisely in terms of what makes them different, rather than abstracting from what they have in common—as we tend to do in the field of scientific research (Stengers, 2005). In this sense, a *creative* ecology of practices (Frichot, 2017) is assumed here as an operative modality that defines its borders in relation to a direct observation of the practice itself and allows one to innovatively grasp and understand architectural practice in its development as a field of scientific investigation.

This new ethnographic wave of studies starts from STS and ANT research, which underlines a fundamental focus on the relational networks of associations in social studies. Indeed, rather than considering the *social* as a specific and identified realm and the context *in which* everything is framed, they start from the point that society comes from operations of re-association and reassembling (Latour, 2005). In these studies, instead of referring to external factors and abstract theoretical frameworks *outside* design, there is an attempt to grasp and trace the connections that allow design works to come into being (Yaneva, 2009) in a pragmatic way. Consequently, the ethnography of architecture is an approach that avoids ideological interpretations and excessive perspectivism in architectural design theory. Instead, critical theory formulations in architecture aim at locating architecture, buildings, and design processes in higher-level theoretical frameworks—as social factors, cultures, and politics—in the search for a richer and more significant understanding of architecture by situating it in a social context in which it is considered to have a place (Yaneva, 2009). The most problematic point for STS and ANT scholars is this concept of a social context as an external domain already given (Latour, 2005) and an attitude that positions architecture into interpretative categories and hidden fields, in which meanings and values are situated, with a will of abstraction and idealization. As a result, critical theory in architecture covers the ideas instead of the practices. Instead, ANT and STS scholars tackle the practices of designers in a pragmatist way (Callon, 1996; Yaneva, 2005 and 2009; Houdart and Minato, 2009) by explicitly proposing a realist, pragmatic method as an alternative approach to the critical one (Yaneva, 2010). Accordingly, they follow architects—and practitioners in general—in their daily routines and actions to unravel the everyday techniques and operations involved in the design process (Yaneva, 2010).

DESIGN – EXAPTATION

Elena Todella - Unpacking Architectural Design Practice *in the Folds* of Decision-Making Processes. An Innovative Mapping Tool

The alternative proposed by looking at and unpacking practices is to define and identify, in a pragmatic way, how architectural practice works and how projects acquire meaning in the practice experience. This means that one must not run into further theoretical interpretations but must instead study and analyze the architectural production in the way it aggregates and relates various entities to avoid pre-given explanations and conceptual frameworks. Starting from some of these assumptions, this paper expands upon an ongoing debate around design research as a scientific field of investigation into architectural practices in a pragmatist way. It does this by deepening some issues, such as the possibilities related to the observation and analysis of architectural practice as an ecology; the output and products of an observation of architectural processes through an ethnographic lens; and the way a mapping methodology can and does convey knowledge in architectural research.

What Do the Folds Allow Me to See?

This research originates from an interest in the decision-making processes of complex urban and architectural transformations, which are dependent on several implications and actors, have a high degree of uncertainty, and are generally complex in terms of the process itself and in the outcomes. These complex processes are often accounted for as a linear sequence of steps and decisions, and causes and effects; however, this linearity is rare, and projects usually do not go straight to buildings without detours, conflicts, and negotiations. Because of this process, this work takes into account precisely these diversions as constituent elements of the decision-making process. To do this, and to witness the folds of the architectural design process, I decided to focus on a practice, with a clear shift in perspective and interests, and try to grasp and trace it in a pragmatic way.

I had the opportunity to research and unfold an architectural design process in this way since I was involved, for over two years, in the Project Team of the *Masterplan* of the Politecnico di Torino urban campuses. Indeed, after being a key player in the transformation processes of some urban sectors, in Politecnico's transformations there has been a slowing down, and some projects have stalled in recent years. To address these difficulties, the Administrative Board of the university activated the *Masterplan* in 2016 to outline alternative transformation strategies, define expansion scenarios, and direct qualification processes for existing spaces.

Furthermore, besides providing the opportunity to participate and have direct access to the ongoing practice in the *Masterplan* on an almost daily basis, my work has also followed two different strands of research. First, my work is positioned within the already mentioned disciplinary debate about the definition of architectural design research as a scientific field through an investigation of practices informed by an ethnographic perspective and "ecology of practice" (Stengers, 2005 and 2010; Yaneva, 2017; Frichot, 2017). Secondly, it is based on an interdisciplinary interest in methods of analysis of decision-making process-es, with particular reference to the entities involved, their role in the process, their interactions, and the objects through which these interactions take place.

Consequently, the aim of this research is to investigate—from the inside—the role of some architectural design practices in relation to the ongoing deci-sion-making processes by exploring the connections between these practices and their results and effects. Indeed, I assume here that it would have not been otherwise possible to observe and witness these connections without having been *in the folds* of the process. Starting from this position, the present research seeks to define whether, in a process observed at the scale of daily practice, it is possible to identify some crucial points, specific strategies, and operational tactics that influence the decision-making level, which may be somehow *invis-ible* on a different scale of indirect observation. This direct observation of the process pays attention to the ordinary and daily practices of architectural design and the related ways in which decisions are made in the real process through interactions on these projects. Starting from the collected data and producing a meticulous reconstruction of the architectural design operations, this research investigates the way in which project operations take place and how they ac-quire meaning and produce effects in the wider decision-making process. This kind of research is qualitative and conducted in close correlation with the con-text in which the phenomenon takes place; this allows for an interpretative ap-proach to be taken in an attempt to capture events that gain specificity in their own moments of occurrence, and in an ecology of practice.

The central question is whether a kind of *oligoptic* (Latour, 2005) observation of the architectural design process from the inside can produce knowledge of the architectural practice in the whole *panoramic* story by following the practice, tracing the materialization of its subsequent operations, and describing the im-plications in the decision-making process. To address this, I trace a taxonomy of multiple actors with different ontologies that interact in a multi-sited and large-scale process. Not only drawings, models, and projects, but also note-taking of Project Team's members, reports, meetings, e-mail, and WhatsApp exchanges, are collected and examined to explore the pragmatic connections between these practices—as a matter of delegating architectural design to several entities—and their effects. Starting from the collected data, a content analysis is the basis for recollecting all the different projects in the whole process of the *Masterplan*.

Therefore, what do the *folds* of this process—on an almost daily basis ob-servation and participation—allow me to see? I recount here a first example of a mapping methodology to analyze the projects, proposed starting from the liter-ature, but also suggesting a personal perspective in managing the data. In this paper, I focus on the perspective I follow in building the maps on two different scales: as a hypertextual archive of the whole process (*panorama*) on the one hand, and as a specific perspective that focuses on episodes (*oligopticon*) as micro-structures of macro-phenomena on the other.

DESIGN – EXAPTATION

Elena Todella - Unpacking Architectural Design Practice *in the Folds* of Decision-Making Processes. An Innovative Mapping Tool

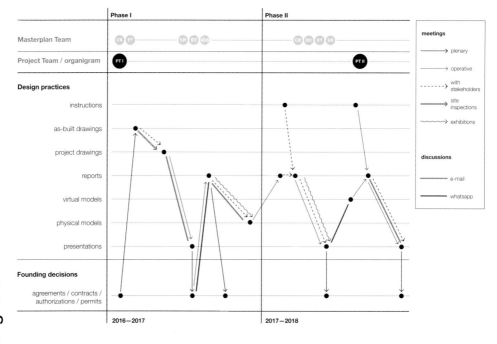

A scheme for mapping a dual perspective on design practices and founding decisions

Mapping the Process: A Panoramic Hypertextual Archive

First, the opportunity to witness the whole process from the inside allowed me to gain access to and trace all the different entities involved—in terms of documents—as an overview and a panorama (Fig. 1). This corpus is then organized from a perspective related to the dichotomic relation between design practices and institutional decisions; indeed, the scheme aims to trace this relation by focusing on three related layers (starting from Armando and Durbiano, 2017, chapter 4): a taxonomy of design practices and productions (i.e., instructions, as-built drawings, project drawings, reports, models, and presentations); a series of founding decisions and effects (i.e., agreements, contracts, authorizations, and permits); and, between these two spheres, the tracing of the exchanges as conflicts, negotiations, and controversies (i.e., meetings and discussion transcriptions).

In this way, the map acts as a hypertextual archive that grasps the complexity of the process as a whole; nevertheless, there is the assumption of a perspective into the relations and exchanges between the inscriptions produced by the architects and the consequent institutive acts. Moreover, it is also possible to focus on any invariant and then generalizable elements as they are repeated.

For example, there is the sequence of media to progressively socialize and then institutionalize the project; the type of arenas in which certain types of products are discussed and negotiated; and the kind and maybe the number of deviations before arriving at a founding decision. To summarize, this overview allows us to follow the way design productions act and connect in a related way to move the process through decisions.

Mapping the Process: Episodes as an Oligoptic Lens

The opportunity to access the whole process from the inside also allowed me to maintain a specific and oligoptic perspective on excerpts of the process, and to go in depth into the investigation of this relation between projects and decisions. Here again, the map with this particular perspective allows us to read the diversions in the exchanges between design practices—as productions and projects—and founding decisions—as effects and decisions—by representing the three related layers I mentioned before (i.e., design practices, founding decisions, and exchanges). Moreover, the reconstruction of the details of specific excerpts leads to the definition of a framework of problems and needs (that is, the specific requests that emerged from the exchanges that are indicated in the links); the identification of the different strategies and operations that the architect carried on; and an attempt to deal with the problems (that can be highlighted from the drawings) to reach certain effects.

As an example, we can see an excerpt of the process of realizing a building with new classrooms that was stopped by the superintendent (Fig. 2) just before the former building was demolished. The kind of instances that emerged from the documents actually reached the effect to restart the process, and can be related to physical aspects (e.g., preservation of the original wall on the main street), but also to quality aspects (e.g., demonstration that in the building, there are no such things to maintain, so the wall is the only aspect to preserve), and so on. Then, all the instances are spilled and spatialized into the products and media through which the practice unfolds in the process, so it is then possible to trace these relations. Finally, again, it is possible to focus on the invariant and generalizable conditions, but on this different scale. For example, there is a sequence between the different media and practices in different moments of the process, a taxonomy of the kind of instances and the related collectives, and a different degree of definition in the several products that follow up in the practice.

Projecting Decisions: Further Developments

So, what I discussed and explored here is a way of narrating and representing architectural operations in an attempt to carry forward a research action across scales. In taking this approach, the mapping methodology allows us to follow and narrate the process to capitalize an experience in operative terms; to iden-

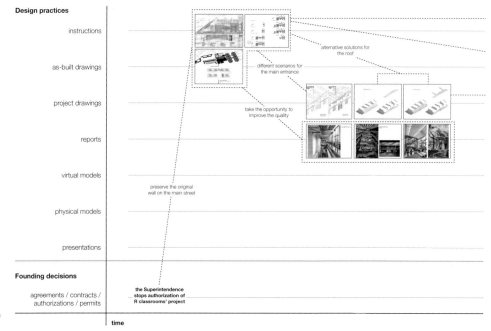

Figure 2
An excerpt of mapping the process through specific episodes

tify specific moves and operations in architectural design with projects as tools for reaching effects; and to make them describable by identifying a tool for description of this kind of process.

Therefore, in this work, drawings, models, reports, and design practices in general are considered as negotiation tools, with the aim of making conflicts and opportunities evident and leading the debate to a possible resolution. Starting from this perspective, the process is shown and analyzed as a sequence of actions and decisions that have recognizable links to trace the related roles of the different entities involved in the process. In terms of perspective, a duality is assumed between design productions and founding decisions as social and institutional objects that are exchanged and negotiated in different arenas. Furthermore, the inside perspective in the process is completely assumed, on the one hand, since it is declared and is essential in terms of collecting data; on the other hand, this kind of mapping tries to move from the singular and specific case to the definition of a replicable map of analysis of potentially different processes. Finally, these maps can be used as tools to investigate what architects do and how projects operate, not only retrospectively, but with the possibility of projecting decisions. Indeed, they could potentially serve as an example of situations in which different media have been used with specific effects or have had certain consequences, so an architect may decide to use the same strategy, or the same sequence of media, to address a specific problem with defined and recognized instances. In this way, it would be possible to deal with not only projects themselves, but also the exchanges and action models aimed at reaching specific effects that an architect can investigate.

References
Armando A., Durbiano G. (2017), *Teoria del progetto architettonico. Dai disegni agli effetti*, Carocci, Roma.
Blau J. (1984), *Architects and Firms: A Sociological Perspective on Architectural Practice*, MIT Press, Cambridge.
Cuff D. (1992), *Architecture: The Story of Practice*, MIT Press, Cambridge.
Callon M. (1996), *Le travail de la conception en architecture*, "Cahiers de la Recherche architecturale," vol. 37, pp. 25–35.
Cuff D. (1992), *Architecture: The Story of Practice*, MIT Press, Cambridge.
Frichot H. (2017), *A Creative Ecology of Practice for Thinking Architecture*, "Ardeth," vol. 1, pp. 139–49.
Geertz C. (1973), *The Interpretation of Cultures: Selected Essays*, Basic Books, New York.
Henderson K. (1991), *Flexible Sketches and Inflexible Databases*, "Science, Technology & Human Values," vol. 16, n. 4, pp. 448–73.
Houdart S., Minato C. (2009), *Kuma Kengo. An Unconventional Monograph*, Donner Lieu, Parigi.
Jacobs J. M., Merriman P. (2011), *Practising Architectures*, "Social & Cultural Geography," vol. 12, n. 3, pp. 211–22.
Latour B. (2005), *Reassembling the Social. An Introduction to Actor-Network-Theory*, Oxford University Press, New York.
Schatzki T. R., Cetina K. K., von Savigny E. (2001), *The Practice Turn in Contemporary Theory*, Routledge, London.
Stengers I. (2005), *Introductory Notes on an Ecology of Practices*, "Cultural Studies Review," vol. 11, pp. 183–96.
Stengers I. (2010), *Cosmopolitiche*, Luca Sossella Editore, Roma.
Yaneva A. (2005), *Scaling Up and Down: Extraction Trials in Architectural Design*, Social Studies of Science, vol. 35, n. 6, pp. 867–94
Yaneva A. (2009), *The Making of a Building: A Pragmatist Approach to Architecture*, Oxford, Peter Lang.
Yaneva A. (2010), *From Reflecting-in-Action Towards Mapping of the Real*, in I. Doucet, N. Janssens (eds.), *Transdisciplinary Knowledge Production in Architecture* and Urbanism, Springer Netherlands, Heidelberg.
Yaneva A. (2017), *Five Ways to Make Architecture Political: An Introduction to the Politics of Design Practice*, Bloomsbury Publishing, Londra.

INNOVATION TRAJECTORIES.
Retracing the History
of Area-Based Initiatives
Caterina Quaglio

Caterina Quaglio is an architect and research fellow at the Future *Urban Legacy* Lab of Politecnico di Torino. She obtained her PhD in "Architecture. History and Project" in July 2020. Since her master's degree and during an internship in Chile, she has worked on the issue of public housing. Her PhD research, developed through in-depth analysis of European case studies, is focused on the policies and practices of urban regeneration of public housing districts. In recent years she has also taken part in several national and international projects related to the field of educational spaces both as a designer and researcher. She is currently participating in a research project developed in collaboration with Fondazione Agnelli focusing on the potential of school spaces in relation to post-pandemic reopening and educational innovation.

A Call for Innovation

At the end of the 1980s, the "concentration of problems in specific urban areas" (Commission of the European Communities, 1993: 12) became a matter of concern for many European cities. To tackle this issue, both national and European institutions developed urban regeneration policies based on the integration of multidisciplinary tools, resources, and projects in predetermined areas. The innovation of practices and procedures was an explicit objective of the so-called area-based initiatives and a central element in the narratives employed by the administrations, as evidenced by the recurrent use of a *new* vocabulary—integration, inclusion, participation, territorialization, etc.—aimed at providing the backdrop for the affirmation of a new approach. According to the advocates of area-based policies, the very act of working in and with a territory would not only foster the advancement of innovative practices, but it would also favor the long-term renewal of the "institutional architecture" behind each project (Bifulco and De Leonardis, 2006: 56). According to Barca et al (2012):

> Underdevelopment traps that limit and inhibit the growth potential of regions or perpetuate social exclusion are the result of a failure of local elites to act and can only be tackled by new knowledge and ideas: the purpose of development policy is to promote them through the interaction of those local groups and the external elites involved in the policy. (139)

In this context, the role of professionals changed. Architects and urbanists, in particular, were confronted with a:

> progressive shift from product-oriented commissions (the drawing up and drafting of plans, projects and programs) to commissions centered on the process, i.e., on the possibility of 'accompanying' projects, policies and interventions well beyond the phase of defining the professional product (Pasqui, 2001: 22).[1]

Moreover, even if spatial transformation remained a key element in urban regeneration programs—often more than publicly admitted—architectural and urban design were no longer considered stand-alone solutions. This variation in the professional demand was mirrored by some important changes in the working practice of designers. On the one hand, they had to constantly negotiate their roles and competencies in a wider interdisciplinary and cross-sectoral work system. On the other hand, they could experiment with new design and planning practices or, more simply, new interpretations of traditional practices.

Starting from the assumption that an over-emphasis on the *newness* of area-based initiatives may lead to overlooking some important aspects for the understanding of this experience, the present essay aims to question innovation on the basis of a close observation of the practices involved and the way they were generated, interpreted, and institutionalized at different levels (Pasqui, 2001: 11). More specifically, the in-depth analysis of three European case studies[2] provides the source material to investigate the forms, directions, and long-term legacies of innovative practices according to two main levels of observation. First, at the individual level, attention will be directed to the trajectories of the experts directly involved in the initiatives as a means of questioning the way professionals can acquire and capitalize on new knowledge throughout the design process. Then, in the following section, the focus will shift to the collective dimension to interrogate the way innovative practices can or cannot affect policies and institutions. Finally, the text tries to retrace the paths of innovation as a process in continuous transition between individual learning and collective capitalization with the aim to complement through this perspective the way area-based programs have usually been presented and evaluated.

<u>Generating Innovation: Learning Through Action</u>

> Innovation is a by-product in itself and, more precisely, a by-product of social learning practices. As far as we know, learning occurs in situations of social interaction characterized by "weak bonds," that is overabundant, plethoric connections, presenting uncertainties that can constitute an occasion and a resource for social invention. (Crosta, 1998: 12)[3]

The production of knowledge *in* action was seen both as a condition and a result of the territorial and cross-sectoral approach of area-based initiatives developed during the 1980s and 1990s. To question professionals' learning processes, however, the present research focuses on the actual implementation of practices in relation to the *collectives* of entities involved in each project rather than on the intentionality of policies. Drawing from Latour (2004: 238), a collective "refers not to an already-established unit but to a procedure for collecting associations of humans and nonhumans". Consequently, the notion of a collective implies the existence of a network of relationships where action is distributed and that may foster individual interactive knowledge. From this standpoint, the addition of new elements and relations to the collective can be taken as a measure of innovation. This pragmatic and relational attitude meets particularly well the idea, typically area-based, that an effective integration of single resources, experiences, and competences can generate results otherwise unattainable.

Even if they are not the only stakeholders engaged in learning processes during the programs, this study adopts the point of view of designers to restrict the scope of the analysis to a specific qualified practice. At a certain level, however, area-based initiatives raised similar challenges for other categories of professionals (e.g., the need to integrate their knowledge and competences in an interdisciplinary collective). Moreover, designers played roles even formally so different in the programs of urban regeneration to make questionable the very delimitation of a precise disciplinary field. Many considerations concerning innovation in design practice can therefore be extended to other professional practices.

The empowerment of professionals from both the public and private sectors was seen as an essential objective of area-based initiatives and a trigger for the renewal of the institutional framework. That is, a crucial node of a process of innovation came into play at the intersection between individual and collective dynamics. Experts were explicitly asked, on the one hand, to revise their working methods for marking a distance from previous experiences. On the other hand, they had to overcome clear-cut disciplinary boundaries to fit the multiplicity of interests and powers emerging from the collectives. In all the programs studied, the design and decision-making process became, indeed, a vehicle for learning, socialization, and professionalization for those practitioners who took an active part in it.

But how did the process of learning happen? And under what conditions did it become the first step in a wider process of innovation? The renewed context in which professionals had to practice not only produced new challenges, but also new stimuli for the activation of processes of "tacit knowing in action," upon which, according to Schön (1983: 49), "the workaday life of the professional" largely depends. The way the professionals involved in the regeneration programs analyzed in the research describe their daily work[4] closely recalls Schön's three forms of "reflective practice": the one produced *in* the course of the action;

the effort of conceptualization made by retrospective reflections *on* the actions developed; and finally, the *ladders of reflections* aimed at capitalizing on an experience for re-using it in action—an example in this sense is the numerous collections of best practices that accompanied the diffusion of area-based policies. Most professionals recognize the value of such fluid learning processes as a viable source of "empowerment-in-practice" (Adams, 1990/1996: 38) and an indispensable complement to technical and disciplinary skills. Accordingly, the employment of soft skills and the capacity to implement projects according to the contingent circumstances of each context have often proved to be as important as technical competencies.

Many factors, both individual and contextual, can, however, influence the actual possibility to learn and, consequently, to innovate. First, according to Crosta (1998: 47), the willingness to learn is itself an attitude that can hardly be predicted or imposed and that has been revealed to be independent from the role played in a project. In addition, as Laino (2012: 192) has pointed out, the more complex and conflictual the process, the more apt it is to enhance fertile confrontations among actors. In the case of area-based initiatives, this directly relates to the features of the collective(s) where professional action takes place. Their scale, level of formalization as official partnerships, internal organization, and institutional position are all elements that played a crucial role in the cases analyzed, affecting the way innovative practices were generated and, even more, propagated.

Time was also found to be a determining factor in individual learning processes. Since urban regeneration initiatives often develop over a long period of time—especially due to large-scale projects of physical transformation—time represents an important and often undervalued resource for the experimentation and appropriation of new methods and tools. More precisely, the innovation of professional practices can occur in two substantially different moments: either during the implementation of a specific project in response to contingent circumstances, or as a long-term learning process through the implementation of durable skills and tools. Accordingly, two main contexts can be affected. On one side, there is territory where the projects perform, common to all stakeholders, and on the other, there are the specific professional contexts where it is designed (e.g., the studio, the public office, etc.). The reciprocal interaction between these two contexts therefore represents a crucial parameter for measuring innovation, which was mostly overlooked in the evaluations of area-based initiatives.

This allows for the introduction of a central issue to the discussion, namely the possibility of transferring individually acquired knowledge to a collective domain. If, in the case of area-based initiatives, the innovation of professional practices largely depends on "judgments of quality for which [the practitioner)] cannot state adequate criteria" or "skills for which he cannot state the rules and procedures" (Schön, 1983: 50), how can this kind of knowledge become transmissible independently from direct experience?

Institutionalizing Innovation. Within and Beyond Contingency

> Adaptive systems that engage in exploration to the exclusion of exploitation are likely to find that they suffer the costs of experimentation without gaining many of its benefits. They exhibit too many undeveloped new ideas and too little distinctive competence. (March, 1991: 71)

The interest in questioning the limits of knowledge transferability lies in the assumption that innovation arises as much from a particular contingency—which defines what is innovative in relation to a specific context—as from the continuous attempt to overcome it (Frassoldati et al, 2020). From this perspective, the implementation of a *new* practice calls into question the overall system of policies and institutions that sets the framework for professionals' work. Only focusing on the network of relations linking these different levels of innovation in practice can be effectively assessed. Even if it will not be possible to address this topic exhaustively, the objective here is to discuss some issues that emerged from the history of area-based initiatives and the analysis of their long-term legacies.

The dissemination of knowledge beyond the individual level can take different forms. In the first stage, the same experts involved in the projects become a vehicle for the osmotic transmission of experimental practices to other contexts or projects. Nevertheless, as Stengers (2005: 193) clearly points out, to do that, professionals must previously be empowered as diplomats, meaning that "the people who empower them have the power to do so, and also the power needed to accept being put at risk by the propositions the diplomats bring back". In the case studies analyzed, the limits imposed by a lack of empowerment—and even a lack of recognition for the work done—often became evident with the completion of the projects.

The embedding of innovative practices also relates to a series of practical operations—which are themselves practices susceptible to innovation—explicitly aimed at building the conditions for capitalizing on the experience gained. It is widely recognized that recording, archiving, and evaluation activities carried out during and after programs' implementation—as strongly sponsored by European institutions—constitute a source of policy learning and institutional innovation (Ferrão, Mourato, 2011: 141). Nevertheless, many scholars also point out that official evaluations could rarely grasp the complexity behind the integrated approach of area-based policies (see Lawless, 2013; Alves, 2017; Agger and Jensen, 2015).

It is precisely when this process of capitalization fully attains its objectives that the experience gained locally can have an impact on a higher level, influencing the development of subsequent policies or programs. This is what at least apparently happened during the 1990s and 2000s, when the area-based approach became an integral part of the mainstream policy narratives (see Barca, 2009). However, the ultimate target of those "conspirators of reform" (C. Jacquier, personal interview, October 16, 2019), who argued for a radical renewal in the way of interpreting and intervening on urban marginality, were the very institutional structures and bureaucracies behind the policies architecture. Using Donolo's (1997: 7) words, even if addressing the evolution of institutions means dealing with "factors of change that are largely unknown to us, that we can only partly control…—like evangelical poverty—institutions will always be with us, for better or worse".[5]

With the aim of better understanding the role of innovation in this complex framework, the microscopic viewpoint adopted in the field research allowed us to put the emphasis on the relations between different dimensions—from the local to the institutional one—rather than on official outcomes. First, the dichotomy top-down/bottom-up does not seem to correspond to the empirical observation of collectives' actions, which are mostly governed by bi-directional and non-deterministic interactions. If under certain conditions—which ones becomes a central question—contingent experiences can affect policy-making processes, this can only happen if, at the same time, public bodies set the structure for professionals' work.

A circular "interactive model" seems to better capture the iterative and discretionary character of the decision-making processes underlying area-based initiatives. If the *policy cycle* is a model already affirmed in political sciences (see Giarelli, 2003), the Latourian *collective's cycles* (Latour, 2004) and Armando and Durbiano's cycles of architectural projects provide the interpretative background to conceptualize innovation in the framework of a succession of tiered sequences of inclusion and/or exclusion of *actants*. In this view, the very notions of top-down/bottom-up can rather be interpreted as "one of the two fundamental ways of reading the exchange movements that occur along the cycles of a design process" (Armando and Durbiano, 2017: 492).[6]

Another interpretative key used to read innovation in area-based initiatives is the dichotomy network/framework. These terms gained particular prominence in the public debate during the 1990s, both as a metaphor of urban phenomena and with reference to institutionally acknowledged realities. The relationship between framework and network lies, for example, at the very heart of the discourse of Quartiers en Crise, a network of European cities that during the 1990s played a central role in bringing the problem of deprived urban areas to public attention:

> Whatever the case may be the relationship between new mechanisms and traditional institutions can be captured in the notions of "network" and "framework." "Framework" corresponds to the image of a compartmentalised, specialised, weakly overlapping, well regulated administrative system featuring a hierarchy of relationships in a command mode and jealously guarding its privileges. Such a system partitions its territory and

its inhabitants according to its own system of status, functions, power and rules but leaves gaps owing to its inflexible nature. It works on the principle that any phenomena which do not conform to this system are simply left out. A "network," on the other hand, does not pretend to cover its territory exhaustively and does not aspire to official recognition. The inter-partner relationships which go to make up the network are ends in themselves; partners belong to many networks and have a range of skills. A network is a flexible system which takes advantage of this multiplicity and thus can maintain its efficiency should certain of its components fail. In other words, the complexity of a network means that it can adapt to changing circumstances and even cause major change. (Commission of the European Communities, 1993: 46)

However, it is added that networks and frameworks

can form a symbiosis, even if it is occasionally conflictual. Partnership organizations, these latter-day Trojan horses, seek to foster this co-existence to regenerate, at the margins, the traditional institutions. The dynamics of this co-existence of frameworks and networks lies at the heart of integrated urban development approaches" (ivi: 46).

If, therefore, the innovation of practices rises from network-based processes, institutional reform is equally important, since only institutions can provide legitimacy to the structural indeterminacy (Crosta, 1998) of networks. What emerges is once again a cyclical process, in which phases of innovative openness alternate with moments of institutionalizing closure (Armando and Durbiano, 2017).

Comparing these perspectives with the findings that emerged from the analysis of the long-term impacts of area-based initiatives, however, it is possible to identify some recurrent criticalities in the processes aiming at the capitalization and institutionalization of innovative practices. First, temporary and purpose-built local partnerships have proved to be very effective in the short term, but they could hardly contaminate ordinary structures. In this case, neither the renewal of individual working practice was followed by the restructuring of procedures and organizations (Castel and Martin, 2012), nor were the results obtained from the programs reused to feed future decision-making and design cycles. What was lacking were the epistemological and material anchors (Agger et al, 2016) necessary to make a singular experience a spendable and enhanceable resource. Consequently, despite a widespread understanding that "macro and micro causes of deprivation, and therefore the necessary remedial polices, are interdependent" (Glennerster et al, 1999), the strategies deployed by professionals often remained confined to the local dimension of area-based initiatives to avoid structural obstacles.

In sum, in the history of area-based policies, the main limitation to innovation lies precisely in the circumvention of the framework's barrier. Without opening the black box of public offices (Tedesco, 2019), it is impossible to fully address the boundaries of innovation in practice. The challenge is therefore to tackle the complexity of the framework head-on. As Atkinson (1998: 82) states:

> We need to lift the veil of official organizations and operations, to delve deeper into the often standard procedures that allow partnerships to function. It is not only a question of recognizing and analyzing the existence of conflicting interests and their interaction, but also of analyzing the way in which the discourses and discursive practices are involved in the very constitution of partnerships the way they operate determine what is "thinkable" and possible.[7]

This does not mean that innovation did not occur at all. Rather, it appeared in the form of contingent yet enduring legacies in the "interstices of 'innovative' urban regeneration actions" (Tedesco, 2011), especially in those circumscribed contexts—e.g., neighborhoods, offices, and social groups—"where public choices and collective behavior interact strongly with the real life of institutions" (Donolo, 1997: 8).[8]

Final Remarks: The Paths of Innovation

The picture emerging from the previous paragraphs does not correspond to the rhetoric of innovation that prevailed in the history of area-based policies. Rather, innovation took the form of a unilineal and often accidental process strongly dependent on individual contingent actions and on the way they propagate inside and outside different collectives. Also, in the long term, innovative practices have produced fragmented and circumscribed effects in particular niches or contexts, rarely affecting the background structure. The result is a re-reading of the history of area-based initiatives in terms of *exaptation* rather than exception (Frassoldati et al, 2020: 14).

This encourages a methodological reflection on the way we look at innovation in professional practices. The risk is to disregard the relevance of long-term and multi-dimensional perspectives in capturing not only the contingent nature of innovation processes, but also their ability to produce lasting epistemological structures. Moreover, the constant emphasis on innovation in public discourse may lead, on the one hand, to overlooking past experiences as a valuable source of knowledge and, on the other, to "obscur[ing] the profound traits of change and the relations with the more general political and social processes" (Pasqui, 2001: 11).[9]

The study of innovation through everyday working practices brings attention to less noticeable and more elusive aspects, such as the actual movement and embedding of innovative practices throughout different contexts. In particular, the interface between individual learning and collective capitalization is advanced as a crucial dimension for assessing innovation as a situated but transmissibility-dependent process. If contamination from below is not accompanied by the "loosening-up of formal governance structures" (Taylor, 2000: 1033), the knowledge acquired is likely to remain relegated to an individual level—thus also subject to the erratic nature of personal trajectories. The precondition for an effective innovation would therefore lie in a revision of the institutional systems of "power" (ibidem) aimed at opening the way to new forms of empowerment in professional practice.

Notes

[1] Original Italian text translated by the author.
[2] The three main case studies of the research are the Développement Social de Quartiers in Orly (1982–ongoing); the New Life for Urban Scotland in Edinburgh (1989–99), and the Programma di Recupero Urbano of Via Artom in Torino (1995–2008).
[3] Original Italian text translated by the author.
[4] See note 2 above.
[5] Original Italian text translated by the author.
[6] The second way is found in the dichotomy of divergence/convergence. Original Italian text translated by the author.
[7] Original French text translated by the author.
[8] Original Italian text translated by the author.
[9] Ibid.

References

Adams, R. (1996 [1990]), *Social Work and Empowerment*, Basingstoke, Hampshire, Macmillan.
Agger, A., Jensen, J. O. (2015), *Area-Based Initiatives-and Their Work in Bonding, Bridging and Linking Social Capital*, "European Planning Studies 2," n. 23, pp. 2045–61.
Agger, A., Roy, P., Leonardsen, Ø. (2016), *Sustaining Area-Based Initiatives by Developing Appropriate "anchors": The Role of Social Capital*, "Planning Theory & Practice," n. 17, pp. 325–43.
Alves, S. (2017), *Assessing the Impact of Area-Based Initiatives in Deprived Neighborhoods: The Example of S. João de Deus in Porto, Portugal*, "Journal of Urban Affairs," n. 39, pp. 381–99.
Armando, A., Durbiano, G. (2017), *Teoria del progetto architettonico: Dai disegni agli effetti*, Roma, Carocci.
Atkinson, R. (1998), *Les aléas de la participation des habitants à la gouvernance urbaine en Europe*, trans. F. Martinet, "Les Annales de la recherche urbaine," n. 80, pp. 74–83.
Barca, F. (2009), *An Agenda for A Reformed Cohesion Policy: A Place-Based Approach to Meeting European Union Challenges and Expectations*, Independent Report prepared at the request of Danuta Hübner, Commissioner for Regional Policy.
Barca, F., McCann, P., Rodríguez-Pose, A. (2012), *The Case for Regional Development Intervention: Place-Based versus Place-Neutral Approaches*, "Journal of Regional Science," n. 52, pp. 134–52.
Bifulco, L., De Leonardis, O. (2006), *Integrazione tra le politiche come opportunità politica*, in C. Donolo (ed.), *Il futuro delle politiche pubbliche*, Milano, Mondadori, pp. 31–58.
Commission of the European Communities (1993), *Quartiers en Crise: Citizenship Laboratories For Europe?*, Directorate General XVI-Regional Policies, Quartiers en Crise Programme 1991–93 FINAL REPORT.
Castel, R., Martin, C. (2012), *Changements et pensées du changement: Échanges avec Robert Castel*, Paris, Découverte.
Crosta, P. L. (1998), *Politiche: quale conoscenza per l'azione territoriale*, Milano, Franco Angeli.
Donolo, C. (1997), *L'intelligenza delle istituzioni*, Milano, Feltrinelli.
Ferrão, J., Mourato, J. (2011), *Evaluation and Spatial Planning in Portugal: From Legal Requirement*

to Source of Policy-Learning and Institutional Innovation, in J. Farinós (ed.), *De la evaluación ambiental estratégica a la evaluación de impacto territorial: Reflexiones acerca de la tarea de evaluación*, Valencia, Universidad de Valencia, pp. 141–66.

Frassoldati, F., Armando, A., Campobenedetto, D., Federighi, V., Barioglio, C., Cesareo, F. (2020), *Design and the Challenge of Change*, "Ardeth" [Online], n. 6, pp. 4–17.

Giarelli, G. (2003), *Il malessere della medicina: Un confronto internazionale*, Milano, Franco Angeli.

Glennerster, H., Lupton, R., Noden, P., Power, A. (1999), *Poverty, Social Exclusion and Neighbourhood: Studying the Area Bases of Social Exclusion*, "CASEpaper," n. 22.

Jacquier, C. (2019, October 16), Personal interview.

Laino, G. (2012), *Il fuoco nel cuore e il diavolo in corpo: La partecipazione come attivazione sociale*, Milano, Franco Angeli.

Latour, B. (2004 [1999]), *Politics of Nature: How to Bring the Sciences into Democracy*, trans. C. Porter, Cambridge, Mass, Harvard University Press.

Lawless, P. (2013), *Reconciling "Bottom-Up" Perspectives with "Top-Down" Change Data in Evaluating Area Regeneration Schemes*, "European Planning Studies," n. 21, pp. 1562–77.

March, J. G. (1991), *Exploration and Exploitation in Organizational Learning*, "Organization Science," n. 2, pp. 71–87.

Pasqui, G. (2001), *Il territorio delle politiche: innovazione sociale e pratiche di pianificazione*, Milano, Franco Angeli.

Schön, D. A. (1983), *The Reflective Practitioner: How Professionals Think in Action*, New York, Basic Books.

Stengers, I. (2005), *Introductory Notes on an Ecology of Practices*, "Cultural Studies Review," n. 11, pp. 183–96.

Tedesco, C. (2011), *Negli interstizi delle azioni "innovative" di rigenerazione urbana*, "Archivio di studi urbani e regionali," v. 100, pp. 82–98.

Taylor, M. (2000), *Communities in the Lead: Power, Organisational Capacity and Social Capital*, "Urban Studies," n. 37, pp. 1019–35.

DESIGN ECHOES.
Four Stories of Projects
That Resonate with Urban Rules
Caterina Barioglio and Daniele Campobenedetto

Caterina Barioglio is Assistant Professor at the Department of Architecture and Design of the Politecnico di Torino. She earned a PhD in History of Architecture and Town Planning in 2016 with a dissertation carried out between Turin and Columbia University in New York City. Bridging history and design, her research relates to urban regeneration processes and urban design, with a main focus on urban morphology and building typologies. Since 2018 she has been a Research Fellow at the interdisciplinary research center Future *Urban Legacy* Lab. She is an Editor of the journal "Architectural Design Theory."

Daniele Campobenedetto is an architect and holds a PhD in History of Architecture and Town Planning from the Politecnico di Torino and in Architecture from Université Paris Est. He is currently an Assistant Professor in Architectural and Urban Design at the Department of Architecture and Design of Politecnico di Torino. His research activities especially investigate urban transformation and urban design in European cities, focusing on architectural typologies and urban rules. He is a Research Fellow of the interdisciplinary research center Future *Urban Legacy* Lab. He is also Journal Manager and Editor of the journal "Architectural Design Theory."

Design Beyond Sites

The effects of architecture extend beyond their localization (Awan et al, 2011). The anthropic modification of the spatial environment produces echoes in terms of urban rules, technical requirements, cultural shifts, and behaviors that travel beyond the place in which the modification occurs. Architectures like Lever House and the Seagram Building, which played a part in the drafting of the 1961 Zoning Resolution in New York, are just some well-known examples of such a phenomenon (Lehnerer, 2009).

Unbuilt projects have similar effects. In particular, projects contribute to forming and destroying urban imaginaries in ways that are difficult to trace. In turn, the debate around imaginaries can foster actual modification of the built environment. The urban visions of Yona Friedman, Moses King, Hugh Ferriss, Paul Maymont, and Eugène Hénard have already been investigated in this sense by contemporary historiography (Cohen, 1995).

While these effects of built and unbuilt projects are part of the outcomes of design, they are hardly considered part of the design process. In most cases, they just occur (as in 1961 New York), while in others, they are intentional (as in 1970s Paris).

How, and through which tools, could these non-local effects of design be recognized? More generally, is it possible to consider localized design as a means of representing and addressing general and comprehensive issues?

Here, we attempt to explore the relationship between architectural projects and urban rules as a way of tackling the theme of design echoes. The correlation between these two terms is widely recognized: on the one hand, architectural projects are not autonomous objects and are developed within regulatory, economic, and social contexts (Marshall, 2011). On the other hand, urban rules are not defined *a priori*, but rather through a continuous stratification, which proceeds by case and adapts to changes (Roncayolo, 2002).

Here, we describe examples of specific architectural projects that played either a direct or indirect role in defining sets of urban rules of any sort applied in different contexts or times compared to those in which these projects have been drafted. This tentative interpretation of these architectural projects suggests a change in the lens through which regulatory and contextual restrictions are interpreted. In other words, we shift from seeing them as a problem to viewing them as possessing potential (Douglas, 2006). What follows are four short stories that provide some hints on how these entanglements have occurred in the cities of Paris and New York in the second half of the 20th-century.

Story 1 - Architectural Project as an Experiment of New/Less Restrictive Urban Rule

How can an architectural project test a change of rules? *MyMicro NY,* the winning project by nArchitects of the adAPT New York City Competition, could be considered an experimental architectural type for multiple dwelling units in New York. Indeed, in physical space, this project tests the change of a crucial building rule: the minimum size of a dwelling unit (Murru, 2020).

It is no coincidence that this exploration was carried out in New York, which has been an American pioneer in housing reforms and innovations in a nation that has continuously faced a severe housing problem since the mid-19th-century. The housing issue calls into question policies and strategies for urban densification. In the city of Manhattan, where hyperdensity is an ongoing topic of public debate, the adAPT NYC experience was part of the policies aimed at accelerating the densification process.

The competition was announced in 2012 by the former Mayor of New York Michael R. Bloomberg. The purpose was to search for new housing options and properly address the changed demography of New York and the different needs of New Yorkers, whose demands were unable to be satisfied by the market. The competition consisted of a pilot program in which designers and developers could imagine innovative ways of living in the dense city. Submitted projects could be assessed as models replicable at the scale of the city to resolve the urgent housing crisis. To accomplish this feat, the municipality allowed for some of the constraints defined by the city's regulations and codes to be overridden.

DESIGN – EXAPTATION

Caterina Barioglio, Daniele Campobenedetto - Design Echoes.
Four Stories of Projects That Resonate with Urban Rules

Participants were allowed to freely design and submit their projects, which defied some of the rules of the Zoning Resolution, such as minimum unit size, bulk, and density limits. In particular, participants were asked to design a new, mixed-use building that had to contain "micro-units," referring to apartments smaller in size than that allowed under then-current regulations.

The winning project, *MyMicro NY,* proposed a prefabricated building composed of 55 micro-units, with common and commercial spaces. The building offered seven different types of units, all ranging between 260 and 360 square feet, to meet different living needs. To proceed with the construction, several rules in New York's Zoning Resolution had to be waived (e.g., maximum number of dwelling units allowed on the plot, lot coverage, height, and setbacks).

The most striking effects of the project are the changes to the minimum dwelling units' size and density. At the time of the competition, the limit of 400 square feet was set as the minimum standard for all the residential units built in New York. Since 2016, when the Zoning Resolution was amended, limits in dwelling unit size have been suspended. In the same amendment, the dwelling density (defined as the ratio between the "maximum residential floor area permitted on the lot" and the "factor for dwelling units") has been increased in certain Zoning Districts by dropping down the density factor from 740 to 680.

<u>Story 2 - Architectural Project as an Opportunity for Dialogue Between Actors</u>

How can architectural projects participate in setting morphological rules? The transformation of central Paris in the 1970s and, in particular, the metamorphosis of the former wholesale market neighborhood at Les Halles provides a case study that unveils elements of the relation between architectural projects and urban rules (Campobenedetto, 2017).

The number of projects for this area reached more than a thousand from the early 1960s to the early 1980s. Still, certain actors played a crucial role in the definition of the final layout for Les Halles. The *Atelier Parisien d'Urbanisme* (Apur), a public urban agency that still exists in Paris, was responsible in particular for the development plans of this area. It is important to remember that in the mid-1960s, the French regulatory system was poorly equipped with the tools necessary to coordinate public and private interventions for urban transformation. In 1967, the *Zone d'Aménagement Concerté* (ZAC) was introduced, and the Atelier was entrusted with the task of drafting the morphological rules—in the form of maximum heights—for the transformation of the area. What is more, again in 1967, a competition was held between six renowned French architects to envision the transformation of the Les Halles neighborhood in view of the demolition of 19th-century market pavilions. The Atelier, in this context, was charged with a two-sided mission: to reconcile the different scenarios that resulted from the 1967 competition, all oriented toward a modern city even with distinctive morphological approaches, and to pave the way for the use of the new tool—the ZAC—approved a few years before. These tasks were accomplished through the *Schéma d'Ossature* (the master plan for the area), an urban project that mediates among the functions at stake at that time which was drafted by architects and engineers of the Atelier in 1969, as well as the morphological parties expressed in the 1967 competition.

The former site of the market pavilions has been replaced with a multilevel public slab covering an extended network of underground spaces that host a mall and other public services, subways, and the regional transport system. On the surface, a mixed program with housing, public services, and an international trade center are hosted in a series of courtyard buildings that surround the central public space.

This project was the tool that allowed the Atelier to acquire the necessary consensus to propose the set of broad morphological rules to the city council (in the form of maximum heights allowed on the site). The first *Schéma d'Ossature* by the Apur was abandoned some years after, but it left on the ground the "Forum des Halles," which recently went through a massive reorganization. This mechanism, in which an urban project plays a crucial role in the definition of urban rules related to the maximum height on the transformation site, is repeated several times after this first experience, and not just in the case of Les Halles. This can be traced as Apur's *modus operandi* in how it repeatedly employs the architectural and urban project as a negotiation tool to set rules on the ground.

Story 3 - Architectural Project as an Anticipation of Urban Rules

How can the architectural project contribute to codifying future morphological rules? In the well-known book *New York 1960* edited by Robert Stern (1995), Sixth Avenue in Manhattan is defined as "the representative street of Twentieth Century Modernist urbanism...." The sense of this statement is particularly clear for those who have walked on the midtown stretch of Sixth Avenue lined by sheer skyscrapers, which looks like a catalog of variants of the tower-in-the-park settlement model.

This ruling urban form makes Sixth Avenue an exemplary case of the New York response to the international second postwar debate around tall buildings and their relationship with the public space (Barioglio, 2021). The Avenue of the Americas—as the street was officially renamed in 1945—is the outcome of an extended urban renewal transformation carried out during the second postwar: the 20-block section from Bryant Park to Central Park turned from a mixed-use area, made up of brownstones and small manufacturing buildings, into one of the most prestigious Midtown corporate corridors. With more than 10 million square feet of rentable spaces built in less than 10 years (1958–65)—a number that more than doubled in the following decade—the Avenue exhibits a wide selection of skyscrapers designed just before, during, and immediately after the entry into force of the Zoning Resolution in 1961. Without delving into the complex system of forces (first technical and socio-economic, and then stylistic) that drove the morphogenesis of the postwar generation of American skyscrapers, it should be noted that the relation between architectural types and urban rules also plays a crucial role. It is widely known that the first Zoning Resolution of New York, established in 1916, had a significant impact on the design of skyscrapers and the urban form. The restrictions on the height and bulk of the buildings through the setback principle, according to the district and the width of the street, favored the spread of *wedding cake* or *ziggurat-shaped* skyscrapers. At that time, if a private owner wanted to exploit the maximum volume allowed on his lot, the shape of the building was, in practice, predetermined by the code.

The adoption of the new code at the beginning of the 1960s changed this situation. With the introduction of the floor area ratio (FAR), the maximum floor area permitted for a building based on the plot size, the new regulation promoted the rise of a different urban fabric. Born with the aim of increasing the amount of light and air at street level and encouraging freedom in the design of tall buildings, the new standards have fostered a tower model that rises in height without interruptions, facing open spaces and public plazas.

Through the 1961 Zoning Resolution, Privately-Owned-Public-Spaces (POPS), open spaces for public use funded and built by private developers within their own lots, were institutionalized. They were encouraged through the practice of *incentive zoning*: the municipality accorded developers an increase in the total floor area of the designed building in exchange for introducing public open spaces on the project lot.

The Time and Life Building is among the first postwar buildings to experiment with the pure prism form that face a corporate plaza: the tower, whose construction is almost contemporary to the Seagram Building, is made up of a monolith that moves backward from the street line to guarantee a large open space on the ground floor that is designed to serve as a public plaza set up with sculptures and fountains. Along 50th Street, a wide *promenade* is created that ideally continues the pedestrian spaces of the Rockefeller Center.

The Equitable Life Assurance Company Building, the Sperry Rand Building, and the Hilton Hotel belong to this generation of "transitional" skyscrapers regulated by the old Zoning Resolution, but that experiment, through the sheer tower model, with different layouts from prewar examples. In this framework, the early skyscrapers on Sixth Avenue contributed to the experimentation and codification of an architectural and urban typology that were to become widespread with the adoption of the 1961 Zoning Resolution.

Story 4 - Architectural Layout as a Reference for Urban Policies

How can architectural projects be systematized in an urban policy? "Des usines ou des bureaux?" (Factories or offices?) was the Hamletic question that, during the second half of the 1970s, animated the debate within the Paris City Council as they dealt with the progressive deindustrialization of the city (Casaletto, 2020). As part of the major urban transformations proposed by the mayor of Paris, Jacques Chirac, and the director of the Apur, Pierre-Yves Ligen, the institution of *Zones Industrielles Urbaines* was promoted. These were sectors with a high percentage of land assigned to production activities. For these areas, the municipality proposed a shared vertical building model—defined as *Hôtel Industriel*—that responded to two needs: the rationalization of land use and the improvement of the integration between production and other activities.

The *Hôtel Industriel* was created to accommodate a productive promiscuity. These buildings require an interior layout based on a division of flows of goods and people. Unlike the *Vertical Factory*, the *Hôtel Industriel* hosts small businesses whose production process avoids a vertical circulation of products.

The policy that fostered the construction of the *Hôtels* was introduced in the late 1970s, with the revision of the *Plan d'Occupation des Sols* (Land Use Plan), which created the *Zones Industrielles Urbaines* (industrial urban zones). This measure would not be effective without the City Council resolution allowing for a 70-years lease-free period or only moderate charges for investors. Results were two-fold: on the one hand, there was an increase in productive activities within the French capital, and on the other hand, the premises were developed for a new building typology.

In 2021, there were 36 *Hôtels Industriels* built within the City of Paris that offered approximately 275,000 square meters of space hosting the activities of small- and medium-sized enterprises. Within the architectural typologies for production activities in the dense urban fabric of European cities, the *Hôtel Industriel* represents neither a singularity nor an *avant-garde*. Indeed, this experience is based on formal models already tested in other contexts. To guarantee moderate rent for workspace, other experiences in Rotterdam and Birmingham, among others, promoted the shared workshop building model. In Paris, already in the 19th-century, a model for production in the dense urban fabric was proposed. This was the *Immeuble Industriel*, a building type that hosted several workshops and production activities in a vertical layout. Also, in this case, workshops were piled up in a building equipped with technical systems (as driving force and hydraulic systems) that allowed for the production of goods and were served by a system of elevators for materials and people circulation.

The echoes of these former applications lie in the spread of a "project of use" (i.e., an intentional projected use of existing buildings according to a given plan). The system of incentives and rules, created in the context of the revision of the Land Use Plan (and related policies), effectively promoted the realization of buildings sharing a common functional layout. Spot experiences of layered workshops in urban contexts—and its peculiar architectural layouts—served as reference, in the late 1970s Paris, for a policy able to produce a recognizable transformation of the built environment.

DESIGN – EXAPTATION

Caterina Barioglio, Daniele Campobenedetto - Design Echoes.
Four Stories of Projects That Resonate with Urban Rules

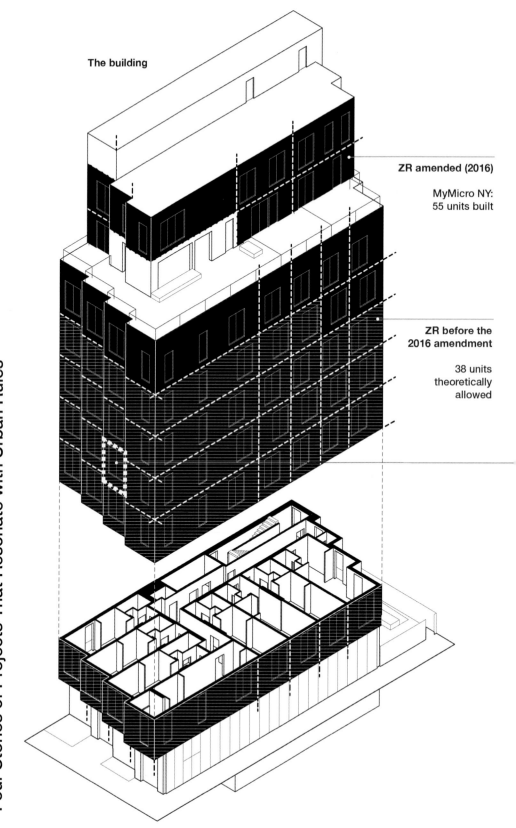

The building

ZR amended (2016)

MyMicro NY:
55 units built

ZR before the
2016 amendment

38 units
theoretically
allowed

A dwelling unit

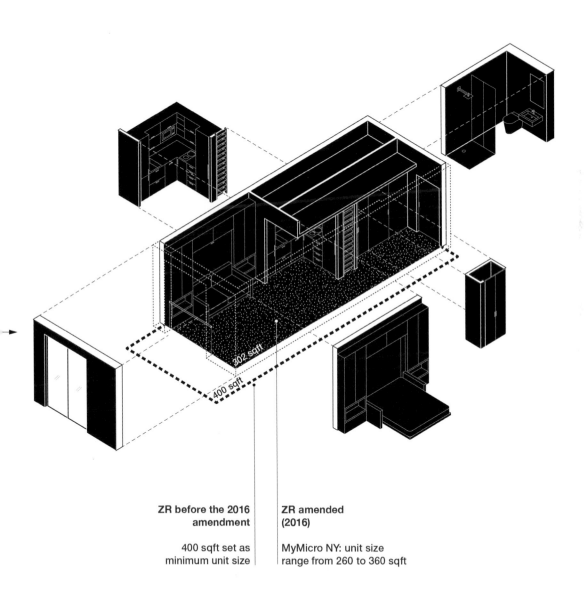

302 sqft

400 sqft

ZR before the 2016 amendment	ZR amended (2016)
400 sqft set as minimum unit size	MyMicro NY: unit size range from 260 to 360 sqft

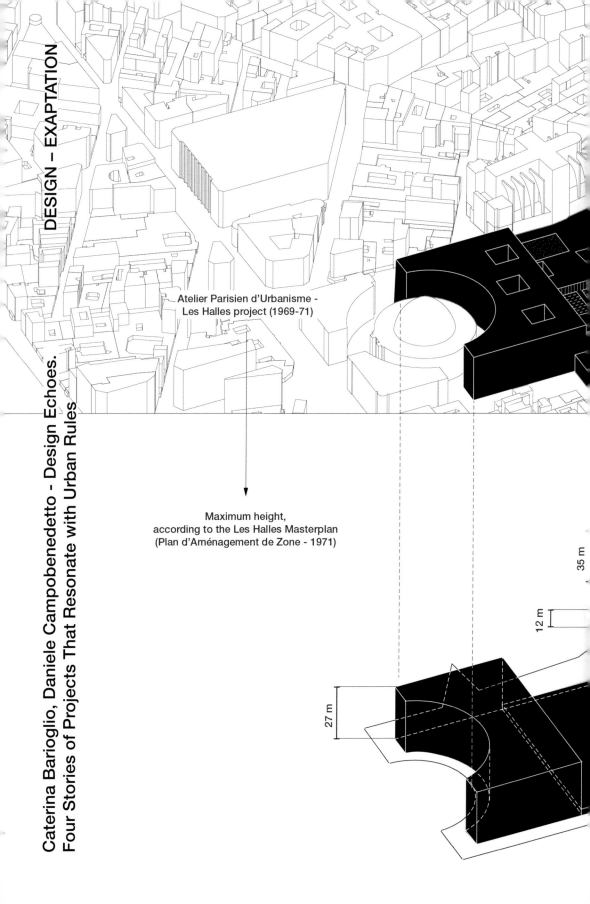

Caterina Barioglio, Daniele Campobenedetto - Design Echoes.
Four Stories of Projects That Resonate with Urban Rules

Atelier Parisien d'Urbanisme -
Les Halles project (1969-71)

Maximum height,
according to the Les Halles Masterplan
(Plan d'Aménagement de Zone - 1971)

35 m

12 m

27 m

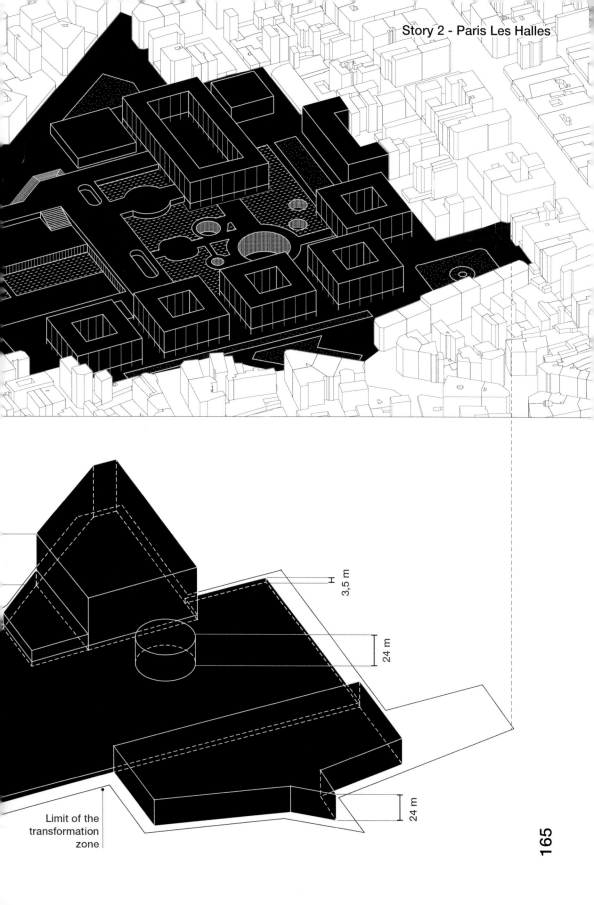

H

3,5 m

24 m

24 m

Limit of the
transformation
zone

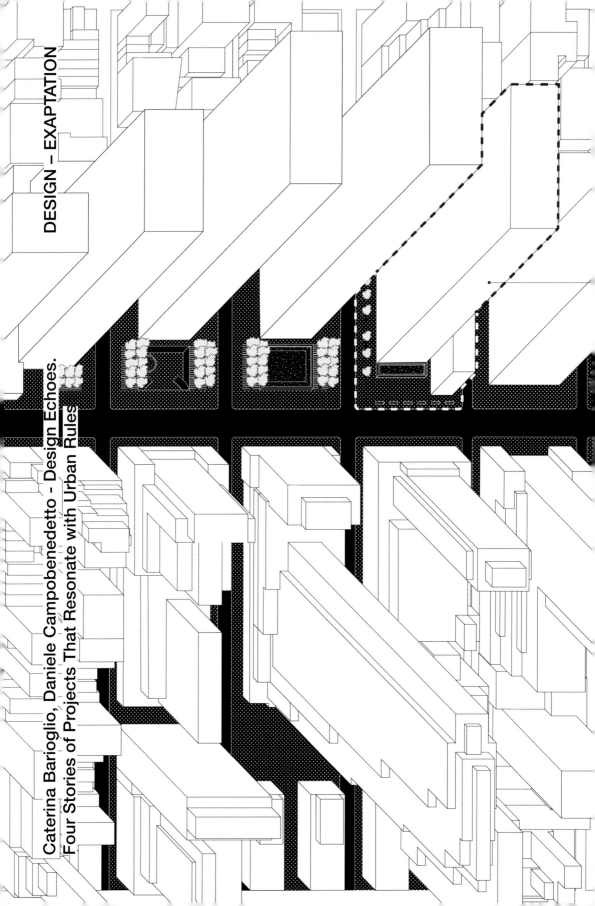

DESIGN – EXAPTATION

Caterina Barioglio, Daniele Campobenedetto - Design Echoes.
Four Stories of Projects That Resonate with Urban Rules

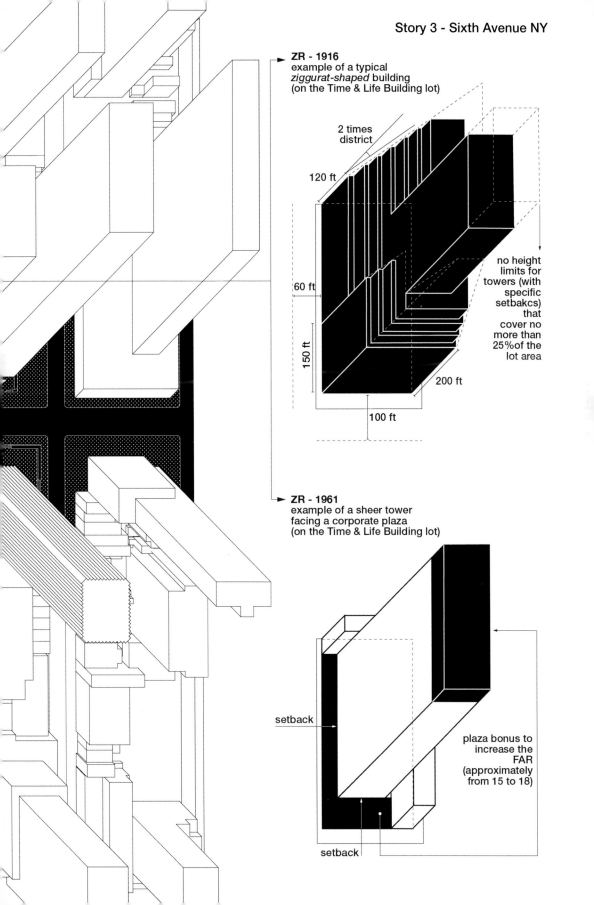

ZR - 1916
example of a typical
ziggurat-shaped building
(on the Time & Life Building lot)

2 times
district

120 ft

no height
limits for
towers (with
specific
setbakcs)
that
cover no
more than
25%of the
lot area

60 ft

150 ft

200 ft

100 ft

ZR - 1961
example of a sheer tower
facing a corporate plaza
(on the Time & Life Building lot)

setback

plaza bonus to
increase the
FAR
(approximately
from 15 to 18)

setback

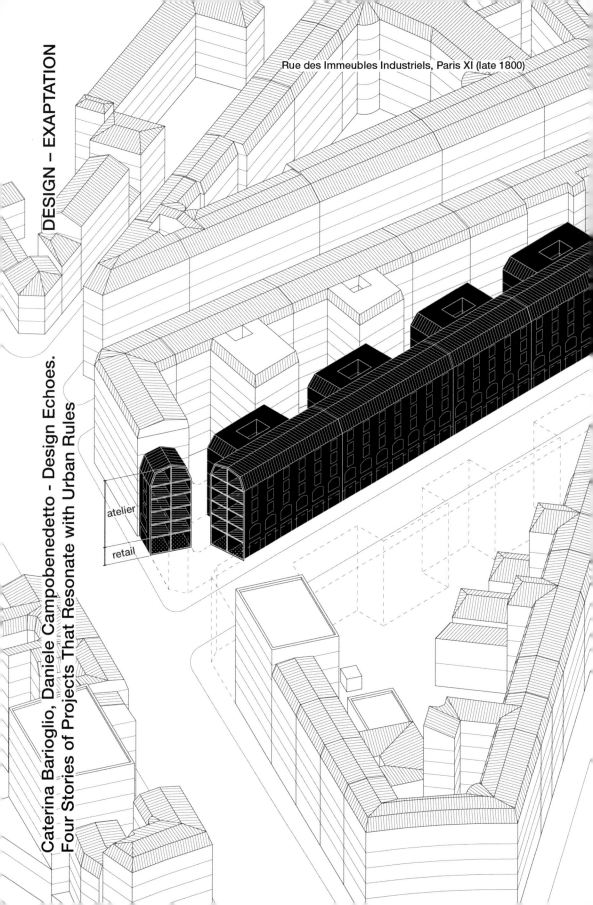

DESIGN – EXAPTATION

Rue des Immeubles Industriels, Paris XI (late 1800)

atelier

retail

Caterina Barioglio, Daniele Campobenedetto - Design Echoes.
Four Stories of Projects That Resonate with Urban Rules

Hôtel Industriel Brûlon-Cîteaux, Paris XII (2008)

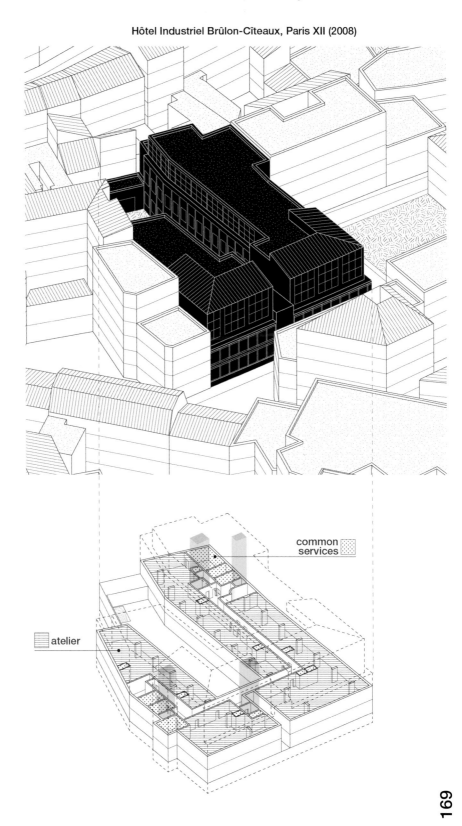

DESIGN – EXAPTATION

Caterina Barioglio, Daniele Campobenedetto - Design Echoes.
Four Stories of Projects That Resonate with Urban Rules

Acknowledgments
Drawings of *Hôtels Industriels* by Davide Casaletto.
Drawings of *MyMicro NY* by Lorenzo Murru.

References
Awan, N., Schneider, T., Till, J. (2011), *Spatial Agency. Other Ways of Doing Architecture*, London, Routledge.
Barioglio, C. (2021), *Avenue of the Americas. New York, biografia di una strada*, Milano, FrancoAngeli.
Campobenedetto, D. (2017), *Paris les Halles. Storie di un futuro conteso*, Milano, FrancoAngeli.
Casaletto, D. (2020), *La produzione dello spazio e lo spazio di produzione. Il caso della politica parigina degli Hotel industriels*, Master's degree thesis: Politecnico di Torino, tutor: Daniele Campobenedetto, co-tutor: Frédéric Bertrand.
Cohen, J. L. (1995), *Scenes of the World to Come. European Architecture and the American Challenge, 1893–1960*, Paris, Flammarion-Pere Castor.
Douglas, J. (2006), *Building Adaptation*, Oxford, Routledge.
Lehnerer, A. (2009), *Grand Urban Rules*, Rotterdam, 010 Publishers.
Marshall, S. (eds) (2011), *Urban Coding and Planning*, London-New York, Routledge.
Murru, L. (2020), *Smallness. 1+11 Contemporary Urban Dwelling Stories*, Master's degree thesis: Politecnico di Torino, tutor: Caterina Barioglio, co-tutor: Richard Plunz.
Roncayolo, M. (2002), *Lectures de villes. Formes et temps*, Marseille, Parenthese.
Stern, R. A. M. et al (1995), *New York 1960. Architecture and Urbanism Between the Second World War and the Bicentennial*, New York, The Monacelli Press.

EXPERIENCING THE POSSIBLE.
The Design of Open Devices
for Modification of Marginal Contexts
Gianfranco Orsenigo

Gianfranco Orsenigo is an architect and PhD in "Architectural, Urban and Interior Design" at Politecnico di Milano. In his research he investigates how architectural design can equip itself to become a key stage in the process of transformation of marginal territories. He is a member of Mapping San Siro, an action-research project in the public housing neighborhood of San Siro in Milan and the co-founder of the office Gru Architetti.

It is customary to think of architectural objects as the outcome of a process that answers to needs and problems. A belief that in recent decades has led architectural practice to be "circumscribed by much more instrumental demands, in which action is determined in reaction to the short-term priorities of clients and the market" (Awan et al, 2011: 29).

The outlook marginalizes the possible contribution of architecture in complex situations. Circumstances where the entanglement of problems and players is so intricate that it makes the situation seem inextricable. Like in the cities' marginal contexts, where the overlapping of critical issues, of fragilities, and the scarcity of resources seem to make any transformation insufficient. Places "where the tension towards change is so high that any possibility of a project is annihilating" (Di Franco, 2019). Complexity and uncertainty push these situations to the margins of the city's transformation processes.

What can the architectural design contribution be in shaking these inert situations, activating a project thinking? What tools should the designer have to help foster a process of reframing the problem to make it treatable (and not necessarily resolvable)? I empirically deal with these questions, through a self-reflexive critique of two researches in action.[1]

#01 Prison Architecture: From Space of Detention to Place of Relationship[2]

January 8, 2013, the European Court of Human Rights condemns Italy—Torreggiani judgment—for the inadequate conditions of decent habitability in the prisons. The obsolescence of buildings and the impossibility of carrying out a comprehensive redevelopment policy characterized the poor condition of the system.

Spring 2015, the Minister of Justice organized the *General States* on the *Penal Executions*, broad reflection on the detention. A thematic table focuses on "architecture and prisons," and it underlines the need to begin a transdisciplinary reflection.

In February 2017, following the General States, a research group from the Department of Architecture and

Urban Studies of Politecnico di Milano started a two-year investigation on both the civil role of the detention space and the possible changes of its inadequacy. The aim is to draw up a strategy of analysis and design understood as a *place of relationships*.

The research uses the Milanese cases and the design explorations to develop a method that frames the plurality of opportunities into an open and strategic plan of long-term. A set of *guidelines for action* is the tool chosen. They would be useful knowledge for those who, every day, work to make Italian prisons more habitable.

The guidelines result from a research process that practices the relationship programmatically. The analysis and design are carried out with inmates and students of architecture through a design studio experience, activated in September 2017. Together, students and inmates designed hypotheses to transform the "waiting time" of execution into a "time of project." Similarly, we activated a dialogue with the administrative and surveillance staff.

The research realized unforeseen artefacts. Programming the studio design, the group met Angelo Aparo, the coordinator of inmates group *Trasgressione.net*. He asked to leave a physical trace of the relationship. So it was organized an internal competition: *Trace of Freedom*. Students and inmates, grouped in teams, have to design a place for meetings with children. In January 2018, a mixed jury selected the *Red little house* as a winner proposal, a wooden pavilion located

Figure 1
The Little Red House and the Pergola in the meetings' garden of Milano-Bolalte Prison.
Photograph © Andrea di Franco.

in the meetings' garden. It was built thanks to a private donation and the work of a cooperative of artisans. It was inaugurated on October 23, 2018.

The experience informs the guidelines, too. They are structured in a *series of principles* that frame a broader design perspective. Follow a *catalog of actions* that describes measures reasonably achievable with the resources and materials available. Each action, described in a chart, combines one space and one practice. Each chart illustrates the expected effect by a title, a diagram, a short text, and a localized project that exemplifies a possible declination. A *matrix* helps to match places, practices, and themes. It is manageable by many entrances, following needs or opportunities of the moment.

The process contributed to building a network across the Milanese prison universe. It is a cooperative network that feeds the local process. The year after, the research built a pergola at the surveillance's request, and the staff became partners in a new research.

#02 West Road Project[3]

June 2017, the *Polisocial Program*[4] announces its annual award. The topic is marginal areas. At that time, *Italia Nostra NGO* and Politecnico researchers discussed a possible cycling path along Via Novara to connect the parks of western Milan and the city center. The call looks like an opportunity to develop the idea.

Spring 2018, *West Road Project* research is financed and begins its activities. The project investigates the form of the public space through slow mobility as an urban and social regeneration tool in marginal areas. The territory investigated hosts an archipelago of run-down and abandoned common spaces and some excellences—three large parks, the stadium, and the network of associations.

The assumption is to experiment with a device able to coordinate a swarm of episodic transformations. WRP chooses the design slogan "*I move well*" as the lens through which both recognize and trigger opportunities and resources. The attempt is to design an *adaptive masterplan* capable of investigating the contingency and transforming the specific occasion into a tool that deals with the general. So the research follows a process that combines general and particular, affecting each other by approximation. On one side, WRP designs an *atlas of habitability*; an updating sketch of a relevant representation of the urban area. On the other side, WRP tries to build an *archive of real experiments*.

04.2018–07.2019 *Farmhouse Case Nuove*, redevelopment of the area in front of the historic building. Interrupted.

06.2018–12.2020 *Quarti Park*, development of a common space in via Quarti public housing estate. Built.

12.2018–10.2019 *Agreement Gigante*, partial redevelopment of via Gigante in San Siro public housing estate. Built.

10.2019–11.2020 *Cadorna Courtyard*, redevelopment of a school courtyard. Built.

10.2019–ongoing *From traffic island to playground*, redevelopment of a traffic space in San Siro.

These experiments are a product of co-design and co-realization processes. Each experience was triggered by different events, saw the involvement of a plurality of subjects, and used different tools and resources. The "shared knowledge" produced is recorded in the masterplan through selective tales of the processes. Each experience becomes an example usable in other situations.

Among the plurality of experiences, it is possible to recognize recurrences regarding the used tools; the events occurred; and the effects of the design action and space's modification. These recurrences can support the

device's effectiveness over time, considering that some territorial and administrative stakeholders are involved in more than one experience.

The desire to make the masterplan an open device for daily action led to experience it in the form of a website. It hosts the *map of possibilities*, places that reveal tensions towards transformation. It is an updating map with the contribution of the inhabitants and local stakeholders. Potentialities can be observed in the *atlas* and activated by reading the *built experiments*. In turn, the new realizations feed into the masterplan, enriching its knowledge.

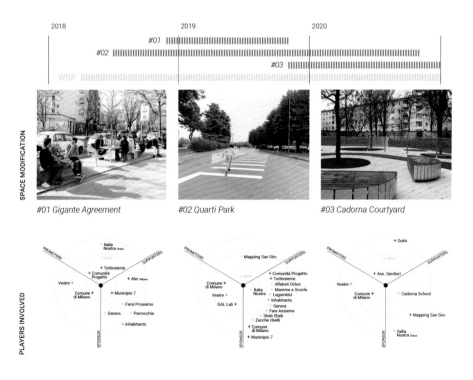

Figure 2

The comparison of three constructed experiments shows how each has specific implementations, but some players, tools, and materials recur, building an attitude to cooperate.

Forward shifts

What drives the research is to find a way to foster actions towards the future in marginal contexts rather than drawing futuristic states hardly achievable. The attempt is to overcome the consolidated procedures that move from the general to the particular, putting them in continuous tension.

The first noticeable shift is to use a *design vision* as a problem-setting tool, to make an entangled situation knowledgeable and manageable. In this view, the project investigates contingency as an opportunity (Till, 2009). Two researches use a guesswork design (design relational places—"I move well") to circumscribe critical issues (high recidivism—degradation of commonplaces), making it an opportunity to imagine alternative scenarios of action achievable.

The second shift is *making together* as a moment of cross-activation of events and players (inhabitants, third sector, and public institutions), and production of *situated learning* (Lave and Wenger 1991). This knowledge is characterized by the relational nature of the production process and the negotiated nature of the meanings attributed to things. We learn about possible transformation doing the transformation. A process influenced by the agency of the documents produced, the objects used, and the spaces modified.

The project moves from a model to a method (third shift) that makes it possible to relate a heterogeneous swarm of actions, places, materials, and peoples within a situated and critical vision. More than a plan, the project seems an "ecology of practices" (Stengers, 2005), a thinking tool that passes from hand to hand. Research is testing the design of *relational devices* — provisional definition — that help distinguish and unite (Morin, 1999) what occurs in time.

Notes
[1] In both researches I was involved from the definition of the program to their conclusion.
[2] A studio financed by a call for basic university research (FARB 2016). https://farbdastucarcere.wordpress.com/
[3] https://www.wrp.polimi.it/
[4] Polisocial is the social responsibility programme at Politecnico di Milano. It finances multidisciplinary society-oriented projects.

References
Awan, N., Schneider, T., Till, J. (2011), *Spatial Agency: Other Ways of Doing Architecture*, Abingdon, Taylor & Francis Ltd.
Di Franco, A. (2019), *La cura del rimosso*, in A. Calderoni, B.Di Palma, A. Nitti e G. Oliva, "Il progetto di architettura come intersezioni di saperi. Per una nozione rinnovata di Patrimonio," Atti del VIII Forum ProArch, pp. 904-9.
Lave, J., Wenger, E. (1991), *Situated Learning: Legitimate Peripheral Partecipation*, Cambridge, Campbridge U.P.
Morin, E. (1993), *Introduzione al pensiero complesso*, trans. M. Corbani, Milano, Sperling & Kupfer.
Stengers, I. (2005), *Introductory Notes on an Ecology of Practices*, "Cultural Studies Review," vol. 11, n. 1, pp. 183-96.
Till, J. (2009), *Architecture Depends*, Cambridge Mass., MIT Press.

POTENTIAL.
Defining, Decoding, and Assessing the Potential in Existing Buildings
Elena Guidetti

Elena Guidetti is an architect and a PhD candidate in "Architecture. History and Project" at Politecnico di Torino, and a PhD fellow at Future Urban Legacy Lab research center. Her PhD research focuses on defining, decoding, and assessing of potential in the architecture field, involving the concepts of embodied energy and morphology and decay. After her graduation at Faculty of Architecture of Ferrara, she worked as freelance architect, as intern in Zimoun contemporary art studio, and as teaching assistant in several design laboratories at the University of Ferrara.

The need to unveil the existing architectural objects both in their actual contingency and their capability to adapt emerges as a crucial issue in the contemporary architectural debate.

Stemming from the roots of the preservationist debate, the research embraces the contemporary theories both related to the adaptive reuse practice, and as to the most innovative approach of "Experimental Preservation," "Postpreservation," and "Counterpreservation."

The concept of *potential* emerges as a commonly used term in this literature, and yet, its univocal meaning is questionable. Evidence suggests that the amount of *potential* is among the most critical design factors within existing buildings. Although the term *potential* varies in literature, there appears to be some agreement among the adaptive reuse field that *potential* refers to the "unexpressed transformability."

The research aims to define, decode, and assess the concept of *transformative potential* in existing buildings following a post-functional perspective. The work intends to define the nebulous concept of *transformative potential* in an operative perspective through its generative elements in the architecture realm.

At first, the literature review focuses on the etymological evolution of this concept across history and knowledge fields. The relevance of the *potential* emerges in philosophy, hard sciences and social sciences. The literature review links the notion of *potential* in post-structuralist philosophy (Delanda, 2002) with the prominent theories from math and physics that have shaped the *potential* as a secular concept.

Starting from other disciplines, the previous analysis and the investigation of the *potential* within the architectural field allow us to propose shared features.

The *potential* acts in a detected force field, and it may be positive or negative; it is multiple and not unique, acting as a function or a flow that needs a trigger element to be activated (Fig. 1). At second, a broad literature review within the field of architecture confirms the relevance of the potential in reuse theory and practice.

The potential in architecture emerges as a transformative power, metaphorically assumed as incompleteness, indeterminacy, or loss (Choay, 1992; Cairns and Jacobs, 2014; DeSilvey, 2020) and the analogical meaning of "chance" or "capability to change." The references to the potential related to existing buildings (Douglas, 2006)—involving the concept of flexibility (Habraken 1990) and transformative patterns (White 1999; Stone and Brooker, 2004)—underlines a kind of *potential* in architecture as the *transformative potential*.

The literature review in architecture studies suggests the *transformative potential* composed by endogenous elements affected by exogenous conditions. The *transformative potential* may express the relationship, both qualitative and quantitative, between spatial elements—size, height, the geometry of plan, configuration pattern, and tectonics of structure—and matter elements—materials and embodied energy—in a trans-scalar and diachronic perspective.

The location of a building—in space and time—structures the exogenous conditions of *transformative potential*. The research will analyze 20 successful adapted buildings across Europe as case studies through their *transformative potential* elements and the multiple reuse interventions.

The case studies selection will consist of architectural objects within various morpho-structural types, as Weberian *ideal types* (Weber, 1949). Each combination between a selection of structural systems and the basic dimensional features—height and

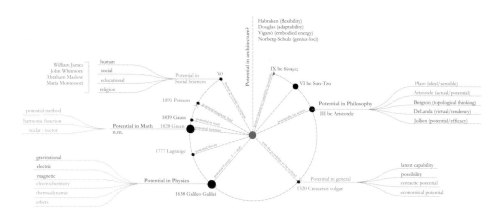

Figure 1
Diachronic analysis on the concept of potential (credits: Elena Guidetti).

size—represents a morpho-structural type. The case studies sample does not comprehend each possible combination, but the scheme may provide a framework capable of enlarging the findings on a morpho-structural type to the whole category.

The classification of buildings in typologies crossed the classical treatises spanning from Vitruvius to Durand. Here, the proposal is to unbuild the classical typological classification in place of a morphological one, assuming the questionable role of the 'new' building over the present sheer amount of built stock.

The post-functional framework is essential to endorse a morphological point of view over a typological one. According to Wachsmann, technological determinism could explain the link between the Gothic cathedral and the industrialized Crystal Palace. Such structural types set analog spatial assets and somehow, a novel classification of the built environment. Buildings are forms, as a critical balance between space and matter (Borie et al 1978, p. 24).

The existing buildings are singular objects connected with their morphological context.

The post-functional framework is an essential condition to lead this analysis. Indeed, the building as an object, free from the contains of function and waiting to be reused represents the perfect stage where the *potential* is relatively maximum.

Such architectural objects faced diverse adaptive reuse approaches, from radical to minimal, that started from a diverse state of decay of the original building. Starting from a particular decay stage may emerge a correlation pattern between the formal starting conditions of a building and its adapting reuse intervention (Fig. 2).

The research methodology leads to the multiple-case-study approach integrating the *morphological analysis* with the existing structure's retroactive-embodied-energy assessment. A critical redrawing of original buildings—highlighting dimensional features and configurational aspects—and graphical analysis of the adaptive reuse project aim to underline relevant links between them.

The critical redraw is part itself of the morphological analysis. The architectural object will be redrawn in its plan, section, and volumetric asset.

The embodied energy analysis aims to place the materials composing the buildings from a broad perspective. The matter addressed in the architectural object has required a certain amount of energy, displaced in the extraction of raw materials, the production of construction components, the transportation, the assemblage on the site, the recurrent maintenance interventions, the demolition, and the eventual recycling of the materials. A part of this energy is still in the existing building, and being able to measure it means to show the amount added, removed, or displaced in the adaptive-reuse process (Jackson, 2005).

Exogenous conditions assessment is both integrated with the urban morphological analysis and the obsolescence calculation. The obsolescence evaluation follows a re-interpretation of Brand's theory of shearing layers

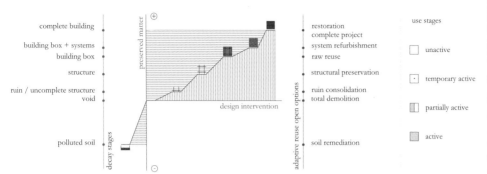

Figure 2
Cross-relationships of the transformative potential (credits: Elena Guidetti).

to address the buildings' evolution across time (Brand, 1995), to underline the decay as an element of *transformative potential*.

Some sub-questions emerge. The concept of *transformative potential* may link morphotype and possible use inherent in the existing form and materials. Both conscious decay approaches and radical design projects may show an analogous *potential* average. Such *transformative potential* increases in the balance between the usage options and the intervention of adaptive reuse. Through which characteristics does an existing architectural object underlie its options for use?

The theoretical objective is to add the concept of *transformative potential* to the current preservationist debate. The novel notion may enlarge the preservation theory following a post-functional perspective in the evaluation of existing buildings.

Despite its exploratory nature, this study offers some insight into the complexity of *transformative potential* as a feature measurable only by setting its domain in physical features such as embodied energy, dimension, obsolescence, and relative location in space. The scale, construction techniques, materials, and volumetric conditions mainly influence its starting potential. However, each adaptive reuse project analyzed stems from such starting asset to several solutions that open up the possibilities, increasing the *transformative potential*. These findings may have significant implications for understanding how to evaluate the *transformative potential* before an adaptive reuse intervention in architectural practice.

The task is to provide a range of *transformative potentials* for the selected morpho-structural types, assessing a "tendency" embedded in the "space of possibilities" for each morpho-structural type chosen in several decay stages. The generalizability of these results is subject to certain limitations. For instance, the small sample may highlight patterns that are not representative in all cases, and the study focuses on a specific kind of *potential*, overlooking many other *potentials* that contribute to decision-making.

Further research may focus on specific types of building with a more extensive selection, to prove the reliability of results.

References
Borie, A., Micheloni, P., Pinon P. (1978), *Forme et Déformation Des Objets Architecturaux et Urbains*, Centre d'études et de recherches architecturales.
Brand, S. (1995), *How Buildings Learn: What Happens After They're Built*, Penguin Publishing Group.
Brooker, G., Stone S. (2004), R*ereadings: Interior Architecture and the Design Principles of Remodelling Existing Buildings*, RIBA Enterprises.
DeSilvey, C. (2017), *Curated Decay*, University of Minnesota Press.
Douglas, J. (2006), *Building Adaptation*, Butterworth-Heinemann.
Habraken, N. J. (1991), *Supports: An Alternative to Mass Housing*, 2th, reprint of the 1972 English edition ed. Urban International Press.
Jackson, M. (2005), *Embodied Energy and Historic Preservation: A Needed Reassessment*, "APT Bulletin: The Journal of Preservation Technology," vol. 36, n. 4, pp. 47–52.
Weber, M., Shils, E., Finch, H.A. (1949), *The Methodology of the Social Sciences*, Free Press.
White, E. T. (n.d.), *Path, Portal, Place*, "Appreciating Public Space in Urban Environments."

DEVELOPING IMAGES INTO VOICES OF CONCERNS.
Some Notes on Using Networked-Images and Participatory Setting for Inquiring into Public Issues

Donato Ricci

Donato Ricci is a designer and researcher. He specializes in the use of Design Methods in Human and Social Sciences. He followed the design aspects of Bruno Latour's AIME project with whom he co-curated the Reset Modernity! exhibition at ZKM Karlsruhe and at the Shanghai Himalayas Museum. He has been involved in the development of the DensityDesign Lab's research programs where he deepened his interest in exploring the role of visual languages and digital data to increase public engagement in complex social issues. He is Assistant Professor of Representação e Conhecimento at the Universidade de Aveiro and part of the SPEAP - Programme in Political Arts. His work has been featured in several conferences and exhibitions, publications, and showcases. He received a silver and a bronze at the Malofiej-Awards, twice a Filaf award, and was selected for the ADI Design Index.

Since its conception, the SciencesPo médialab has been involved in the description of socio-technical public issues.[1] To further an approach taking advantage of the empirical capacities embedded in digital activities[2] (Rogers, 2013), the lab blended together methods that come from three distinct traditions—social science, computer science, and design research. On the one hand, design research contributed to investigate specific issues tracing their liveliness, describing their evolving dynamics, and mapping the actors' alliances and oppositions by producing digital tools and graphical means (Ricci, 2010). On the other, it contributed to question the traditional dichotomy opposing qualitative and quantitative methods (Latour et al, 2012), renewing the role of public participation in social research (Venturini et al, 2015) and opening up the research beyond academic environments (Ricci, 2019). On a broader panorama, these contributions are part of the increased permeability between Sciences and Technology Studies and "inventive" (Lury and Wakeford, 2012) approaches re-distributing the agency of research between a growing set of actors (Lezaun et al, 2017), tools, and data-sources.

Furthering the invention and innovation of social research methods is becoming increasingly necessary if we pay attention to the multiplication of digital objects and formats that contribute to the constructions of ways of *seeing* and *perceiving, producing,* and *practicing* the material worlds we inhabit. One of the new challenges, for example, resides in the use of pictorial content for the descriptions of the social, now that the vast majority of social media have become image-centric platforms (Faulkner et al, 2018). The dynamics of producing and accessing, distributing, and viewing *networked* visual contents (Niederer, 2018: 20) embedded pictorial components in almost every social activity.

This contribution proposes a collective and participatory research approach, called *developing,* to investigate and, at the same time, repurpose the *networked* qualities of on-line images to inquire into public issues. To illustrate and expose its aims, the text details a project called *DEPT.—Describing the Present Tense* as unfolded in the cities of Rijeka, Porto, and Paris sharing the opportunity and the need of using digital visual materials coming from social and digital networks—Google Street view, Airbnb, Twitter—to describe and intervene into urban public issues.

The *developing* register, in its shortest definition, could be condensed as follows: it collects on-line images—as objects of articulation and meaningful expressions of social issues; it transforms them into a progressive cascade of visual artefacts—as tests of the computational and algorithmic technologies on-line images are enmeshed in; and, at once, it constructs around them a public enquiry—as discursive feedback operations on the social issue that triggered the entire process.

Using networked-image for the study of social issues

The opportunity for experimenting and testing a new register for social research and public participation was offered by a set of different situations knotted with the dynamics of on-line image production and circulation:

Presenting, within a network of media-activists in the city of Rijeka, some reflections about the role of visual practices for addressing cultural and political issues, we[3] have been invited at inquiring[4] how the complex identity of the city (Jesné, 2013) could have mutated or been muted by the European Capital of Culture program. We directed our attention to the very skin of the city: its visual richness as captured by the "poor images" (Steyerl, 2014) of Google Street View. Knowing that it would have been myopic *just* to *show* if and how the skin of the city is changing through the Google's nine-eyed cameras for "capturing the world" (Anguelov et al, 2010), we had to address how the same technology blooms into controversial issues—so extensively *revealed* by many artistic projects (Ertaud, 2016)—of surveillance and control, and privacy and labor exploitation (Zuboff, 2015). Hence, we extracted the pictures using Google's proprietary API and processed them with the Object Detection Algorithms usually applied to Street-view images for socio-economic profiling (Gebru et al, 2017).

Extending, in the frame of our teaching activities, our academic interests about the intersections of platform economies (Srnicek, 2017) and urban fabric (Graham, 2010), we set up an event[5] during the Porto Design Biennale. It addressed the issue of the digitally impulsed urban gentrification (Wachsmuth and Weisler, 2018). We quested to describe the aesthetic mutations of domestic spaces through the city's Airbnb listings, images, and the objects they contained. Acknowledging that it would have been neglectful *just* to visually *recompose* the private imaginaries pushed by digital home rental marketplaces we had to have a technical grip on how Airbnb's computational technique—so neatly *exposed* by a multiplicity of digital and critical projects[6]—fosters an apparent growing sameness (Pavoni and Mubi Brighenti, 2017) of the "private spaces we share" (Ricci et al, 2020). So, we exploited image-sets circulating among Airbnb-watchers[7] and simulated the vector-embedding model (Grbovic and Cheng, 2018; Yao, 2018) the company uses for classification and sorting purposes of its listings.

Sharing, in a cycle of seminars about digital methods and urban studies, a tweets dataset related to the urban-nature in Paris (Ricci et al, 2017), we have been called to justify why a portion of the set—meant to account for "nature's" 's entanglement with broader social issues (de Biase and Ricci, 2018)—contained photos of rats. We seized the opportunity[8] to repurpose this ambiguous collection of images to render the necessity to negotiate our living spaces with a broader cosmos of "neglected things" (Puig de la Bellacasa, 2017) and living beings. Recognizing that it would have been rash *just* to *trace* how the Parisian urban-nature is stretching and bending imaginaries, we had to rebuild the *experience* of the multi-layered structure of social-media (Cardon et al, 2019), produced by algorithmic processes, make conversations cross (Pariser, 2011), and pictures being manipulated (@bascule, 2020; Theis and Wang, 2018). Thus, a backend tool tapping into the API,[9] an Image Cropping algorithm, and a custom trained Natural Language Processing model along an interface emulator[10] have been used to mimic how Twitter makes sense of both text and images.

Visualizations and analysis

We identified, with our referents in the different cities, the sources and the entry points for extracting data and pictures from digital platforms or social media—specific Google Maps paths in Rijeka; extension and definition of the urban boundaries in Porto; bags of words for retrieving the tweets in Paris, and took the responsibility to start to analyse and visually render the corpora. Going back and forth between classical data-visualisation (see Fig. 1) and media-visualization, we started to observe objects, frequencies along the street of Rijeka (see Fig. 2); to detail territorial correlations among objects composing domestic moods and atmospheres in Porto (see Fig. 3); and to discern discursive intersections of topics and visual imaginaries related to the un-wanted nature in Paris.

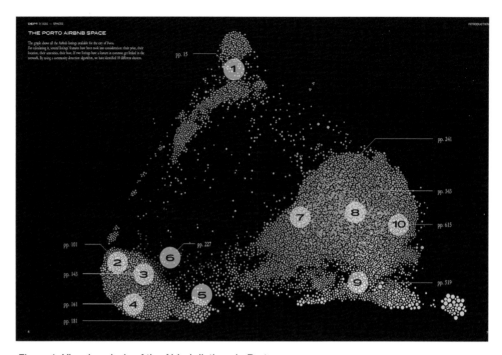

Figure 1: Visual analysis of the Airbnb listings in Porto.
CC BY-NC, the author.

All the graphical artifacts we produced in the first exploratory phase belong to visual information compression technologies requiring expert training for unfolding the content shaped by their format. Instead, the people we were collaborating with were unevenly versed in literacy, articulacy, numeracy, graphicacy: the competencies required to deal with data-intensive visual artifacts (Monmonier, 1993). This undermined the possibility to use intricate visualizations in our further participatory activities. We were looking for malleable graphical expressions to activate a process of collective manipulation aimed at *saying* something *with* them—express how on-line images reground into personal understandings of the issue under inquiry—and *doing* something *through* them—trigger a process of self-description of the communities we were working with. We were to invent a publication format informed both by our analysis of the *networked*-quality and the *bulk*-experience of the corpora; tuned to the on-line content it had to hold and enrolled in the production of new potential meanings.

Designing this new format was everything but forthright: How to bring them from the inside of our *laboratory* to the outside of our collective inquiries' participatory *settings*?

<u>Catalogs and conversations</u>

By re-exploring histories of media-related practices and impulsed by the reading of Hanke te Heesen (2014) works, we identified in the format of the catalogues a possible solution. A specific root of this format could be placed in the 19th century's newspaper-clipping industry, producing image and text corpora dispatched as catalogs, albums or dossiers: intermediary visual formats enrolled in a vast spectrum of material and intellectual practices.[11] The proper pertinence of such a format was further provided by realizing that some of these information-processing practices have been reinstituted by artificial-intelligence-geared services. Image-banks sell computationally indexed dossiers of images[12] to companies; consumers' desktop and mobile applications identify, index, crop, move, and rearrange the contents we take, share, and download in our daily activities, to produce "automagically" (Biersdorfer, 2019) catalogs and albums[13] (see Fig. 4).

We have, therefore, cought in catalogs the possibility of, literally, downloading, expanding, and developing the analytical compression of the first part of our study. Classification and frequencies of the objects encountered in the city of Rijeka; probabilities of association for the object of the domestic landscape of Porto; patterns of sharing and topic of discussion about the rats in Paris (see Fig. 5) could have been appreciated by leafing through the pages of materially printed objects.

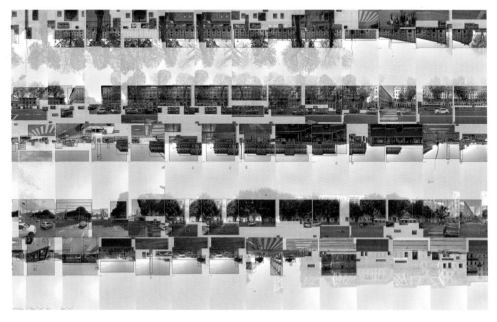

Figure 2: Object Detection on Google Street View images in Rijeka
CC BY-NC, the author.

Donato Ricci - Developing Images into Voices of Concerns

Figure 3: Vector embeddings of the Airbnb-listing images clusters
CC BY-NC, the author.

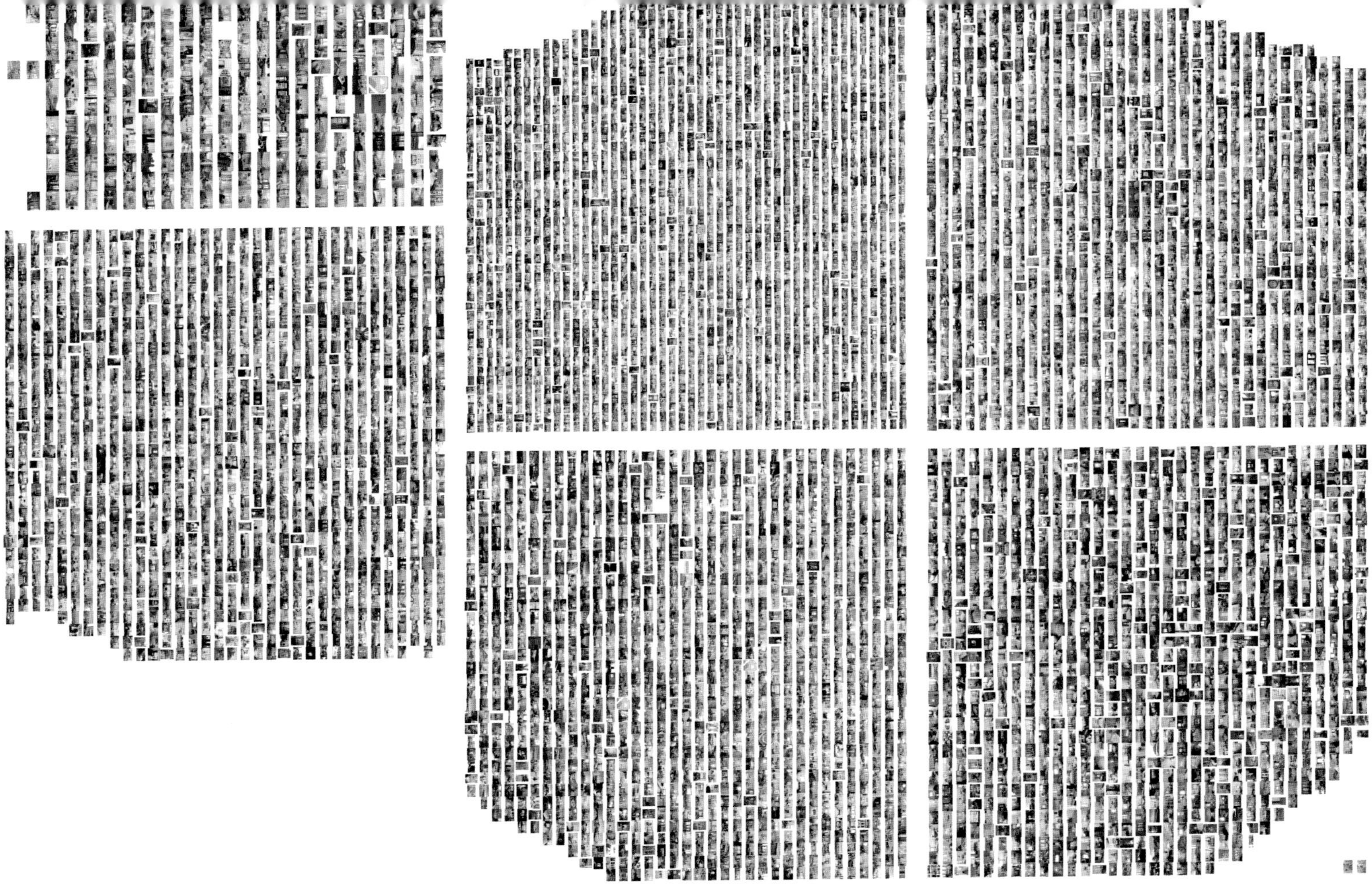

Figure 4: Spread from the catalog used in Porto containing the Airbnb listing and the objects identified in them.

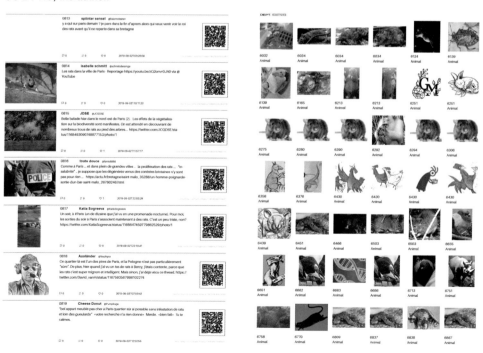

Figure 5: Spread from the catalog used in Paris containing the full tweets and the images shared over social media.

We hoped that through the catalogs, *through* and *with* the image contained, people would narrate the issue they were facing in their cities, unfold their understandings, point of interests, and future possibilities. In each iteration of the DEPT. project, the participants, one at time, were invited to join a table where two members of our team were sitting (see Fig. 6). One holding the catalog. The other, introduced as a testimony and notetaker of the dialogue to come. Few questions were asked to the participants: in Rijeka, the path they traveled the most; the location, the square meters, the number of people living in their apartment in Porto; in Paris, a few keywords describing their relationship to nature. These few bits of information were useful to open the catalog at a specific chapter: the one that had most probabilities[14] to *correspond* to the participant. The catalog, then, was handed, the participant left alone with some further guidelines, cheaply printed on an A4. The exploration lasted, usually, for more than 30 minutes.[15]

Long conversations started, by the descriptions of the atmospheres encountered; extended through an appreciation of the visual materials' (mis)alignment with personal experiences; concluded with a recognition of the specific role that pictures played, as actual objects, in the participants' everydayness. Eventually, the notes were re-read to the participant asking if there was anything else to add. The notes, along with the pictures and the annotations layered on the catalogs, were rearranged as *tableaux*.

Figure 6: DEPT. Rieka table with participants discussing and annotating the catalog.
CC BY-NC, the author.

Tableaux and narratives

The *Tableaux* have been conceived as visual *chimaeras* composed of images scraped and cropped, indexed by algorithm, annotated by hand, layered with the participants' personal narratives (see Fig. 7). We came to call them *tableaux* since the term latches itself on the specific *genre* produced by formally arranging visual content to provide and reveal argumentative structures (Bender and Marrinan, 2010). Defined by composition—strata, overlap, and juxtaposition—of individual items, *tableaux* gather together separate and disparate—chronologically, spatially, cognitively, or technologically—phenomena. They provided overviews not by simplification and abstraction but by detailing fragments, articulating different scales and perspectives held together by compositional principles. *Tableaux* inscribed, provisionally, the personal experiences developed with the corpora through the catalogs (see Fig. 8). In Rijeka, the Google Street View's aesthetic appreciation developed into grounded reflections about the capabilities of these "poor" photos to be faithful testimony of the city's demised industrialized identity rather than stylized Instagram ones. The same appreciation

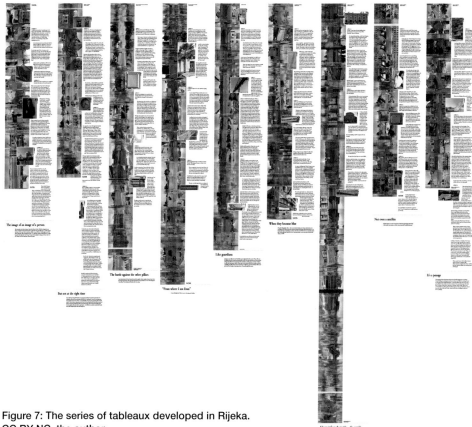

Figure 7: The series of tableaux developed in Rijeka.
CC BY-NC, the author.

resulted in arguments addressing the impossibility of Google's machinery to explore some part of the city, thus impacting the possible futures of these places. In Porto, pictures of the clocks pointing always at the same hour; the ashtrays systematically missing in the pictures have been revelatory of the injunctions the platform produces towards its user both in terms of the aesthetic—the pictures were took always with the same light conditions—and behaviors—no party allowed, no smoking allowed, thus, no ashtray.

As a material trace of the process, at the end of the dialogues, we handed the participants the printed version of their *tableau*. We hung them together upon the walls. Originally, we thought of this as the conclusive gesture of the collective experience able to start the final collective debriefing. Nevertheless, something else, independent and parallel, was systematically happening when testing the procedure. The participants had a small interest in the methodological or epistemological aspects, even lesser in a condensed or distilled meta-narrative of the experience. Instead, they were turning their attention, by their murmuring voices and brouhaha, towards a finer understanding of that which was contained in the others' *tableaux*.

Figure 8: Annotated tableaux in Porto
CC BY-NC, the author.

Scores and voices

After mazy ruminations, we tested some active interventions by the help of speculative praxes (Debaise and Stengers, 2015). Far from being practices of pure invention—abstract projections of a world disconnected from any grip on reality—speculative gestures propose *reprises* and (re)constructions of events unfolding in present and localized situations. Untied from the burden of representation, intensifying the sense of the possible, speculative gesture promises to act as embedded tests for the "redeployment of the real" (Pihet, 2017). More than simple reorganizations of a reality already at hand, they invite to actively manipulate them to reach a greater amplitude and consistency. For us, speculations meant to modify the apprehension of the collective experience through narrative and performative magnification.

We took, then, the *tableaux* off the wall. We re-distributed them to the participants. We started a new process of interrogation of these materials. The participants were, and we along with them, invited to read each other's stories aloud; to highlight the passages in or out of phase with their personal experiences; to re-write the images on which those stories were built. These non-analytical and non-representational[16] ways of questioning our visual materials, borrowed by the techniques of the theater, have been *improvised* to accept and cultivate a partial but mutual sensitivity among the participants. Each of the *tableaux* dis-

Figure 9: Exercises of performance and writing in Rijeka, Porto and Paris
CC BY-NC, the author.

closed its provisional and biased, individual, and subjective nature. Through the reading exercises, the content of the *tableaux* were retraveled and inspected to find tensions and partial connections with the other ones.

Once these points were identified, we started another set of exercises to write down a score: a document accounting for, as the murmurs of informal conversations, the alignment of various individual experiences altogether with the moments and the reasons for their possible divergences. Sort of non-mechanical montages, the scores mixed different levels of our whole experiences: single images of the corpora; reflections about the role of digital platforms in the urban realm; effects of algorithms in personal and collective lives. Eventually, the scores (see Fig. 9) were rendered as a voice standing for a localized and shared understanding of the issue under inquiry: performed by its very actors; video exhibited in Rijeka; radio broadcasted in Porto; texted in Paris.

In this last (more-than) visual object we designed, single manifestations of interest toward the issue faced in the different cities have been articulated through and with the images, diffused without dissolving in the community's voice (see Fig. 10). Made out of the empirical materials collected and produced all along the development register, it emerged as the product of collaborative and affective processes. It is through this object that we, finally, engaged with the discussions and the debrief of the experience and its significance.

Figure 10: The score and its final performance exhibit in Rijeka
CC BY-NC, the author.

Visibilization and Visualization

What can be offered here, as the final discussion, is feedbacking onto the mo-
tivations that brought into existence the DEPT. project: our desire to make our
usual visualizations, maps, and diagrams to exist more. Existing as the extension of their presence and action in the world: what could be said *with* and done
through them rather than just read and seen *in* them.

As Tim Ingold (2013) beautifully described, after his reading of Vilém Flusser's
(1995) argument about what to design as a practice entails, an "object" to exist
requires a full "choreography" around and for its "performance" in the world.
Objects are more "traps" than solutions. To make our objects—our visualizations—perform outside the lab, we trapped ourselves in the constructions of
their condition of use and existence. Each "performance" required us to design
a new "object" and its "choreography." To extend and care for our data- and
media-visualizations we had to develop the catalogs. They required the *tableaux*
to be conceived. They itched us to produce the scores. They had to be provided
with a voice to exist. Each of these sequential objects, composing our register,
is the result of an explicit and radical transformative act. Every object is the
legitimation of the following and the denaturalization of the previous one. Each
of them is a memorandum and a promise. The chain they compose wishes to
overcome hard boundaries between the domains of the visual and verbal; the representational and the performative; the research laboratory and the public setting.

We took the opportunity to experiment otherwise with the cultural and technical practices needed to produce the context of use, the meaning, and the
interpretation of digital and visual instances of social processes. To this extent,
the DEPT. projects is, first and foremost, an experiment on designing *visibilization* affordances of data-intensive procedures—the capability for a sensitive
rendering of awareness and affections—rather than on the *visualization* ones—
the pure optical manifestation. We accepted the risk to cope with a register that
the more it advanced, the more it became situated and contingent. The more
it developed, the less its results were distinguishable from the techniques, the
methods, the situations, and the people providing for their existence and caring for their performance. The more the register advanced, the less we could
withdraw. We have been trapped in dependencies of languages, of relationship
networks, of frictions between broad data treatment and micro-histories. Making our objects exist has been to experience the intensities, the pressures, and
the reactions they triggered. By rewiring infrastructures of circulation, putting in
motion fixed images, and tweaking the experience of revelation, we developed
a fabric that trapped ourselves in.

Notes

[1] Often the two terms are used interchangeably. The distinction between them lies in the type of objects and situations they express. While the term 'controversy' addresses scientific and technological contested objects, 'issue' refers to wider and less specific situations of disagreement.

[2] A less data-and digital-intense version, linked to the need to train students in the observation and description of socio-technical debates, is still active in the lab under the FORCCAST program. Its most recent iterations along with its results are available at http://controverses.org (see de Mourat & Ricci 2021).

[3] DEPT. is based on a multiplicity of artistic and academic experiences, in which the core team has been involved for more than five years. Its members are: Donato Ricci, member of the médialab SciencesPo and design researcher; Duncan Evennou, actor; calibro, a multidisciplinary design studio in the field of digital data experiments; Benoît Verjat, designer.

[4] The event was held at Drugo More. It was called "OUT THERE: Exploring the invitations to act in the public space by material signs." It took place between November 15-17, 2019. It was realized in the framework of Refleks program. It involved 15 participants.

[5] The event was held at UPTEC Baixa and at the STOP shopping mall and funded under the Porto Design Biennale program. It was called "IN HERE: Engaging in the rituals of domestic spaces through the stories of their objects." It took place between December 2-8, 2019. It involved 55 participants.

[6] See, inter alia, the artistic production of (ÅYR, 2014; Berkes, 2016; Freier, 2017; Schmidt, 2019).

[7] (Inside Airbnb: Porto. Adding Data to the Debate., 2019)

[8] The event was planned at Les Plateaux Sauvages in collaboration with the ESAD theatre school. It was called "HEREUNDER: Digging into the emotional responses to the city's most unwanted living beings." It involved 13 participants from February 17-28. Meant to scale up at the city level it was interrupted by the lockdown due to the COVID pandemic.

[9] The tool is available at https://medialab.sciencespo.fr/en/tools/gazouilloire.

[10] The tool is available at https://medialab.sciencespo.fr/outils/catwalk.

[11] Companies, as the "Argus de la Presse" in Paris, by centralizing the acquisition of world-wide newspapers and setting up a long chain of work, spanning from the keywords identification inside articles and advertisement, to their indexation untill the actual paper cutting, flourished by producing corpora of image and texts. Fig. 4-5.

[12] Take as an example the partnership that Getty Images built with AI companies such as Veritone and Cortex for collecting images and suggesting new ones to be used for advertisement purposes.

[13] From Google Photos to MacOS and iOS Photo these manipulations run hidden. They become evident, with their potentially harmful bias, once they "glitch" (Meunier et al, 2019)—as the infamous case of Google Photos labeling Black people as "gorillas" (Noble, 2018)—manifesting the traces that have become invisible in the process of rendering something visible.

[14] The reproduction of the algorithmic processes used in each specific digital domain of our corpora granted us the possibility to identify it. For example, for the iteration in Porto we built an interface, mimicking the Airbnb one where the user enters the information and gets the chapter containing the listing most similar to the apartment of the participant.

[15] There are great similarities with photo-elicitation methods rooted in anthropology (Collier & Collier, 1986), sociology (Harper, 2002), and artistic practices (Ketelle, 2010). Nevertheless, the classical way of deploying these methods is to select and work only with one or a few pictures carefully selected before the encounter with the participants in the inquiries.

[16] Under the umbrella term of "non-representational" theories are assembled a variegated set of methods and approaches to sense the politics of everyday life by the means of active and embodied experience (Thrift, 2008). To the extent of the relationship between theater and social research it is worth noting that the most recent experiments are going well beyond the simple performance and staging of researches (Turner, 1982) or the use of the stage as a productive metaphor (Goffman, 1990). A new prolific strand of hybrid approaches is impulsing the stage and the theater, broadly conceived, as a space for the research and the setting for producing empirical and affective relationships with the research materials. See (Giordano & Pierotti, 2020).

Anguelov, D., Dulong, C., Filip, D., Frueh, C., Lafon, S., Lyon, R., Ogale, A., Vincent, L., Weaver, J. (2010), *Google Street View: Capturing the World at Street Level*, "Computer," vol. 43, n. 6, pp. 32–8. https://doi.org/10.1109/MC.2010.170.

@bascule, T. A. (2020, October 20), *Trying a horrible experiment...[...]* [Twitter]. Available at: https://twitter.com/bascule/status/1307440596668182528.

Bender, J., Marrinan, M. (2010), *The Culture of Diagram*, "Standford University Press." Stanford University Press.

Biersdorfer, J. D. (2019, April 10), Organizing Your Unwieldy Photo Collection Is Easier Than You Think (Published 2019), "The New York Times." Available at: https://www.nytimes.com/2019/04/10/technology/personaltech/photo-organizing-apps.html.

Cardon, D., Cointet, J.-P., Ooghe, B., Plique, G. (2019), *Unfolding the Multi-Layered Structure of the French Mediascape*, Institut Montaigne.

Collier, J., Collier, M. (1986), *Visual anthropology: Photography as a research method* (Rev. and expanded ed), University of New Mexico Press.

de Biase, A., Ricci, D. (2018), *Articuler les temps et les présences de la nature urbaine: Une méthode contemporaine*, S. Marry (Ed.), "Territoires durables: De la recherche à la conception," Editions Parenthèses/ADEME, pp. 33–50.

de Mourat, R., Ricci, D. (2021), *Mettre en forme l'enquête*, C. Seurat, T. Tari (Eds.), "Controverses mode d'emploi," Presses de Sciences Po, pp. 289–96.

Debaise, D., Stengers, I. (Eds.) (2015), *Gestes spéculatifs: Colloque de Cerisy*, Les Presses du réel.

Ertaud, G. (2016), *Google Street View comme domaine d'actions: Éléments pour une conduite* [UR2 UFRALC - Université de Rennes 2 - UFR Arts, Lettres, Communication]. Available at: https://dumas.ccsd.cnrs.fr/dumas-02368801.

Faulkner, S., Vis, F., D'Orazio, F. (2018), *Analysing Social Media Images*, J. Burgess, A. Marwick, T. Poell, "The SAGE Handbook of Social Media," SAGE Publications Ltd, pp. 160–78. Available at: https://doi.org/10.4135/9781473984066.n10.

Flusser, V. (1995), *On the Word Design: An Etymological Essay* (J. Cullars, Trans.), "Design Issues," vol. 11, n. 3, pp. 50–3. Available at: https://doi.org/10.2307/1511771.

Giordano, C., Pierotti, G. (2020), *Getting Caught: A Collaboration On- and Offstage between Theatre and Anthropology*, "TDR/The Drama Review," vol. 64, n. 1, pp. 88–106. Available at: https://doi.org/10.1162/dram_a_00897.

Goffman, E. (1990), *The presentation of self in everyday life* (Nachdr.), Doubleday.

Graham, M. (2010), *Neogeography and the Palimpsests of Place: Web 2.0 and the Construction of a Virtual Earth*, "Tijdschrift Voor Economische En Sociale Geografie," vol. 101 n. 4, pp. 422–36. Available at: https://doi.org/10.1111/j.1467-9663.2009.00563.x.

Harper, D. (2002), T*alking about pictures: A case for photo elicitation*, "Visual Studies," vol. 17, n. 1, pp. 13–26. Available at: https://doi.org/10.1080/14725860220137345.

Heesen, A. te. (2014), *The newspaper clipping: A modern paper object* (L. Lantz, Trans.), Manchester University Press.

Ingold, T. (2013), *Making. Archaeology, art and architecture*, Routledge.

Inside Airbnb: Porto. Adding data to the debate (2019), [Data set] "Inside Airbnb.» Available at: http://insideairbnb.com/porto.

Jesné, F. (2013), *Fiume/Rijeka 1919: Question nationale, expérimentations politiques et contrôle social dans un cadre urbain*, "Cahiers de La Méditerranée,» vol. 86, pp. 85–96. Available at: https://doi.org/10.4000/cdlm.6850.

Ketelle, D. (2010), *The Ground They Walk on Photography and Narrative Inquiry*, "Qualitative Report,» vol. 15, n. 3, pp. 547–68.

Latour, B., Jensen, P., Venturini, T., Grauwin, S., Boullier, D. (2012), '*The whole is always smaller than its parts': A digital test of Gabriel Tardes' monads*, "The British Journal of Sociology," vol. 63, n. 4, pp. 590–615. Available at: https://doi.org/10.1111/j.1468-4446.2012.01428.x.

Lezaun, J., Marres, N., Tironi, M. (2017), *Experiments in participation*, C. Miller, E. Smitt-Doer, U. Felt, R. Fouche (Eds.), "Handbook of Science and Technology Studies" (Vol. 4), MIT Press. Available at: https://mitpress.mit.edu/.

Lury, C., Wakeford, N. (Eds.). (2012), *Inventive Methods: The Happening of the Social*, Routledge.

Meunier, A., Ricci, D., Cardon, D., Crépel, M. (2019), *Les glitchs, ces moments où les algorithmes tremblent,* "Techniques Culture,» vol. 72, n. 2, pp. 200–3.

Monmonier, M. S. (1993), *Mapping it out: Expository cartography for the humanities and social sciences*, University of Chicago Press.

Niederer, S. (2018), *Networked images: Visual methodologies for the digital age*, Hogeschool van Amsterdam.

Noble, S. U. (2018), *Algorithms of oppression: How search engines reinforce racism*, New York University Press.

Pariser, E. (2011), *The filter bubble: What the Internet is hiding from you*, Penguin Press.

Pavoni, A., Mubi Brighenti, A. (2017), *Airspacing the City. Where Technophysics Meets Atmoculture*, G. Tsagdis, S. Lindberg (Eds.), "Intersections. At the Technophysics of Space."

Pihet, V. (2017), *Speculative Narration. A Conversation with Valérie Pihet, Didier Debaise, Katrin Solhdju and Fabrizio Terranova*, "PARSE, 7.» Available at: https://parsejournal.com/article/speculative-narration/.

Puig de la Bellacasa, M. (2017), *Matters of care: speculative ethics in more than human worlds*, University of Minnesota Press.

Ricci, D. (2019), *Tensing the Present. An annotated anthology of design techniques to compose political representations*, "Diseña," vol. 14.

Ricci, D. (2010), *Seeing what they are saying: Diagrams for socio-technical controversies*, D. Durling, R. Bousbaci, L.-L. Chen, P. Gauthier, T. Poldma, S. Rowoth-Stokes, E. Stolterman (Eds.), "DRS2010 — Design & Complexity proceedings."

Ricci, D., calibro, óbelo (2020), *Cozy/Flat*, L. Tozzi (Ed.), "City Killers. Per una critica del turismo," Libria / Campo, pp. 45–50.

Ricci, D., Colombo, G., Meunier, A., Brilli, A. (2017). *Designing Digital Methods to monitor and inform Urban Policy. The case of Paris and its Urban Nature initiative*, "3rd International Conference on Public Policy (ICPP3)."

Rogers, R. (2013), *Digital Methods*, The MIT Press.

Srnicek, N. (2017), *Platform capitalism*, Polity.

Steyerl, H. (2014), *Proxy Politics: Signal and Noise*, "E-Flux Journal," vol. 60.

Theis, L., Wang, Z. (2018), *Speedy Neural Networks for Smart Auto-Cropping of Images*. Available at: https://blog.twitter.com/engineering/en_us/topics/infrastructure/2018/Smart-Auto-Cropping-of-Images.html.

Thrift, N. J. (2008), *Non-representational theory: Space, politics, affect*, Routledge.

Turner, V. W. (1982), *From ritual to theatre: The human seriousness of play*, Performing Arts Journal Publications.

Venturini, T., Ricci, D., Mauri, M., Kimbell, L., Meunier, A. (2015), *Designing Controversies and their Publics*, "Design Issues," vol. 31, n. 3, pp. 74–87. Available at: https://doi.org/10.1162/DESI_a_00340.

Wachsmuth, D., Weisler, A. (2018), *Airbnb and the rent gap: Gentrification through the sharing economy,* "Environment and Planning A: Economy and Space," vol. 50, n. 6, 1147–70. Available at: https://doi.org/10.1177/0308518X18778038.

Zuboff, S. (2015), *Big other: Surveillance capitalism and the prospects of an information civilization*, "Journal of Information Technology," vol. 30, n. 1, pp. 75–89. Available at: https://doi.org/10.1057/jit.2015.5.

The Environmental Architect. Reflections on Media Performativity
Lidia Gasperoni

The environmental architect is responsible for experimenting with the manifold effects of the spatial constitution and impacting on it. This experimentation is the challenge for the designer as a producer of architectural artifacts, expanding her role regarding the architectural significance of complex processes. In order to reveal these complex inter-relations, the environmental architect uses different media in their performative capacity. Media are generative, producing architecture in the design process but also performative impacting on the environment. In the first part of this essay, I will introduce the notion of mediality in architecture. In the second part, I will stress the relevance of performativity theory in order to distinguish between means and media. I will conclude by outlining the importance of providing an account of media performativity when it comes to implement-ing the modes of experimentation of the environmental architect.

The New Planning Paradigm between Experimental Practice and Regulatory Framework
Ambra Migliorisi

Cities are dealing with a schizophrenic situation: on one hand the disparity between the increase of forces of globalization, population growth, and advancing technology; on the other the fragmentation of the urban territory with an increment in vacant lots and disused buildings. Within this context, activities are changing faster than the physical environment, reducing the power of traditional urban design instruments and providing gaps for experimentation to flourish. A reflection on the actuality of the redevelopment strategies reveals how the rigidity of the regulatory framework contributes to slow down the propulsive drive of those hypotheses that, due to their experimental nature, are not suitable for an immediate re-traceability within the existing regulatory grids. The paper attempts to give a new legal context of reference to contemporary urban practices, an-swering not only to the disarmament of architecture in our urban landscape, but also to a possible advancement of the design culture.

Andean Heterotopia. Disruptive Innovation in El Alto
Marco Paladines

This article begins with a description of the emergence of the Alteño building type and the Neo-Andean and Transformer styles, which triggered a disruption of the collective expectations and the urban landscape of the peripheral but developing city of El Alto. The second part narrates the confluence of different accumulation processes that made this innovation economically sustainable and publicly legitimate, and finally realized by identity-seeking clients, creative constructors, and skilled workers. The last part interprets this emergent architecture as heterotopic and as a performative claim for aesthetical autonomy in the public space.

The AA Project on the City. Architecture in Transition
Maria Fedorchenko

The visual essay analyzes the work of the research-design studio on the European City that ran at the Architectural Association, School of Architecture, since 2010. It is curated into two sequential chapters. First, I contemplate how we tackle clashes between old and new cities, institutions and artifacts, testing ideas for cultural and architectural "depositories." Then, I suggest we can use real urban contexts to expose deeper, long-term disciplinary tensions — leading to works on deliberately "dis-continuous" urban models and transitional elements. Overall, we seek broader speculative urban projects that go beyond previous oppositions and mediations, and operate across levels and scales.

THE ENVIRONMENTAL ARCHITECT.
Reflections on Media Performativity
Lidia Gasperoni

Lidia Gasperoni is a research and teaching associate at the Department of Architectural Theory at the Institute of Architecture of the TU Berlin. She has studied philosophy in Rome, Freiburg im Breisgau, and Berlin, and received her doctorate in philosophy at the TU Berlin. Her research focuses on aesthetics, philosophy of architecture, media philosophy, and Anthropocene theories.

Who is the architect today? What is her/his role in society, in rethinking the city, in the so-called profession, in university teaching and research, and in those roles that she/he already plays by defining herself/himself as such (or not)? Certainly, the architect is not only a designer of the built environment; her/his field of action is broader and more complex. What is often referred to as the crisis of the architect's profession, almost lost between theory and engineering, hides the appearance of a much broader capacity for action on the part of the architect who designs the environment. This figure, whom I would dare to call an environmental architect, should not be equated with the very important and worthy figure of the architect who raises the primary question of respect for the environment, and therefore of an architectural practice aimed at protecting it and preventing it from being eradicated. The environmental architect is in a more general way the one who, in addition (or prior) to the construction, makes up the environment by perceiving it, understanding it, and bringing it to new light with her/his design practices. This new architectural agency concerns also the analysis and documentation of building processes, which are collectors of many different levels of society and culture. The project in this case brings architectural processes to new light, showing the complexity of their impact. In this regard, it is very important to distinguish the concept of design, as the act of producing architecture in the narrow sense, from the concept of a project, which concerns, in a wider sense, all real and potential "effects" produced by architecture (Armando and Durbiano, 2017: 73) and in which also documents are grasped in their performativity (Ferraris, 2014: 301). Architecture results from the project, which cannot be reduced only to the intentions of the designer but is a social reality constituted by many agents of different kinds.

The main aim of this essay is to highlight the performative function of the architectural project according the attitude, through which the environmental architect analyzes, transforms, and discloses our environment. This topic is an essential part of rethinking the performative pragmatics of the project according its capacity to develop a shared environment. Theory in this case has the task of outlining this new sense of the project. Its question emerges from practice, but as a theory it also has the task of posing questions to practice and, starting from its analytical tools, trying to expand the range of practical action. The theoretical work is not merely explanatory or descriptive; dealing with conceptual features it should have the critical relevance of increasing the relevance of practices. Systematizing certain aspects of the architectural project, the theory of performativity can help us to understand how we can increase the impact of architecture today. This empowerment cannot avoid, in some respects, the mediality of the project, which is a condition of the possibility of the unfolding of architecture in a sensible—i.e. perceivable and, more importantly, communicable—form.

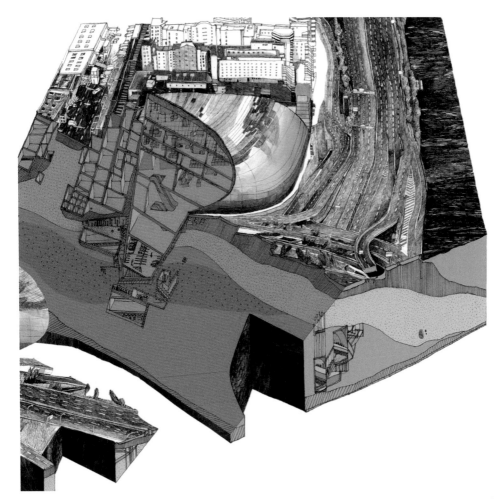

Figure 1
Éva Le Roi, Coupe!, 2018

THE ARCHITECT IS NOT ONLY A DESIGNER OF THE BUILT ENVIRONMENT; HER/HIS FIELD OF ACTION IS BROADER AND MORE COMPLEX

Media are no longer considered just tools that are accessories to content or merely artistic experimentations; rather, they are the mediators through which content comes to constitution. Without media, as performative practices, content would also lose its relevance. Without these practices, complex factual situations on a large scale would not be able to reach a new level of synthesis. In this sense, the practices perform the project and realize it.

The mediality of architecture

Architectural projects depend on mediality. In design in the narrow sense, different media are used one after the other and side by side, so that every final presentation in the context of a design seminar, a competition, or a commission is a string of media that are simultaneously valid and ultimately represent a multimedia product. This constant interaction between media makes architectural design a perceptible media prism of a complex process of constitution. Design processes are potentially accessible in any medium, and it is well known that there are architects who favor certain media and, in whose work, a specific media language can be recognized—we can think of the model works of Frei Otto, the painterly drawings of Aldo Rossi, and the diagrammatic drawings of Zaha Hadid. Generally speaking, media make architecture perceptible through their connection to the senses. Consequently, media must not be decoupled from their function of making things sensible, which in this case consists in making architectural meaning perceptible. As a discipline of design, architecture sensitizes spaces through media, which contain a specific aesthetic knowledge, constituting real spaces of our experience. In this sense, architecture cannot do without an aesthetic theory that deals with the process of constitution perceiving the environment. Aesthetics thus makes way for new reflection on the sensual expression of our environmental positionality: Rather than consisting in passive perception, human cognition is active in perception, shaping its object through different sensual media, such as images, texts, diagrams, and bodily practices. In this regard, architecture should implement its intrinsic relation to perception, going beyond the primacy of visual cognition—as Juhani Pallasmaa points out in his work (2012: 19).
   Media are also the generative paths of meaning in the broader sense of design as project. In design-driven research, the centrality of media leads the way to a wide approach to architectural design, to experimenting with processes of design, the aim of which is not limited to building production. This aspect also concerns the recent applications of ethnographic and cartographic methods to architecture, which attempt to reveal the complexity of architectural processes, identifying "different ways of gaining knowledge about a building" (Yaneva, 2009: 5) and about the multilayered essence of the built environment as a new way of making the earth—as the work of Éva Le Roi shows (Fig. 1). In these recent approaches, research content depends essentially on the media that make content perceivable and communicable. And because the content has to be revealed and not just represented, researchers are looking for new media, for new aesthetic practices, which constitute meaning and embedding hybrid practices—such as bureaucratic documents, interviews, and process sheets.

The constitution of meaning is inventive not in the sense of a genial act in the mind of the producer. It is not understood as a creative-mystical moment—a kind of black box—that is hardly documented, while the execution and presentation of the original concept are seen as mere processes of reproduction and adaptation. From the perspective of a performative attitude, the processes of execution, building, adaptation, and conservation also represent a space for generative reflection, within which the project must constantly be unfolded. The environmental architect is in this respect like a researcher who uses design practices to constitute the complex reality of the environment. As a researcher, the environmental architect must rethink the media of architecture, finding appropriate practices to bring the project to light and to verify its impact.

In another context, Alexander von Humboldt's work is paradigmatic of this inventive, generative approach to media practices. His geographic diagrammatic paintings in "Kosmos" are new inventions of poetic and aesthetic media revealing natural phenomena—as the "Géographie des Plantes Équinoxiales," an intermixture of data and image, shows (Fig. 2). The transmission of knowledge cannot be separated from its aesthetic experience, which permeates different scientific practices. Humboldt was aware that his representations were the only form of documentation in the countries he visited, and he explored the aesthetic boundaries between art and science to show how closely the two are connected. In this sense, his paintings are not representations but rather creative practices

Figure 2
Alexander von Humboldt, Géographie des Plantes Équinoxiales, 1807

of knowledge that combine the analytical function of the diagrammatic with a pictorial act in a new medium. Knowledge thus depends on the performative practice of the environmental constitution.

In a similar way, architectural media should therefore be regarded as practices of unfolding space in every dimension of perception. The extent to which certain media enable the unfolding of architectural meaning, and how they can lead to a new conceptual and material understanding of architecture, has often been left to the individual competencies of designers in offices and teachers in design seminars. The focus on the performativity of media—also discussed in "Media Agency" (Barlieb and Gasperoni, 2020)—is therefore both a theoretical and a practical proposal to bring to light the generative and performative function of media in architectural design and to create an institutional and scientific role for them in architectural practice. The notion of performativity is often abused, but it retains a relevant meaning if we explore and take seriously its philosophical implications.

Performativity: "Not all means are media"

The theory of performativity allows us to introduce new elements to the debate on the role of architecture in the constitution of the environment through a specific mediality. It allows us to define an attitude in architecture that, beyond the mere representation of a primary content, idea, or intuition, constitutes it in the design process itself, creating a new type of representation. The theory of performativity thus allows us to conceive an innovative pragmatics of design as a laboratory in which significance is constituted—a significance that depends on (too often undistinguished) "tools," "means," and "media." The theory of performativity allows us to distinguish between these different notions of mediation, emphasizing the generative path of design, and thus of the project.

In "Art as Experience," John Dewey describes two possible means:

> "There are two kinds of means. One is external to that which is accomplished; the other kind is taken up into the consequences produced and remains immanent in them. … But the moment we say 'media,' we refer to means that are incorporated in the outcome."

The first kind of means corresponds to a purely instrumental attitude towards an outcome, in which the process is understood as a mere means to an end. The second, on the other hand, implies an attitude that is not indifferent to the process; the process is a medium for constituting the outcome itself. Thus, Dewey states: "Not all means are also media" (Dewey, 2005: 205).

Simply put, we can compare this to traveling: we can view travel as a purely instrumental path to a goal or as a part of the traveling itself. We can travel in order to reach a destination, thus understanding the journey itself as purely instrumental, or we can travel somewhere and at the same time consider the journey an essential part of the outcome. In the first case, the journey is only a means to an end; in the second case, the journey is part of the goal—or, as Dewey puts it, "means and end coalesce" (Dewey, 2005: 205).

These two forms of travel are exemplary of two different ways of life or attitudes that can also be transferred to the context of mediality: we can understand the media practices used in design and representation processes—such as models, pictures, drawings, photos, texts—as mere instruments, regarding them merely as means to the end of the final product, or we can understand them as part of the design journey, through which a product reaches realization and in the course of which our way of perceiving and thinking about architectural space is constituted in the first place. While in the first case media are pure tools, in the second case they play an active part in the design process and are thus a prerequisite for experimenting with the qualities hidden in space, and thus in the sociopolitical sphere as well. According to Dewey, in their externality, means merely define the mechanical and have an unaesthetic quality insofar as the relevant things are simply denoted without being essentially constituted by the tools. Media, by contrast, are immanent in things and constitute their meaning— paradigmatically, we cannot separate Humboldt's diagrammatic paintings from the information they embed.

This approach to media also changes our attitude towards project failures and bureaucracy. From the point of view of the first (instrumental) attitude, they appear as mere obstacles to the planned procedure, while from the point of view of the second (performative) attitude, they can be seen as moments of discovery through which the process changes, which can lead to new, initially unplanned developments. In order to clearly distinguish the performative attitude outlined in this way from a merely instrumental use of tools, it is advisable in the first case to speak of media, which always involve a performative element, while the traditional instrumental attitude corresponds to the concept of means.

In this sense, all practices employed in design processes, but also in the processes of unfolding the project in the first place, are no longer considered neutral objective means, probes, or sensors; rather, they are understood in their agency and are an integral part of the design process. This different consideration of instruments contains two fundamental aspects: the first concerns the media as sensible modalities that structure and articulate meaning. The second aspect concerns the attitude of the designer, as an environmental architect, towards instruments. If it is performative, the instruments will be media, enriching the complexity of the project; otherwise, the means will just be implemented for the sake of representation. These two aspects also play a crucial part in theories of performativity in philosophy, in theater, and in gender studies. Applying the concept of performative practices to the field of physics and gender studies, for instance, Karen Barad's theory is both a media theory and a critique of representationalism. As she suggests concerning also the predominance of words in the determination of phenomena,

> "unlike representationalism, which positions us above or outside the world we allegedly merely reflect on, a performative account insists on understanding thinking, observing, and theorizing as practices of engagement with, and as part of, the world in which we have our being" (Barad, 2007: 133).

Above all, this performative understanding changes our perception of practices that are not mere instruments of observation, or apparatuses that "can be used as neutral probes of the natural world," but rather "boundary-drawing-practices" that materially reconfigure the world again and again: "apparatuses are not mere observing instruments but boundary-drawing practices—specific material (re)configurings of the world—which come to matter" (Barad, 2007: 140). In this sense, media practices are also specific materializations of meaning. The focus on these boundary-drawing practices is the main topic of Barad's posthumanistic account, the goal of which is not the demonization of humans but rather a critique of the anthropocentric perspective that grounds this materialization process and—I would add—the conception of creative acts as generated only by genial minds. In this regard, the focus on boundary-drawing practices is compatible with a humanistic topic that aims to emphasize the human capacity to cross borders through media practices. As Giancarlo De Carlo stresses, rethinking the role of humanists who visit the Roman temples:

> "they are not pedants who measure them in order to be able to reproduce them as they are, they are not typologists; they are people who have decided to devote themselves to moving borders and dealing with them even in the most diverse and unimaginable conditions, so that their work becomes an opportunity and a tool for stimulating the imagination, and finally to be inclusive and not exclusive, that is, not to exclude other elements and other cultures, but to include them and measure themselves against the new contradiction. And this enriches enormously not only the human spirit but also the creative capacity of human beings" (De Carlo, 2019: 116–117).

With this focus on boundary-drawing practices as performative media, the creative capacity is also the way in which the environmental architect deals with the interdependency of the different processes by which artifacts and their environmental effects are materialized—as Colomina and Wigley point out in the book "Are we human?" (2016). This approach depends intrinsically on the practices of materialization, but the architect acts performatively looking differently at practices, to view them as media for crossing boundaries and not just as tools of the introspective imagination.

The capacity for experimentation

The critique of representationalism opens up an epistemological level when it comes to the fundamental attitude we take when experimenting with media practices. The environmental architect should be a performative and critical humanist, including in the case of so-called "techniques." In architectural design, technical applications are pre-programmed for designers and therefore offer limited possibilities in terms of architectural representation that the designers themselves rarely control. A performative attitude can lead to a change of media or, ideally, to intervention by the designers at the level of programming.

In this sense, on the media agency approach, the designers are not only users but also hackers of mediality (Cannaerts, 2020: 179): they are capable not only of using technical apparatuses in terms of their medial quality but also of transforming and modeling them. In this way, they develop the architectural design generatively rather than merely implementing it technically in order to find new forms of architectural knowledge that explores space. The function of sensorics could became an object of experimentation within space; this is also the aim of a semi-mobile sensing device called "Jambalaya" (Fig. 3), which was produced 2016 by Barlieb, Müllauer, Cannaerts, and Prang for Fieldstations Berlin. This device, which contains GPS, temperature, air pressure, gas, and wind sensors, was used for collecting data on and around Teufelsberg in Berlin. This exploration of space is not merely quantitative; it tries to constitute a

Figure 3
Field Station Berlin (Christophe Barlieb, Sebastian Müllauer, Corneel Cannaerts, Holger Prang), Jambalaya, 2016

complex sensorics in order to approach spaces as fields of complex perception and environmental impact.

This kind of practice thus shows that design is part of our sensual perception and constitution of the environment, dealing with geology, anthropology, media studies, sociology, and many other disciplines. A new practice of aesthetic knowledge opens up the generative space of architecture, a paradigmatic example of which are the score drawings and notations of Lawrence Halprin (Fig. 4). The American landscape architect conceived his own system of notation to analyze, understand, and design the embodiment properties of architectural interventions. Design cannot be separated from aesthetic understanding through practices that in turn performatively animate the built space and generate as productive ecology a new approach to landscape.

Exploring the boundaries between the conventional representation and the experimental exploration of our living space is the task of designers as inventors of space-generating practices that also have a common, shared dimension. The

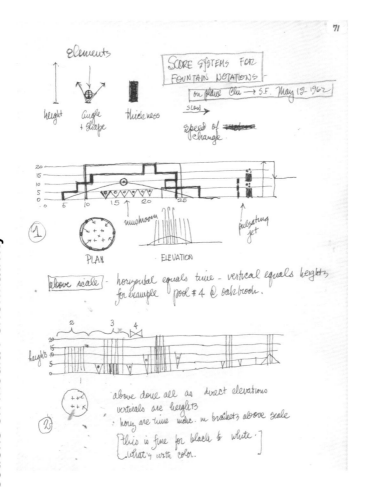

Figure 4
Lawrence Halprin, Ira
Keller Fountain ,1970

experiments with children performed by the Italian architect Riccardo Dalisi show that the performative power of design exceeds architectural representation. With his animation architecture, he invented a performative practice in the 1970s that consisted of drawings and model works to explore a living space beyond representation with children. Dalisi is a producer of practices that attempt to discover latent aspects of perception in collective memory in order to develop a common language of space. This results in a change to the function of practices, which, rather than merely being technical competencies of designers, are already present in our perception of space, in our sense of space, even in children (Fig. 5). Thus, they cannot be reduced to a mere instructive representation; they must be attributed to the much richer area of the figurative, which contains manifold dimensions of perception. In this sense, locality represents the sensual place of the imagination, which can and should be explored quantitatively and qualitatively with all of the senses. Locality is the field in which perception, descriptiveness, and re-conceptualization of the environ-

Figure 5
Riccardo Dalisi,
Architettura d'animazione,
Rione Traiano, Napoli,
1971-1975

ment become the generative laboratory of designers—a laboratory that is exemplified by the "spatial agency" (Awan et al, 2011) of interdisciplinary groups like Haus-Rucker-Co, Raumlabor, and Constructlab. Design already takes place in the perception of space and in all the (aesthetic, cultural, sociological, environmental) dimensions that local space potentially contains within itself.

The experimental approach contains an aesthetic component that lies in the relationship between the perception and the design of our living space. This approach is generative creating new sensible forms and articulations of the environment. But from a performative point of view, the complex relationships with which the designer deals should be renegotiated. In this regard, the architectural project is the production of effects and social realities. Experimental practices, which at first glance aestheticize and de-functionalize architecture, are the essential part also of the architecture that seeks to become aware of its environmental constitution. But in order to be not just generative rather performative, experimental practices should impact by changing the environment, with which they are dealing. It is not sufficient to create a new practice to obtain an environmental impact. This needs an effect producing changes. That is the reason why it is very urgent to question the role of architectural practices dealing with the Anthropocene and the climate emergency: these phenomena need not only the implementation of building techniques, but rather performative practices and strategies in order to renegotiate the manifold connections within the environment.

References
Armando, A., Durbiano, G. (2017), *Teoria del progetto architettonico. Dai disegni agli effetti*, Roma, Carocci.
Awan, N., Schneider, T., Till, J. (2011), *Spatial Agency: Other Ways of Doing Architecture*, Oxon, Taylor & Francis Ltd.
Barad, K. (2007), *Meeting the Universe Halfway*, Duke University Press.
Barlieb, C., Gasperoni, L. (2020), *Media Agency. Neue Ansätze zur Medialität in der Architektur*, Bielefeld, transcript.
Cannaerts, C. (2020), *Hacking Agency: Digitale Fabrikation als Entwurfsmedium*, in C. Barlieb, L. Gasperoni (eds.), "Media Agency. Neue Ansätze zur Medialität in der Architektur," Bielefeld, transcript, pp. 179–196.
Colomina B., Wigley, M. (2016), *Are We Human?*, Lars Müller Publishers.
De Carlo, G. (2019), *La città e il territorio*, Macerata, Quodlibet.
Dewey, J. (1934/2005), *Art as Experience*, New York, TarcherPerigee.
Ferraris, M. (2012), *Documentality: Why It is Necessary to Leave Traces*, New York, Fordham University Press.
Pallasmaa, J. (2012), *The Eyes of the Skin. Architecture and the Senses*, Chichester, John Wiley & Sons.
Yaneva, A. (2009), *The Making of a Building: A Pragmatic Approach to Architecture*, Oxford, Peter Lang AG.

THE NEW PLANNING PARADIGM BETWEEN EXPERIMENTAL PRACTICE AND REGULATORY FRAMEWORK

Ambra Migliorisi

Ambra Migliorisi obtained her PhD at Sapienza University of Rome in 2021, where she researches new project paradigms and disciplinary frameworks related to urban regeneration and temporary uses. She holds a master's degree in Architecture from the University of Ferrara where she authored a thesis in urban studies, policies, and abandoned heritage in collaboration with the FAUUSP of Sao Paulo.

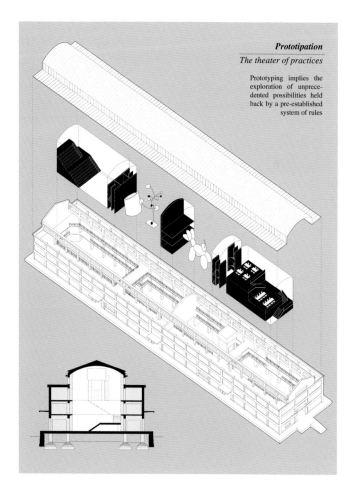

Prototipation

The theater of practices

Prototyping implies the exploration of unprecedented possibilities held back by a pre-established system of rules

Figure 1
The temporary activation of the former railway yard in Bologna, in a state of abandonment since 2012, as the trigger phase of the enhancement process for the area (Source: Prototipation ©Performa A+U).

A COMPLEX OF THEORETICAL POSITIONS FAILS TO UNDERSTAND THE CONTEMPORARY DYNAMICS OF TRANSFORMATION

The Plan and its Modern legacy

Cities are dealing with a schizophrenic situation: on the one hand the increase of forces of globalization, population growth, and advancing technology testifies their establishment within international global processes; on the other, production migration, priority given to infrastructural urban transformation, and more specifically, the financial crisis that hit the real estate sector since 2008, cause an unstable fragmentation of the urban territory with an increment in vacancy rates and an increase of abandoned lots and disused buildings. All these factors deeply affect the expectations and needs of the inhabitants and generate a new urban condition that the current planning paradigm seems to address. The impotence of the disciplinary apparatus emerges when it represents a complex of theoretical positions that fails to understand the contemporary dynamics of transformation, continuing to exercise its function in the absence of the conditions that can justify its forecasts. The current lack of resources for the completion of urban plans and the inability of the masterplan to meet the needs for which it was designed question the spatial, temporal, and economic dimensions of design, undermining the "heroic" attitude that guided Modern planning.

The urban planning discipline of uses, applying its own function by establishing what (uses), how (methods of intervention), and when (validity of the forecasts) to transform the territory, indirectly imposes this "presidium" also on those areas that are configured today as "dead capital" (Marzot, 2012: 29), or rather inactive vacant buildings and abandoned areas. Doing so, it encloses their potential energies and capacities within a conventional mandate that limits their role and availability, excluding a considerable part of the building stock from any form of transformative forecast. Those hypotheses that determine to claim an active role in the transformation of space, due to their experimental nature, are not suitable for an immediate re-traceability within the existing regulatory grids. Left without a functional identity and deprived of the possibility of being temporarily employed, vacant buildings and abandoned areas, end up becoming "planned waste" (Marini, 2008: 189).

In order to free any attempt to anchor the kaleidoscopic social reality, so sensitive to the context, to an idealistic condition, to which the rigid normative structure seems to tend, it is necessary to recognize what Wittgenstein calls the "friction of the reality."

> "We have got on to slippery ice where there is no friction and so in a certain sense the conditions are ideal, but also, just because of that, we are unable to walk. We want to walk: so we need *friction*. Back to the rough ground!" (Wittgenstein, 1953: 46).

This "intellectual desublimation" (Wittgenstein et al, 1981: VIII) helps to de-objectify the *a-priori* form that structures the normative paradigm in order to attend more at the real world. This means rendering visible the hidden mechanisms in the production of urban space, or rather the role of the practice in the design process.

The concrete experimentation on the existing city could enable city planning to avoid preconceived spatial models (the "ideal conditions") and functional assignments, offering the chance to rescue back the original primacy of architecture both over the priority given to the infrastructural-oriented urban development and the techno-bureaucratic administration of the territory.

<u>An overturning of perspective between the Plan and the architectural project</u>

The culture of urban recycling, in the persistent search for the legitimizing conditions, through the identification of research and practice, seems to be the only strategy capable of bringing the planning back into the context of a process able to find its self-regulation system through its own making.

The de-activation of the prescriptive character of the regulatory instrument would be the pre-requisite to recognize architecture as an *in itinere* process, by its nature attempted and unpredictable, and would entail the recognition of a transitory regime that finally admits the institution of a "meanwhile use." It is in this time-in-between of old and new use, that it is possible to experience projects and activities that can offer new scenarios to existing unused heritage, mobilizing various actors and recognizing new categories of social subjects.

Besides on public policy, the development of meanwhile uses calls for an articulated reflection on the role of the agency of the architectural project.

Taking note of the conventional territorial management tools failure, it re-introduces the possibility of an active experimentation on existing spaces as a substantial moment of testing the quality of the forecasts on those areas. More specifically, the theme of temporariness allows to prototype what will be the possibilities of the strategic vision for a future transformation and makes possible to experiment, through trial and error, spatial and functional solutions.

The temporary activation of the Ravone former railway yard in Bologna, in a state of abandonment since 2012, is a recent Italian case study that demonstrates how the experimentation becomes a trigger phase for the enhancement of the area (Fig. 1). Recognized as successful, the Ravone's innovation in practice is orienting urban planning procedures to be capable of adopting the solicitation of change coming from new hypotheses, establishing an important overturning of prospective between the Plan and the architectural project (Gullì and Migliorisi, 2020) (Fig. 2).

Finally, if the project is at the same time the instrument (as previously said it is a method of inquiry) and the final goal of architecture, it could be argued that boundaries within poiesis (the sequence of operations aimed at achieving an objective) and *praxis* (an activity whose purpose is identified with the activity itself), according to the traditional Aristotele's definition, have become porous so that it is possible to rethink the contemporary project culture starting from this hybridization. Founded on the concrete experience

Ambra Migliorisi – The New Planning Paradigm Between
Experimental Practice and Regulatory Framework

Figure 2
In the absence of operational guidelines, the current masterplan of temporary uses for the Ravone
former railway yard in Bologna is made as an official agreement and drive to a deep reshaping
of the city's urban regulatory instruments, to guarantee a higher feasibility of the experimental
interventions (Dumbo Space, Bologna (Italy) ©Dumbospace).

of contemporaneity, the project becomes that action that finds its fulfillment in its making but also it has itself as the real final product, since its activity is finalized to its production.

On processuality, autonomy, and documentality

The project is nothing more than an outcome, always revisable (in a logic of actions and reactions), of an internal dynamic made of a continuous interaction between subjectivities that claim a role in the transformation of a space. Its "making" emerges in the attempt to govern this process with respect to which a convergence of general interests is established. The project becomes, then, the synthesis of this interaction, or rather a process. Affirming the experimental function of architecture as a practice and recognizing the project as an ongoing process, by its nature not predictable, can help to prefigure alternative scenarios, conforming them to the real needs of the city. Thinking in procedural terms means, then, implying the transformability of spaces and their ability to absorb, in a constant dynamic of adaptation, the challenges of contemporaneity.

According to Modernity, the discipline of architecture finds its final goal in getting rid of all forms of conditioning, where the autonomy is the outcome. However, in order to be able to claim the spaces in a transformative key, this process of dissolution is necessary but not a sufficient premise. Through a purely abstract functionalist legislation, Modernity has introduced conditioning factors that do not allow

any action to innovate the architectural discipline. So, if that of Modernity is a project of autonomy, it is unfinished since it lacks the last act of liberation from a normative paradigm that prevents certain degrees of experimentation, both in forms and behaviors. That of autonomy becomes a misunderstanding that the themes of regeneration and recycling are able to remove. Reclaiming the spaces in a transformative key, or rather declaring to be ready to inherit certain places through a transformation, they aim at freeing them from those constraints that compromise experimentation.

Finally, recognizing the ability of the phenomena to highlight a gap in the legislative context creates the conditions for a new documentality. This is possible only by bringing back the architectural project as the foundation of the regulation, reaffirming its primacy in addressing the system of rules. The urban fabric and buildings, with their prototypical value, constitute the origin on which to define a methodological practice: this synthesis represents the starting point to outline strategic guidelines to which conform the regulatory framework.

References
Gulli, L., Migliorisi, A. (2020), *Promises and uncertainties of temporary uses in Emilia-Romagna*, "Lo Squaderno," n. 55.
Marini, S. (2008), *Spazi bianchi. Progettare lo scarto*, "L'architettura e le sue declinazioni," Iperesto Edizioni, Verona.
Marzot, N. (2012), *Re-Loaded buildings. Interfacce innovative per la mappatura del patrimonio edilizio inutilizzato*, "Paesaggio urbano," n. 2.
Wittgenstein, L. (1981), *Osservazioni sui colori*, Einaudi, Torino.
Wittgenstein, L. (1953), *Philosophical investigations*, "GEM Anscombe," n. 261.

ANDEAN HETEROTOPIA.
Disruptive Innovation in El Alto
Marco Paladines

Marco Paladines is sociologist with a mention in Political Science from the Catholic University of Ecuador, Quito, with a thesis on Latin American Political, Cultural and Literary Thought. He then moved to Berlin, where he finished a Master's in Social Science at Humboldt University with a thesis on The Mediality of Architecture as a Social Communication Medium and the Concept of Atmosphere. Now he is a member of the Graduate School *Innovation Society Today* at Technical University Berlin. He is also developing his PhD project at the Chair for Architectural Theory in the same University. His current research project concerns Contemporary Indigenous Architecture in El Alto, Bolivia. The main topics are Indigenous Knowledge and Practices, Innovation by Other Means in Architecture, and Hermeneutical Analysis of Architectural Photography.

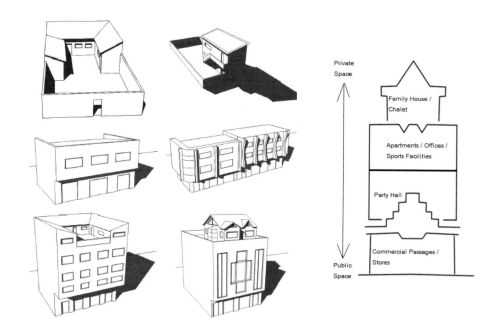

Figures 1 (left)
Different stages in the Alteño type formation process (Cárdenas et al, 2010).

FIgure 2 (right)
Section with a typical distribution of spaces (Sketch by Maria Continillo).

Emergent Architecture

In the last decades, the self-recognized indigenous city of El Alto has transformed itself from an impoverished periphery of La Paz, Bolivia's seat of government, into an economically vibrant, and politically autonomous urban center. This development created an environment for architectural innovation in the last 15 years, consisting of different emerging and competing *styles*[1] (e.g., *Neo-Andean, Transformer, World-Eclecticism*), based on the same building *type*, the *Alteño type*.[2]

The *Alteño type* established itself as a fashionable choice after a relatively anonymous and distributed process in different neighborhoods of the city. It has developed in stages, according to the economic capacity of the owners (Fig. 1). Constructed with modern materials (reinforced concrete columns, lightened concrete slabs, cemented brick walls, and glass windows on aluminum profiles), this type adjusts to the city's rectangula\r grid patterns. The internal spatial organization responds to context-related and socially defined functions: it combines economic activity on the ground floor, followed upwards by double-height party halls with internal balconies, apartments, offices, or sports facilities, and finally, on top of four to seven stories, a family house with two or three more stories (Fig. 2).

At the peak of the type formation, stylistic features on facades and interiors took more importance as semiotic mediums for the conformation of (individual and collective) identity forms. In this way, experimental design and construction practices, regulated through negotiations between clients and constructors, triggered a notable disruption of El Alto's urban landscape,[3] until then dominated by unfinished-looking, red brick buildings. As relatively stabilized styles, *Neo-Andean*, first, and *Transformers*, later, made it to national and international media, short documentaries, and traveler's chronicles, attracting the attention of tourists, artists, professional architects, anthropologists, and sociologists.

It was mainly the Aymara[4] constructor Freddy Mamani, who developed *Neo-Andean* style. His meticulous work reinterprets elements typically considered indigenous or Andean, particularly, the shapes from Tiwanaku[5] iconography and the Andean Cross or Chakana, as well as the intense color patterns of Awayus[6] (Fig. 3). The style met well the expectations of clients who desired the recognition of their cultural identity, giving them concrete presence in the public space. After the success of *Neo-Andean*, Santos Churata, another Aymara constructor, took a different path: he developed a style devoted to the Hollywood series *Transformers* (Fig. 4) and other high-tech fictions such as *Iron Man*. He met the expectation of clients (and their children), who wanted to see the architectural realization of their admired techno-fictions.

Building Heterotopias

What exactly made the emergence of *Neo-Andean* or *Transformer* possible? At an architectural level, the coincidence of creative and experimental

Figure 3
A detail of the ornaments inside a Neo-Andean building. The nuanced color pattern resembles an Awayu, the squared cross is the Chakana, and the figure in its center is a Tiwanaku puma (photograph by author).

Marco Paladines - Andean Heterotopia.
Disruptive Innovation in El Alto

constructors, talented workforce, and relatively wealthy clients is notorious. However, what is the social side of this coincidence?

Aymara clients in El Alto are nodes of networks driving self-organized and alternative processes of capital accumulation (Tassi, 2012). As market actors, specially dedicated to commerce, clients have reached a magnitude of resources in the last decade and a half that makes possible a surplus, and even luxurious spending on architecture. This accumulation overlaps with the accumulation of legitimacy for the Aymara, and particularly the *Alteños* within them, in the context of the Bolivian nation. Political events such as the autonomy of El Alto in 1988, the Gas War in 2003, and the election of Evo Morales as first indigenous president of Bolivia in 2005, provided legitimacy to the Aymara in the public sphere, and with it, the opportunity to express their own identity (also in architecture). Finally, economic sufficiency and public legitimacy encountered skilled workers and creative constructors, who broke with the established aesthetic values.

In this manner, *Neo-Andean* style gave a possible answer to the demands and possibilities conforming the social conjuncture in El Alto after 2005.

Transformers, on the other hand, seized the momentum of the innovation environment to turn high-tech science fiction figures into a decorative style for housing Aymara families and their businesses. While *Neo-Andean* gave expression to a wider demand for recognition in a country with a long-term colonial history, *Transformers* liberated this expressive dimension of architecture from attachments to a specific collective identity (by reinforcing the presence of Hollywood influenced imaginaries, at least temporarily). Both styles, nonetheless, correspond culturally and temporally to a trend in El Alto, which as such, was criticized by some academic architects in La Paz, who perceive it as homogeneous, superficial, and as a tribute to bad taste (Cárdenas et al, 2010: 56).

Far from being homogeneous, the shared *Alteño* type takes different orientations when it comes to style. El Alto's *World-Eclecticism* cites roofs, ornaments, and domes from Arabic, Chinese, or European provenience, and many clients develop with constructors a very personal or familiar style. Contrary to the interpretation of academic architects mentioned above, I propose that the innovation

Figure 4
The Galvatron building inspired in the character with the same name from the Transformers (photograph by author).

conjuncture in El Alto, by means of a creative translation of traditional and futuristic, Aymara and cosmopolitan elements into architectural spaces, actualizes a *heterotopy,*[7] enacting a heterogeneously constructed present. An actual space, which is *other.* And performs it, in relation to the western architectural imagination and to the hegemonic cultural values in the Andean region.

Disruptive Architectural Innovation

Alteño type in combination with the heterogeneous styles described above disrupted both, the expectations on urbanism in a place assumed as peripheral, and its urban landscape. This disruption epitomizes a claim for autonomy in the definition of what good taste is, which in itself connects to a wider but nonetheless situated struggle for recognition through the search of bigger economic, political, and aesthetic autonomy in El Alto. Additionally, the fact that *Alteño type* arranges a minimum functional structure with a maximum customizable style favors its proliferation, while *styles*, distinguishable by the kind of their referential inspiration, allow carrying demands for identity recognition to the public space for a durable period.

Furthermore, it is plausible to argue that the intersection or juxtaposition of several differentiated accumulation processes, when facing a critical point, requires creativity and experimental action in order to turn merely incremental transformation into disruptive change. In the specific case of El Alto, it seems that accumulated economic wealth and public legiti-

macy were not enough for disruptive innovation; creative action was necessary for challenging what was stylistically established, and for making, on the basis of the already accumulated, *another* construction possible.

Notes

[1] Here I follow Alejo's classification of aesthetical references (2019: 9) but introduce minor changes to it.

[2] Cárdenas (2010: 54) describes the process of this type formation. Although this type, or variations of it, are also present in other areas in the region, it has a special prominence in El Alto, where it most probably originated, and therefore I suggest calling the type after the city.

[3] So much, that the German broadcaster Deutsche Welle called it "the architectonic revolution of the Andes."

[4] Aymara is the name of the biggest indigenous nationality in Bolivia, also present in Peru and Chile.

[5] Tiwanaku is the name of an antique civilization (from around 200 or 300 BC) and of the remaining archaeological site. It is located a few kilometers to the north of El Alto.

[6] Awayu is the name of a textile object with colorful patterns. It is of everyday use in the Andean region.

[7] The concept of heterotopia was crafted by Michel Foucault and defined as "a kind of effectively enacted utopia in which […] all the other real sites that can be found within the culture, are simultaneously represented, contested, and inverted." (Foucault, 1984: 3).

References

Alejo, G. (2019), *Arquitectura Aymara: de la Urbanidad a la Posmodernidad*, "Pukara," n. 149, pp. 7–10.

Cárdenas, R. et al (2010), *Arquitecturas Emergentes en El Alto*, La Paz, PIEB.

Deutsche Welle (2018), *La revolución arquitectónica de los Andes*, online video: https://youtu.be/K2CEQsdrHdc

Foucault, M. (1984 [1967]), *Of Other Spaces: Utopias and Heterotopias*. Available at: : https://web.mit.edu/allanmc/www/foucault1.pdf

Tassi, N. (2012), *La Otra Cara del Mercado*, La Paz, I. S. Ecuménico Andino de Teología.

THE AA PROJECT ON THE CITY.
Architecture in Transition
Maria Fedorchenko

Maria Fedorchenko is a Unit Tutor at the AA, where she has also taught History and Theory Studies, Housing and Urbanism, and Visiting School programs. She has held teaching positions at UC Berkeley, UCLA, and California College of the Arts. Primarily an educator and theorist, focusing on diagram and infrastructure, she is also a co-founder of Plakat, an urban consultant, and co-director of Karta Architecture.

This body of work is part of a larger project on the European City, developed at the Architectural Association, School of Architecture. It has run in the framework of several Intermediate and Diploma design units, since 2010. It is primary concerned with the bi-directional relationship between architecture and the city. The sampling of the student projects below focuses on the transformation of historical contexts, redefining the role of architectural culture and design in that process. More generally, our work directly responds to a number of persistent problems when it comes to architectural approach to transitional cities. Going beyond apparent clashes between old and new, preserved and transformed, we question the fitting cultural agencies for such proposals and seek to define new programmatic briefs to sustain the ongoing exchange between urban realms, architecture, and the city, as well as phases of individual projects. And we seek contingent and adaptable design models, creating dynamic prototypes of future architectural artifacts within our experimental laboratories.

This selection of student project is best introduced in two distinct chapters, each composed of two thematic sub-clusters. The first chapter tries to unpack the common tensions between old and new urban contexts, cultural institutions, and architectural monuments. The research exposes new relations between history and modernity—moving from initial ruptures and oppositions, to longer life-cycles, and ultimately to dynamic models for continuous transformation. They also prompt the move of cultural agencies and institutions from more passive roles to more active ones. However, for us to notice more subtleties in the students' response, it is best we try and separate the two sub-clusters within the chapter.

[**Fig. 1 ↓**] The first cluster "Shadow Cities and Anti-Museums" is more invested in splintered urban identity, memory, and visual image. Several projects consider what the current cultural institutions—such as the ubiquitous museums—contribute to the city-wide divides. To mitigate the issue, they often propose to include the possible counter-bodies and often focus on the possible future subject "journeys" that could cut across the initial "sharp" boundaries between sites, typological diagrams, and interior elements—while calling our attention to the transfer points (such as portals, gateways, bridges, etc.).

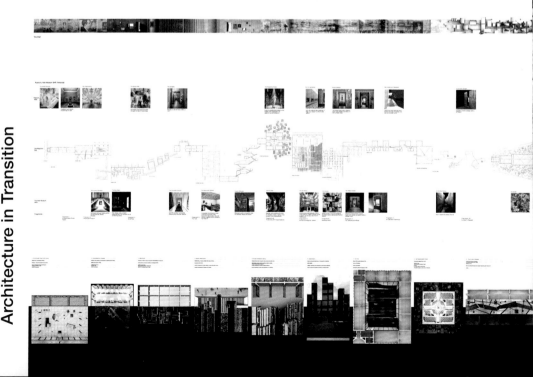

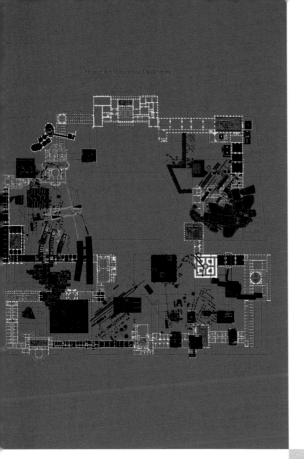

Moscow Art Museum Plan Site Collapsed

[**Fig. 3 ↓**] We could detect these shifts by looking at the second cluster: "Cultural Depositories and Exchanges." This cluster of project is also in part triggered by particular urban issues in their built contexts. This time, it is the traumatic legacies of Moscow and Berlin—marked by brutal erasures, imposed identities, and rapid renewal. And their primarily focus tends to drift from memory, preservation, all the way to amnesia and destruction. They suggest that we could strive to "preserve" the history, and the process of cyclical construction and re-construction of the city. These slightly re-configured cultural project continue to explore the future fate of urban monuments and visual landmarks. But they do so by articulating the more direct exchange "loops" that exist between architecture and the city. This body of work also reacts to the peculiar tendencies towards cyclical "restoration" and "remake" (that result in resurrected Cathedrals and masquerading Palaces, and other breeds of "zombie" architecture).

[**Fig. 2 ↑**] Many times, in response to the jarring ideological leaps and over-rides in the Russian history, the first step is to remodel the city as a paradoxical co-existence of several different "cities." The "division" of the city into "surface" and "shadow" worlds here begins to unfold. We imagined the less-restricted "flow" of cultural artifacts—liberated from the planning regimes, institutional networks, and curatorial control. It is here that we notice these "mis-placed," "extra-institutional," "anti-curatorial" moments—such as glimpsed in indiscriminate art "dumps" and storage "silos," accessible archives, and immersive columbaria. Moving forward, we start to question the tendency to approach the city as formulated in dialectic terms, mediated using collage or montage techniques. Furthermore, we sought ways to go beyond merely inter-linking or hybridizing existing cultural typologies by shifting away from more generally understood "cultural artifacts" from different fields, onto the distinctly architectural content of the city.

[**Fig. 4 →**] Unlike the typological "basis" of the preceding cluster, their cultural visions arise directly from some of the most symptomatic, "accursed" sites (subject to construction / destruction / reconstruction). These dysfunctional sequences and disruptive transformations become some of the most important organization diagrams at the core of the project. However, they tend to embrace the idea of the conflicted site from the very start. We can note their tendency towards the animated structures and evanescent imagery, as if continuously "under construction." These are featured in their "Ruin Cities," traversed via "Liquid Streetscape" and "Blur Bridges."

[**Fig. 5 ↓**] But how do these project reconfigure the cultural agencies, outside of the existing institutional circuits? I suggest we should explore new models for the architectural "depositories," able to accept, alter, and release diverse content back into the city, and into the collective imaginary. While initially inspired by the infrastructural ideas of transit (as road bridges, rail stations, production lines), they are assembled first and foremost as invisible "diagrammatic machines." These are primarily conceptual devices that capture the cultural processes that ran behind the scenes.

[**Fig. 6 ↘**] We become most curious in the bizarre "by-products" of their cultural processors—captured in such drawings as "Rivers of Facades," "Parades of Monsters," "Cascades of Chimeras." This cluster of work resulted in a number of valuable lessons for the unit. We accepted that the idea of the evolving city requires more than simple opposition and mediations. We attempted to pursue a new chapter of the trans-disciplinary project on the city. We primarily seek to emphasize the importance of conceiving and maintaining extensive "flow spaces," carrying seeds of the future projects on urban form.

This second chapter of the unit's work on the European city delves deeper into long-term architectural tensions, linked to transitions between urban frameworks, design elements, and modes of representation. We play further with sequential, coincident, and alternating temporal dimensions within the city. A different use of cultural analogies such as "archives" or "cemeteries," stands for the particular historical "layer" of the city and to condense further conceptual "sub-cities." And we declare more explicit research briefs on the so-called "Meta-Elements"—some of the most essential, consistent, yet evolving components of the European city across contexts and times.

[**Fig. 7 ↓**] The first sub-cluster of works—"Dis-continuous Cities and Archives" – allows us to build upon our earlier hypotheses, developing models for the European city as 'dis-continuous' not only in space but also in time. In an attempt to conceptually stretch the urban domain, many project consider the current built city as its only one possible version. This is often accomplished by creating several "virtual copies" and cultural doppelgangers. These conceptual "mirroring" of the city is captured as dissimilar "archives," to capture alternative histories and suppressed futures (releasing those victims of ideologies, or "orphans of modernity" onto the cartographic "gameboard."

[**Fig. 8 →**] Overall, this cluster of work starts to register the evolution of our interests as a unit. It reinforces our focus on the "expanded" disciplinary project that extends beyond a single place or a moment in time, draws on both "artificial excavations," disciplinary "variations," and visionary projections. However, the early struggles with oppositions and mediations between urban domains and "archives" are slowly superseded with the projects that operate mainly via discrete, specific points upon the urban map.

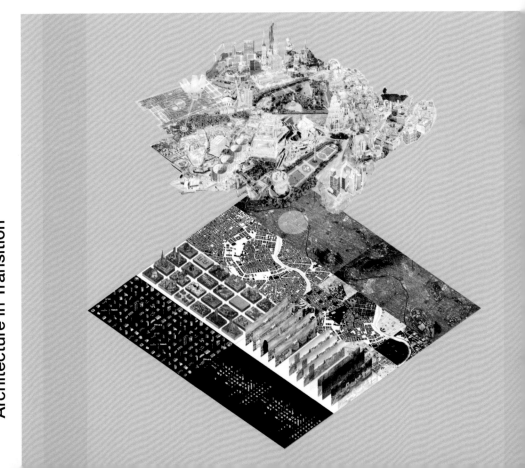

Casa Colombo

Markets of Rialto

Fish-hunting Hooks

Palazzo Mocenigo

Molino Stucky

Fondaco de Tedeschi

Santa Lucia

Dogana da Mar

Piazzale Roma

Arsenal

San Marco

Padiglione

TRANSFORMATIVE

CIRCULATIVE

NEGATIVE

PARASITIC

[**Fig. 9 →**] Further, the study of the history of the "Interrupted," "Extended," and "Multi-Channel" disciplinary cities (recall Roma Interrota or Piranesi Variations), inspire the use of the urban surface as an ideological battlefield and an architectural playground. However, these are not merely theoretical collisions between built and cultural realms, dissimilar archives, and architectural landmarks. They make more pragmatic proposals to incorporate ostracized and peripheral histories when we revitalize the over-protected historical centers (such as in Paris).

Yet invariably, these early battles and direct "attacks" give way to more peaceful coexistences, especially once we notice the addition of the zones and lines mediation. Gradually, these 'lines' become more diagrammatic, implying the wider infrastructure of "flow and exchange" that extends beyond the single city or urban culture.

Further shifts of focus are registered in the final sub-cluster of projects—"Re-enactments and Visual Apparata." At this stage, we start to question how architectural landmarks could perform both as a "stabilizer" as well as an "agitator"—for the urban structure, cultural identity, and the collective memory and imagery. We focus more on the complex origins, life-cycles, and wider influences of notable architectural structures—that could start to perform as 'Meta-Elements.' This sub-cluster also attempts to respond to a number of deeper design challenges.

By focusing yet again on singular architectural landmarks, they would like to restore the architecture's ability to affect directly the processes of urban transformation, on its own terms. Furthermore, while committed to the design trajectories of their select structures, they also try to maintain the more intellectually consistent, "Slow" project on the city. And by looking into the history of the city and the discipline, they also try ways of working that respect both old and new methods and techniques, suggesting future possibility of accessing the kind of a-temporal, and multiplied 'design intelligence.'

So let's briefly summarize the key design approaches that characterize this particular cluster. First of all, many projects unpack complex processes of cultural exchange—including import and export of architectural typologies, morphologies, and styles. These processes help to unlock new futures of their locations (even for such an artificially frozen, touristic city such as Venice). The time-less, local landmarks are exposed as fleeting moments, common illusions, and masked impostors. With this, they probe the deeper undercurrents of historical fictions and "re-enactments" of architectural influences that crisscross European territory.

[**Fig. 10 →**] Thus exposed mechanisms of importation, assimilation and incorporation of various external influences could be also seen as potent tools for affecting other, new contexts, cities, and artifacts. We begin to test the possibility of additional, semi-autonomous design contexts.

These interim, "limbo spaces" are open to both historical excavations and fictional projections, analytical reduction, and speculative expansion. The life-cycles of recurring Landmarks become the means to construct further paradoxical, both culturally specific and architecturally generic, unrestricted "Edge-zones" and borderline "Liberlands."

And finally, these dynamic sites are further refracted, not only using cultural narratives but also visual representation.

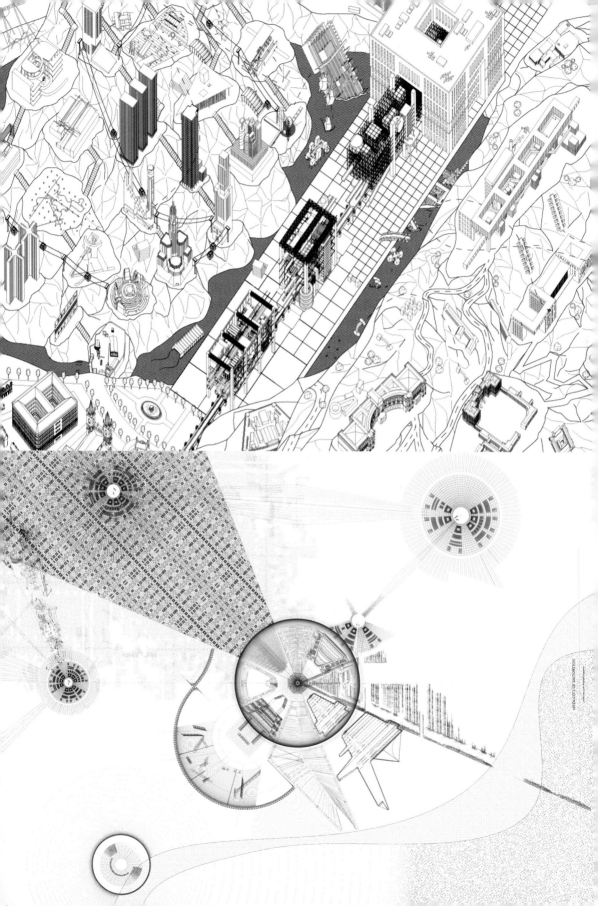

IMAGE CREDITS:
Cover figure: Alessandro Magliani, "City of Morphologies"
Figure 1: Olympia Simopoulou, "Museums Anti-Museums – Transcript"
Figure 2: Olympia Simopoulou, "Museum Anti-Museum – Double Loop Block"
Figure 3: Gleb Sheykin, "River of Facades – Berlin"
Figure 4: Vidhya Pushpanathan, "The Depository of Forgotten Monuments – Patriarshiy Bridge as the Depository Framework"
Figure 5: Sebastian Tiew, "Memory Palace – The Factory Axonometric"
Figure 6: Gleb Sheykin, "The River of Facades – Flow Space Composites"
Figure 7: Olympia Simopoulou, "Anachronic Artefact Collider – Vienna"
Figure 8: Olimpia Presutti, "Transitional City – Venice"
Figure 9: Lloyds Lee, "Vienna Mega-District"
Figure 10: Lorenzo Luzzi, "Tuscan Special – Map"
Figure 11: Lorenzo Luzzi, "Tuscan Special – Spiral of Transformation"
Figure 12: Alessandro Magliani, "The Objects Against the Canon – Milan"

[**Fig. 11** ←] These projects most succeed in "de-contextualizing" the artifact from the real limitations of cultural traditions and built sites. Rather, they insert them into much more complex space-time matrices. They maintain the in-direct relationships between narrative and space, form and image, geometry and imagination. This second chapter also suggests a number of general results. We should continue re-conceptualizing the Time of the City—working with negotiable archives of malleable artifacts. Their simultaneous presence suggests the possibility of designing within the laminated cartography "eternal present." Overall, we could note a few general lessons. The wide-spread 'animation' of artefacts in these projects could ultimately shake up the way we view the set histories, fixed images, and preserved heritage. Armed with an expanded arsenal of conceptual and visual tools, we can adapt our future methodologies and design processes to the changing nature of the Urban Project. And this is only a small selection of the student projects that make up the larger unit's Project on the City. There are many links between these briefs and other chapters in the unit's archive that tackle 'transitions' at the level of urban diagrams as well as disciplinary methods.

[**Fig. 12** →] For example, 'dis-continuity' could be also explored as extensive "journeys" across several areas and cities in Italy (from Milan to Venice, in this case). We could consider fates of these "roaming" Meta-Elements that keep interacting with different frameworks and contexts. In such projects, we also compare the distilled Canonical and the blurred Post-Canonical, emergent project on Form. These are new disciplinary research briefs, drawn out as inherent yet suppressed aspects of Italian urban history.

But that is already a different story, to be told elsewhere, at another time.

POSTFACE: THE LOVE OF INNOVATION
Albena Yaneva

POSTFACE: THE LOVE OF INNOVATION
Albena Yaneva

Albena Yaneva is Professor of Architectural Theory at the University of Manchester, UK. She has worked at Princeton School of Architecture, Parsons, Politecnico di Turino, and held the prestigious Lise Meitner Visiting Chair at Lund, Sweden. She is the author of: *The Making of a Building* (2009), *Made by the OMA: An Ethnography of Design* (2009), *Mapping Controversies in Architecture* (2012), *Five Ways to Make Architecture Political. An Introduction to the Politics of Design Practice* (2017), *Crafting History: Archiving and the Quest for Architectural Legacy* (2020), and *The New Architecture of Science: Learning from Graphene* (2020), co-authored with Sir Kostya S. Novoselov. Her work has been translated into German, Italian, Spanish, French, Portuguese, Thai, Polish, Turkish and Japanese. Yaneva is the recipient of the RIBA President's award for outstanding research.

We cannot imagine a society that is not built by things—IT technologies, trains, telegraph cables, cars, but also—we might add—buildings and infrastructure. We cannot understand societies and how they work, without an understanding of these things and how they shape our everyday life, without unravelling the meaning of innovation. Therefore, it becomes important to study the process of technological and architectural innovations. The socio-technical studies of innovation (Akrich, 1992; Akrich et al, 2002; Callon, 1986) developed in the 1980s in the aftermath of structuralism, advocated a new approach to innovation where the modernist divide between the "subjective" and "objective" dimensions of technologies was entirely abandoned in favour of the idea of mediation, of translation, of network of practice. Drawing inspiration from this body of work, the volume *Innovation in Practice* explores the agency of the architectural project and questions the meaning of innovation in architectural practice: what does it mean to innovate in architecture today? What are the technologies, the tactics and the documentary techniques that drive innovations in design process? How does innovation happen in practice? To understand the rationale behind this nexus of questions, let us clarify some key concepts from innovation theory that shed light on the relationship between design technologies and social processes, and the meaning of architectural innovation.

Innovation as a War of Interpretations

In the early 1960s, an iconic high-tech automated subway system known as Aramis, was developed in France. Designed as a Personal Rapid Transportation (PRT) system, it was poised to dethrone the automobile as the future of transportation. This system was supposed to combine the efficiency of an automated train with the convenience of personal transport. It implied walking into a car, entering your destination into a computer onboard, and walking out a few minutes later. A combination of private cars and public transportation that was to be accomplished by programming the individual cars to autonomously link up into trains when traveling in a group, and then splitting off onto branching paths as per the rider's destination. An innovative line of technology, mechanically inventive and politically relevant, it had so much promise.

Intrigued by this highly complex technological project, the French sociologist Bruno Latour analyzed the Aramis innovation as it wended from its inception as an innovative inevitability to its eventual end. Throughout his account, which is also a narrative experiment mixing criticism and fiction, he engaged with the historical and social aspects of the project as well as the technical aspects (Latour, 1996). Interviewing engineers, bureaucrats, and politicians in order to address the central question "Who killed Aramis"? Latour investigated, like a detective, the failures in the socio-technical network that surrounded the concept of Aramis. The exploration of this question allowed him to bring his rhetorical resources to bear on his argument regarding the inclusion of nonhumans such as motors, chips, and PRT systems into his theoretical sociological network as actors in their own right. The concept of Aramis is enticing, but its execution proved to be rather complex.

As a prototype, Aramis was at the mercy of its makers—a diverse group, ranging from industrial kinematicians and satellite engineers to sympathetic bureaucrats and the Mayor of Paris. They could not agree on what Aramis was supposed to do and their views as to what killed Aramis ranged from fundamental technical failures to cynical political manoeuvring. After 50 interviews and a year of fieldwork, Latour gathered not only one explanation but at least 20 different interpretations of the project that remain inseparable from the project itself.

> "To study Aramis, we also have to explain how certain points of view, certain *perspectives*, certain interpretations, have not had the means to impose themselves so as to become objects on which others have a simple point of view. So we have to pass from relativism to relationism ... The war of interpretations continues for Aramis; there are only perspectives, but these are not brought to bear on anything stable, since *no perspective has been able to stabilize the state of things to its own profit*." (Latour, 1996: 79) [emphasis added]

It is difficult to arrive at one interpretation, the correct explanation as to who or what killed Aramis. The sum of the interpretations of Aramis is hard to make, since there is no common intersection and hence no distinction between the interpretations and the object to be interpreted. Aramis remains a story, an argument, a quasi-object that circulates as a token in fewer and fewer hands. After 15 years, millions of francs, and the participation of dozens of governmental and private institutions the project was abandoned as a failure.

Innovation as a Network of Practice

The irony of the Aramis case is that the main engineers behind the project really believed in the epistemological myth of a technology fully independent from society. Latour demonstrated that this is a pragmatic absurdity. To end the dualism of Society and Technology, and the partition between materialist and culturalist or sociological accounts, he engaged in *a symmetrical anthropology of technology*. Shifting attention to the network of practices and following the trail of actors involved with Aramis, Latour concluded that Aramis was not deliberately "killed." There was no perpetrator, no guilty party. There was no Aramis affair, scandal, or public controversy. Rather, its trajectory "depends not on the context but on the people who do the work of contextualizing" (Latour, 1996: 50). The individuals and the interest groups involved in its conception and creation failed to "love" it, they stopped the negotiations, the research, and they abandoned it; or, in other words, they failed to engage with the concept of Aramis in a fashion that would make it a dynamic actor within the network of practice.

The case of Aramis demonstrates forcefully that the social construction of artifacts/technologies and by extension buildings and infrastructure, should be understood together with the technical construction of society. Rather than positioning the object (Technology) at one of the extremities while the social would be at the opposite (the pole of Society), Latour demonstrated that the body of the social is actively constituted by technologies (Latour, 1993). Technologies exist as institutionalized transaction between humans and nonhumans. In this process of transaction elements of the human actors' interests (bureaucrats, politicians, funders, and others) are reshaped and translated, while nonhuman competences are upgraded, shifted, folded, or merged. Therefore, *the process of innovation becomes accountable if we follow simultaneously the translations of human and nonhuman competences* instead of only following the displacements of the intentions of the human actors and their multiple interpretations, the perspectives.

Therefore, the real locus of enquiry for the researcher of innovation processes is neither the technical object itself, nor the social interests and subjective interpretations of different human actors. The locus of enquiry is to be found in the exchanges between the translated interests of humans and the delegated competences of nonhumans. As long as this exchange goes on, a project is alive and remains a possibility.

The thing we are looking for is not a human thing, nor is it an inhuman thing. It offers, rather, *a continuous passage, a commerce, an interchange, between what humans inscribe in it and what it prescribes to humans*. It translates the one into the other. This thing is the nonhuman version of people, it is the human version of things, twice displaced. What should it be called? Neither object nor subject. An instituted object, quasi-object, quasi-subject, a thing that possesses body and soul indissolubly. The soul of machines constitutes the social element. (Latour, 1996: 213) [emphasis added]

The thing, the project, as witnessed here, is a contested gathering of many conflicting demands; a disputed assemblage of humans and nonhumans. Paradoxically, many design objects often appear as things and not as mere objects; in design studies, new design artifacts are often a contested territory and their study cannot be reduced to a simple description of what they are materially, of how they function, and what they mean (Latour, 2004). As soon as a project is interrupted, or fails, it dies, and we obtain, on the one hand, a social assembly of quarrelling human actors and, on the other, a stack of documents, and a pile of idle and rapidly decaying technical parts. As Latour stated, "The distinction between objects and subjects is not primordial, it does not designate different domains in the world: it is rooted in the fracture of action" (Latour, 1999: 26). That fracture of action, that failure of the technical gesture, separates what is blended together in the repetitive act of making or in the use of the technological artifact. That is why in its normal functioning technology is an abstract system, often invisible; when it fails, it becomes visible, concrete, actual.

Taking inspiration from Latour's anthropology of technology, it becomes important to study the *work of innovation in architectural practice*, as well as the work of success and failure symmetrically. This would require scrutinizing carefully the documentary exchange in both successful and unrealized projects (Armando and Durbiano, 2017), the failed design projects (Yaneva, 2009), the unbuilt and highly controversial urban plans, the technological failure in urban contexts (Simondon, 1989). Both to study the work designers perform on the representation of users, but also, equally, the work they do on the representation of the design object itself (its agency, what it does, how it is perceived and apprehended). Scrutinizing the object and the user, their relationship and the effects that the object generates on relevant social groups, is another way to introduce symmetrical thinking in design research.

Innovation *in* Practice: The Escape from Perspective

Architectural theory commonly embraces an understanding of buildings as having an objective reality "out there" while a number of subjective perspectives *to* the building are being expressed, compared, weighted, and reconciled.

This interpretation can be termed "perspectival flexibility" and points to the fact that design generates physical reality that has *a meaning* for many different actors (users, planners, citizen groups). Designers have *a perspective*; they acknowledge also *the perspectives of others* and their points of view to the objective reality of built forms.

Taking a step away from the dominant perspectivalism in architectural theory, *Innovation in Practice* aims at foregrounding the practicalities, materiality, and events in various architectural processes of innovation. If we focus on the practices of making, negotiating, decision-making, drawing, fabricating; if the actions of urban practitioners (designers, planners, renovators, builders, contractors) are foregrounded, buildings will cease to be passive objects that can be understood and interpreted from various perspectives. The analysis would escape perspective. Buildings will not be seen any longer as symbols; they will rather become a part of what is done in design, construction, and dwelling. This will place the analysis within an "aperspectival objectivity" (Daston, 1992; Daston and Galison, 2007) of built form. One that shifts the source of variability from the many subjective viewpoints (in the perspectival view) to the multiple realities of design process.

Inspired by a pragmatist philosophy of process each essay in this volume unearths a palette of implicit theories about the meaning and the tactics of architectural innovation and its network of practice. Scrutinizing different sites of innovation, the volume takes the reader to the heart of these places through empirical accounts of the work of contextualizing innovation and the various sets of techniques through which architectural innovation is performed. *Innovation* emerges here not as an attribute of Architecture, but as an active underlying dimension of architectural practices that can only be grasped by following *how* they unfold. It is to be constantly negotiated, translated, scrutinized, probed and assembled in such a fashion that would make it a dynamic actor within the network of practice; it is to be "loved." And it can only succeed if it is "loved."

References

Akrich, M. (1992), *The De-scription of Technical Objects*, "Shaping Technology/Building Society: Studies in Sociotechnical Change," edited by W.E. Bijker and J. Law. Cambridge, MA, MIT Press, pp. 205–24.

Akrich, M., Callon, M., Latour, B. (2002), *The Key to Success in Innovation, Part I: The Art of Interessement*, "International Journal of Innovation Management," vol. 6, n. 2, pp. 187–206.

Armando, A., Durbiano, G. (2017), *Teoria del progetto architettonico: dai disegni agli effetti*, Roma, Carocci.

Callon, M. (1986), *The Sociology of an Actor-Network: The Case of the Electric Vehicle*, "Mapping the Dynamics of Science and Technology," edited by M. Callon, J. Law and A. Rip, Basingstoke, MacMillan, pp. 19–34.

Daston, L. (1992), *Objectivity and the Escape from Perspective*, "Social Studies of Science," n. 22, pp. 597–618.

Daston, L., Galison, P. (2007), *Objectivity*, Cambridge, MA, MIT Press.

Latour, B. (1993), *Ethnography of 'High-tech': About the Aramis Case*, "Technological Choices – Transformations in Material Culture since the Neolithic," edited by P. Lemonnier, London, Routledge and Kegan Paul, pp. 372–98.

Latour, B. (1996), *Aramis, or the Love of Technology*, trans. by C. Porter, Boston, Harvard University Press.

Latour, B. (2004), *Why has Critique Run Out of Steam? From Matters of Fact to Matters of Concern*, Critical Inquiry, vol. 30, n. 2, pp. 225–48.

Latour, B. (1999), *Factures/Fractures: From the Concept of Network to the Concept of Attachment*, "RES," n. 36, pp. 20-32.

Simondon, G. (1989), *Du mode d'existence des objets techniques*, (réédition avec postface et préface), Paris, Aubier.

Yaneva, A. (2009), *The Making of a Building: A Pragmatist Approach to Architecture*, Oxford, Peter Lang.

Published by Applied Research and Design Publishing, an imprint of ORO Editions.
Gordon Goff: Publisher

www.appliedresearchanddesign.com
info@appliedresearchanddesign.com

Funding for this publication was provided by the Department of Architecture and Design at Politecnico di Torino.

Book Design: Valeria Federighi, Caterina Quaglio, Elena Todella
Cover Design: Dalila Tondo
Project Manager: Jake Anderson

10 9 8 7 6 5 4 3 2 1 First Edition

ISBN: 978-1-954081-55-0

Color Separations and Printing: ORO Group Ltd.
Printed in China.

AR+D Publishing makes a continuous effort to minimize the overall carbon footprint of its publications. As part of this goal, AR+D, in association with Global ReLeaf, arranges to plant trees to replace those used in the manufacturing of the paper produced for its books. Global ReLeaf is an international campaign run by American Forests, one of the world's oldest nonprofit conservation organizations. Global ReLeaf is American Forests' education and action program that helps individuals, organizations, agencies, and corporations improve the local and global environment by planting and caring for trees.